≡CONTENTS

SWAN'S HOW TO PICK THE RIGHT PEOPLE PROGRAM

William S. Swan, Ph.D.

written with

Phillip Margulies
Maxine Rosaler
and
Hilary S. Kayle

WILEY

JOHN WILEY & SONS

New York • Chichester • Brisbane • Toronto • Singapore

This publication is designed to provide accurate and
authoritative information in regard to the subject
matter covered. It is sold with the understanding that
the publisher is not engaged in rendering legal, accounting,
or other professional service. If legal advice or other
expert assistance is required, the services of a competent
professional person should be sought. *From a Declaration
of Principles jointly adopted by a Committee of the
American Bar Association and a Committee of Publishers.*

Library of Congress Cataloging in Publication Data
Swan, William S.
  Swan's how to pick the right people program.

  Bibliography: p.
  1. Employment interviewing. 2. Employee selection.
I. Title. II. Title: How to pick the right people
program.
HF5549.5.I6S95   1989   658.3'112   88-27888
ISBN 0-471-62189-7
ISBN 0-471-62188-9 (paper)

Printed in the United States of America
10 9 8 7 6 5 4 3 2 1

PREFACE

$\mathbf{N}$o matter how much money companies devote to office space and manufacturing sites, the factor that makes the greatest difference to the success of an organization (and for that matter, the factor that accounts for the lion's share of the cost) is still people. Whatever your business or profession, there's no better way to increase productivity, profitability, and morale than to hire the right person—the first time.

Yet selecting the right people is a skill few managers master. Even human resource professionals who interview candidates daily have found the task can be stressful and full of risk.

My intensive two-day How to Pick the Right People seminars and in-house workshops are designed to fill that gap. For the past 12 years I have trained over 15,000 human resource professionals, recruiters, systems and data processing managers, engineering managers, lawyers, and sales managers in just about every imaginable industry. They have all been provided with a proven way to hire more productive employees, reduce costly errors, and attract top candidates. The selection interview techniques I present in my seminar are simple and easily put into practice. They are based on years of research and in-depth work with organizations of all sizes and types. The emphasis throughout is on providing the tools managers need to make their own successful, real-life hiring decisions.

In this book I've tried to compile every practical and helpful insight that has been learned from 20 years of research on the interview—everything that I present in my seminar—and put it into a step-by-step presentation.

You'll learn:

- ☐ How to analyze the job requirements and relate them to the assets and limitations of each candidate.
- ☐ How to use a logical, immediately applicable interviewing format that won't cramp your style or limit the spontaneity of the candidate.
- ☐ How to create the atmosphere that gets more and better information from the candidate.
- ☐ How to ferret out crucial information that might otherwise have been hidden or missed.
- ☐ How to conduct a thorough—and legal—interview that stays within Equal Employment Opportunity guidelines.
- ☐ How to get talented candidates to say yes when you make them an offer.

HOW TO USE THIS BOOK

This book is meant to be both a practical guide and a reference. If you've never had any formal training in the interview process, it would be well worth your while to read it from cover to cover. If you have had training, it still might not be a bad idea to read it all, but in any case there arc individual chapters that may answer questions you still have about the process, or help you to brush up on some fine points.

With this dual purpose in mind, I've tried to make it easy for you to get to the information you need. Most of the chapters focus on an individual interview issue or skill, and the titles of the chapters clearly describe exactly what is covered in them. In addition, the book is divided into five parts. At the beginning of each part is a summary page which will define for you the contents of every chapter in that part. So if the table of contents doesn't tell you where to find a topic, one of the summary pages will. There is also an index in the back of the book for your convenience.

WHAT'S IN IT

Much of the difficulty in developing effective skills in the selection interview stems from the fact that the interview isn't really one skill done well—it's an amalgam of many discreet skills. To really understand what goes on in a good selection interview you have to study these techniques separately; but when it comes to putting the techniques into practice in the interview itself, you've got to deploy them all as an integrated whole. In the pages that follow, I'm going to take the selection interview apart like a fine Swiss watch—and then, before your eyes, piece by piece, I'll put it back together again.

As we go along, I'll use numerous examples and demonstrations to dramatize the power of these individual techniques and tactics when used in combination—putting together, in effect, what we've taken apart to study.

I believe that this book will make a real difference in the effectiveness of your interviews. The methodology presented here has been proven effective by careful field testing and by its continuous use by thousands of managers in major corporations. I recommend it as the most reliable and practical tool you can find to guide you in your quest to pick the right people for you and your organization.

WILLIAM S. SWAN, PH.D.

New York, New York
February 1989

≡ INTRODUCTION

THE INTERVIEW "GAME" AND ITS COACHES

Almost every job candidate has had the opportunity to receive some form of coaching in interviewing skills. College seniors, MBA candidates, and other students have had the opportunity to attend a course in interviewing, often with videotape feedback, offered by their placement office. Senior executives are carefully coached by the search firms that send them to you, or have gone through outplacement counseling, which includes training and advice on how to handle themselves in the interview. At the very least, anyone can go to their local bookstore and pick up a book to learn the basics of "how to be a better applicant" in an interview.

The experts who coach or instruct these job candidates are in the habit of telling their clients that the interview is a game. There is a playing field (usually your office with a desk and two chairs), a time limit (anywhere from 30 minutes to two hours), and a basic format of questions and answers. As with any other game, there is a strong element of competition. To reach their goals, these experts say, the job candidates must reveal only those things about themselves that will make them appear to be ideal for the job and hide whatever qualities might make them appear less than ideal; it is up to the interviewers to find out whether the candidates are telling the truth.

Although the idea of the interview as a game is not one that I endorse, let me proceed for the moment as if it were. Perhaps by looking at it from the perspective of those who characterize it as such we will be able to learn something about what's wrong with the interview as it is commonly practiced. It is the business of these advisors to take advantage of the interviewer's mistakes, so they pay close attention to them.

WHAT THE "HOW TO GET A JOB" BOOKS SAY ABOUT THE INTERVIEW

There are over 20 "How to Get a Job" books published each year. Here are a few of the things they have to say about the interview process. If, like most of us, you have ever played on the other side of the interview game, some of these ideas should already be familiar to you.

> *"A basic principle of good interviewing is to get the Prospective Employer to do most of the talking . . ."*[1]

> *"Follow the interviewer's lead—your way. This means that instead of answering his questions in the precise sense he means them, you use them as an opening to say what you want."*[2]

---

[1] *The Executive's Guide to Finding a Superior Job* by William A. Cohen, Amacom, 1978.
[2] *Get the Right Job Now! An Insider's Guide to What the Employer Is Looking for and How To Convince Him You've Got It* by Jeffrey Eisen, Ph.D.

*"Most executives do not know how to handle or conduct inter-
views. . . . It will be easy for you to take command of the situation and
maneuver the discussion to your advantage . . ."*[3]

"You'll encounter more inept interviewers than any other kind."[4]

As you read through a stack of these books a caricature
emerges not only of the managers who are conducting the
interviews, but of the individuals they are hiring—the ideal
candidate who is sure to please the interviewer.

If what these books are saying has any validity at all,
then it would seem that when it comes to the interview,
managers are hiring candidates for all the wrong reasons.

Managers often hire people like themselves. "Isn't an
employer's hidden agenda to hire someone like himself?"
the author of *Go Hire Yourself An Employer* asks rhetori-
cally, and he answers: "Often."[5]

Managers supposedly hire only attractive people. "If you
are overweight by more than 10 pounds, either go on a diet,
get a brilliant tailor, or else resign yourself to the fact that
heavyweights usually don't get too many job offers—very
few at the upper levels."[6]

Managers—it would appear—hire candidates who dress
well for the interview; people who are personable and articulate; who smile a lot; who have spent a lot of time rehears-
ing their answers to the 10 most frequently asked questions;
who have researched the company and absorbed a great deal
of superficial information about it that at first glance might
seem very impressive, but probably wouldn't stand up under
very close scrutiny.

The employees hired using these criteria are not necessarily always the wrong people for the job—but they would be

[3]*Ten Weeks to a Better Job* by Stanleigh B. McDonald, Doubleday & Company, New York,
1972.
[4]*How to Get the Job that's Right for You* by Ben Greco, Dow Jones-Irwin, Inc., New York,
1975.
[5]*Go Hire Yourself An Employer* by Richard K. Irish, Anchor Books, Anchor Press/Double-
day, New York, 1973.
[6]*The Professional Job Search Program: How To Market Yourself* by Burton E. Lipman,
John Wiley & Sons, New York, 1983.

much more likely to be the right people if a more systematic method had been used to pick them.

THE CONSEQUENCES OF HIRING MISTAKES

The picture sketched above is undoubtedly a jaundiced, and somewhat distorted by the books' need to score dramatic points. Nevertheless, there is some truth in the perceptions of those who imagine themselves to be on the opposing side of what they consider the interview game. When it comes to helping us understand exactly why interviewers prove to be so ineffective, these books are not as useful (after all, they are more interested in exploiting the phenomenon than explaining it). Some suggest that the source of the interviewer's ineffectiveness is attributable to underlying confusion. Others say that the cause is a system of values that can be easily manipulated.

When we consult the interviewers themselves, a completely different picture emerges. I have met thousands of executives through my work as an consulting psychologist and in the course of presenting my seminar on the interview process; for the most part, individuals rarely admit to hiring decisions based on irrational factors. They never admit to rewarding a candidate with a job in appreciation for a good sense of humor, or as a tribute to a firm handshake and good eye contact, or the candidates' resemblance to a previously successful employee. A little more often, but still not very often, they admit instinct or intuition was the primary basis for decisions, the consequences of which can cost their organization hundreds of thousands of dollars. When I ask managers to describe the process by which they arrive at their hiring decisions, they usually mention a careful review of the job description, an in-depth review of the candidate's work experience, and a weighing of pros and cons.

Yet, consider young Mark, that powerhouse accountant, who kept saying "Super" and practically lifted the desk off the floor a couple of times during the interview in sheer enthusiasm for what he described so articulately as "a challenging spot for a self-starter who's willing to have rewards tied to productivity,"... Six months after he was hired, and, let's face it, since about a week after orientation, Mark has been brooding like Hamlet and walking around the office halls without lifting his feet off the ground. This, apparently, is the real Mark. This is what he was like all along.

And the programmer analyst—steady, loyal, Sam "my priorities are to do whatever I can to help your department achieve its goals...." Sam, who during the course of the interview convinced us and was convinced himself that he would find a permanent home in our organization—Sam left two months ago.

Oh, yes, and there was the famous case of Beverly. Beverly had proved with her incredibly impressive résumé and the direct over-the-phone testimony of her previous employers that she was a proven star performer—a high achiever with a track record of success. Of Beverly, it develops after nearly two years, just the opposite is true. She seems to be incapable of doing anything except get other people to do the work for her and claim the credit for herself.

These are examples, broadly sketched, but drawn from real life, of the kinds of hiring mistakes that are made by managers who haven't had the opportunity to develop the necessary techniques and skills of interviewing. If you have not yourself been responsible for such disasters, you may have had to work with them on a day-to-day basis. Arguably, there are hiring mistakes far worse than these, the invisible ones, the ones that go unnoticed—the people who are neither grossly incompetent nor particularly uncooperative, the people who go on functioning at marginal levels for years.

Those employees are the "false positives," the people who were hired and shouldn't have been. Another less visible, but no less important consequence of ineffective interviewing are the "false negatives"—candidates who could have been quite effective in the job and weren't hired. These are the individuals who went to work for the competition, perhaps, or in another field entirely and made valuable contributions there. Because grossly bad matches are only a small part of the picture, because there is no measure for opportunities lost, the costs of mishirings nationwide—or even companywide—are impossible to calculate. However, factoring in salary, wasted benefits, placement fees, training costs, time wasted by interviewers, relocation costs, the effects on fellow employees, and, most of all, the reduced efficiency and opportunities lost due to the actual inferior work of the person who should never have been hired in the first place—the cost of this mistake may be measured in tens to hundreds of thousands of dollars per hire.

RESEARCH ON THE INTERVIEW

The interview is perhaps the most intensively researched interaction found in any area of business. This research began in World War II when, in a very short period of time, on an unprecedentedly vast scale, decisions had to be made about selecting people for the military and determining the roles and responsibilities they should have once they were in. Who should be involved in intelligence operations? Or public relations? Or the Signal Core? It became clear that the time-honored military solution to the problem, which as we know is to say: "Okay, we need a body here—you: go here," regardless of an individual's background, training, and experience, could no longer be relied on.

Studies initiated at that time on all aspects of selection procedures, including the interview, established the groundwork for our current knowledge of the selection process. During the fifties, research was sponsored by large organizations such as AT&T, by universities, and by consulting firms staffed by industrial psychologists. During those decades the pattern was for industrial psychologists, serving as consultants, to take over for management the

role of interviewing and selecting candidates, espec
senior-level hiring and evaluation of salespersonᴸ.
late seventies and eighties, however, as equal opportunity
issues and cost containment became increasingly important,
corporations have moved toward making their own hiring
decisions, without the help of outside consultants—and
the emphasis of the research on the interview has shifted
to the interview process as conducted by managers and
supervisors.

According to the research on the selection process over
the last 45 years, the interview, as it is usually conducted, is
an ineffectual selection device. The typical interview, conducted even by intelligent, highly motivated, conscientious—but untrained—interviewers, is often no better than
chance—no better than flipping a coin—at predicting how
someone is going to behave in the future on the job. And yet
that is what we as interviewers are asked to predict. In a
relatively narrow window of time (30 minutes to 45 minutes,
typically) we hope to make judgments about a candidate's
technical competence, knowledge base, experience, analytical ability, logic, common sense, and ability to learn
quickly. In addition, we also hope to assess such intangible
but crucial factors as initiative and motivation. Is the
candidate going to work well on a small project team? Can
you count on this individual to get things done on time?
There are so many things you want to be able to assess in
the interview, yet the interview is notoriously inaccurate at
making these predictions, despite all the effort interviewers
put into it.

Yet, the research also shows that the interview can answer these questions validly, and that it is possible to
conduct effective interviews with a high degree of predictive
accuracy. What is at fault in bad interviewing is neither
confusion as to goals, nor a flawed set of values. The only
things missing are the tools, the well-thought-out systematic
methods for obtaining pertinent information and properly
assessing it once obtained.

I ═══ THE PROCESS OF PICKING THE RIGHT PEOPLE

Before we examine the individual skills that make up an accurate and effective job interview, I'd like to step back and take a look at the interview as a whole. That way the individual elements will make more sense as we examine them one by one.

Clarifying goals is usually a good way to get a complex task in perspective. In Chapter 1, "Anatomy of the Effective Interview," I'll enumerate and briefly discuss all of the skills covered intensively in the remainder of the book, as well as review the purposes of the interview.

Then, in the light of those necessary skills and purposes, I'll discuss what usually goes wrong: Chapter 2, "Common Errors Made by Interviewers."

If you are tempted to read this book in no particular order, it would be helpful to review Chapter 1 first. Topics you might have passed over may intrigue you once you see the way they interact with other skills.

1 ANATOMY OF THE EFFECTIVE INTERVIEW

Whether you are a vice president of marketing in a multinational pharmaceutical company, or a sales manager for a software design firm employing 30 people—in fact if you occupy any position above the entry level in your chosen field—you will at some time in your career be called on to conduct a selection interview. Audit managers hire auditors, sales managers hire salespersons, systems managers hire programmers: everyone above that first layer of the pyramid, everyone in a supervisory position over anyone else, is likely to be involved in the selection process. If just one person reports to you, chances are you will have interviewed that person, even if only as part of a series of interviews.

Where is most of the interviewing being done today? You might guess that it would be in expanding industries. And to be sure, constant, increased selection interviewing is being carried out by defense contractors, chemical companies, computer software companies, and so on. On the other hand, a tremendous amount of hiring goes on in industries like the automobile industry, where, even though many blue-collar workers have been laid off, the need for engineers and systems analysts is greater than ever. A company in a shrinking industry may have to do lots of hiring because its composition is changing while its gets leaner and more efficient. Federal, state, and local government agencies are continually hiring new employees at every level.

Organizations nowadays are very concerned about excellence, ethics, being effective, the quality of their relationships with their customers, being efficient and organized and lean and productive in a competitive marketplace. In order to be effective in those arenas, having the right people in the right spots and selecting them properly is critical.

Given the critical importance of effective hiring, one would think that a high proportion of people involved in the interview process would get some training. Yet, that is rarely the case. I've learned from my own experience in nine years of conducting my How to Pick the Right People seminars, from presentations I've made at conferences, and discussions I've had with clients, no more than 10–12 percent of those actively involved in hiring new employees have received any kind of formal training on how to conduct an interview.

Most managers or supervisors were introduced to the interview process with the words: "There are two candidates coming in tomorrow morning, the first one at 11 o'clock, the second at 12; interview them, tell me what you think, and do a good job."

It seems odd, doesn't it, that while you would never be expected to perform any of your other professional duties without some sort of plan or guidance, selecting the person with the skills and knowledge and character traits neces-

sary to perform a particular job function—a critical component of the success of any organization—is often left to trial
and error and chance? Interviewers usually have no more
than their everyday social conversational skills to rely on.
For those few who have had some training, the form it
usually takes—sitting in and watching someone else do
it—isn't particularly effective. Obviously, for someone who
has never interviewed before, some exposure to the interview process is better than none at all. However, even if the
person you were watching was an expert, there would be too
many things going on for you to be able to digest them and
apply them in a systematic way.

The interview is not just one skill done well, but a dozen
or so skills and techniques working together simultaneously. All the research conducted on interviewing in the
past 45 years supports the conclusion that about twelve
independent factors, when united, will make up the most
effective possible interview. These factors form the core of
this book and my How to Pick the Right People seminars,
but before I introduce them I would like to review the
complex task the interview represents.

What are the goals of the interview? At first glance, they
would appear to be straightforward enough. Clearly, you
want to Get Information (review the candidate's background as a basis for predicting how well the candidate
would function on the job); Give Information (tell the
candidate about the job); and Promote Goodwill (make sure
that candidates leave feeling they have been fully heard and
fairly treated). Although these goals may be straightforward, what it takes to accomplish them is very complex.

GETTING INFORMATION

Here are some of the problems in getting information. If we
are going to arrive at a valid prediction of someone's future
behavior on a job, what information should be collected?
How deep should you probe? How do you test the validity

and accuracy of the information? Is the candidate telling you the truth? How can you control a candidate who has had a two-week course on "How to Handle the Interview"? How do you organize and analyze the information you've collected so that you and others involved in the interview process can make decisions about the candidate's ability to perform the job?

GIVING INFORMATION

The process of giving information is also more complicated than it would seem at first. For example, most interviewers start the interview by providing information about the job or organization to break the ice and make the candidate feel comfortable. This can be a serious mistake. There are three reasons for deferring at least a detailed description of the job until after you have finished reviewing the candidate's background. For one thing, it tends to contaminate the interview—many candidates will tell you what they think you want to hear, because you've already told them what you're looking for.

Another problem with giving information too soon is that you might very well be wasting time on inappropriate candidates. By the end of the interview you might know enough to decide that you're not very interested in this particular candidate, and a brief overview of the job would be sufficient.

If, on the other hand, the candidate looks promising, it would be more persuasive to tailor your presentation based on what you've learned in the last 30–45 minutes. Because you're in a competitive marketplace, you want to be sure that you get that talented person to say yes once you make the offer. You can be in a much better position to assure that response if you know enough about the candidate to tailor your "sales" presentation to that person's needs. For all these reasons, interviewers should furnish details about the job after they've probed to get information about the candidate's background, interests, needs, and abilities.

PROMOTING GOODWILL

Promoting goodwill must not be just a courtesy. It serves an important business purpose. How many candidates do you need to interview for a specific job in order to hire a new employee? Two? Ten? On average, 10–20 percent of all candidates actually interviewed end up working for you. The other 80–90 percent go to work for competitors or are out in the business community; they may be potential users of your products or services; they can influence the decisions of others. They carry with them an attitude about your organization based on their one human contact: the interview. To those people you are the organization. It's an irrational way to evaluate a complex organization, but that's how people react, and that's why it's important to make sure that each candidate feels that he or she has been fully heard and fairly treated. Not only will this result in good public relations—since 80 or 90 percent of these candidates will take their views about your organization wherever they go—it will also lead to a decrease in the number of unfounded Equal Employment Opportunity complaints. You might end up saving yourself the headache of the unnecessary legal complexities that can be brought on by unsuccessful candidates who are mistakenly under the impression that they were not given a fair and complete hearing.

KEY ELEMENTS OF AN EFFECTIVE INTERVIEW

In order to learn how to conduct an interview that achieves these purposes, it is necessary to first study all its elements individually. It is my intention here to take you step-by-step through the interview process to enable you to pick up the needed skills. Before we begin, I would like to outline for you the ten elements that comprise this effective interview that we've heard so much about by now. You might say that I'm about to take the interview apart and array its pieces before you. In the course of this book, I'll put it together again, piece by piece, before your eyes. All of these elements will be treated in depth; some of them are so complex that they'll be broken down into subcomponents and discussed in a series of chapters. When the last piece is back in place, the effective interview will stand before you complete, and you'll understand it because you'll know it from the inside out.

In the meantime, let's take a look at those basic elements which, working in cooperation, make for the interview that yields the most accurate and relevant information, and maximizes your chance of getting the candidate of choice to say "yes" to a job offer.

They are:

1. Preparing for the interview

2. Building the proper atmosphere

3. Organizing and controlling the interview

4. Probing and listening techniques

5. Presenting information effectively and closing properly

6. Note-taking techniques

7. Organizing and interpreting information

8. Report writing and documentation

9. Managing sequential interviewing—When several interviewers will see the same candidate

10. Conducting fair and legal interviews

Remember: Although the best method to learn these techniques is to examine them separately, in the interview they are woven together. Yet each component is critical. You can't make up for a shortcut in one area by doing a better job in one of the other areas. Once you've taken a shortcut, the loss is irretrievable. If you take too many shortcuts in too many areas, you might as well line up the candidates according to height and pick the tallest or shortest for all the accuracy the interview will have!

PREPARING FOR THE INTERVIEW

In Part II of this book I'm going to show you how to take a job—any job—and break it down into its component requirements, so that you will be able to focus in on exactly what you should be looking for during the interview. Then I'm going to show you a quick and easy way—a rational way—to organize these factors. With a clear picture of the job requirements, you will find the meaning of what candidates say jumping out at you during the interview.

But preparation for the interview will also go beyond this one area of concern. You'll learn what to do with résumés, how to handle scheduling, where the interview should be conducted, and more. Efficiency and preparation are closely related issues. If you're properly prepared, then in a relatively narrow window of time, 30–45 minutes, more or less, you can make pretty accurate judgments about how a candidate will behave in the future on a job. If you're not properly prepared, you could spend two hours with that individual and still be unable to make the most accurate judgments.

BUILDING THE PROPER ATMOSPHERE

There is an approach to interviewing that attempts to test the candidate's mettle by putting him or her under stress. How would you like to be told, at the beginning of an important interview, "Do something that will infuriate me!" As bold and aggressive as this technique might appear, it really does not effectively accomplish its intended aim, since the kind of stress you create by making the interview an ordeal has little to do with the stress the candidate would encounter on a job. It is also disastrous for everything else you want to achieve in the interview.

Under the heading "Building the Proper Atmosphere," I'll consider a practical way to develop the type of atmosphere that is most likely to elicit the most subtle information from candidates. Such an atmosphere will encourage candidates to be open, spontaneous and natural, so that they will furnish you with accurate data—not just a rehearsed and prepared presentation, or a presentation constricted by their nervousness. Of course, if all we did was make candidates comfortable, the interview might end up being one of the "goody-two shoes" variety. We're not looking for that. You will conduct a highly organized and comprehensive interview, not permitting the candidate to pick and choose what to discuss—and you will be able to test and validate the information the candidate gives you. I am confident we will have a structure that will allow the interviewer to collect significant information. But everything must proceed in an atmosphere that encourages the candidate to open up, to emerge in subtle detail. Neglecting that, structure and probing techniques aren't as effective.

ORGANIZING AND CONTROLLING THE INTERVIEW

In this book, I will present an overall strategy for organizing and conducting an effective interview. Twenty years of research and field testing have resulted in an actual plan of topics to cover, the order in which they are to be covered, and a description of the kind of sequencing and timing that should be used. This strategy is not as rigid as it may at first appear. It merely outlines a proven plan for you to work with, which you will modify and adapt to your special circumstances.

Once the overall strategy is in place, I will provide you with specific tactics to implement this strategy—a set of key, well-researched questions; the core questions for you to ask in each of the areas of the applicant's background that you are investigating with the help of the interview structure. Again, you need not be limited to those questions, but they will give you a sure, sound way to proceed.

In my list of questions you will not find questions like: "Tell me about yourself." "Why should we hire you?" "What can you do for us?" "Where do you think you'll be in the next three to five years if you were to come on board?" I do not wish to imply that you are doing anything inappropriate or silly if you are presently asking similar questions. The problem with questions like these is that they're just not very helpful. Ask them of ten candidates, and eight of them will give you pretty much the same answer. They just don't do a very good job of differentiating one person from another—not to mention that people are most likely to have rehearsed their answers to these questions, especially if they are right out of a college placement office's course on the interview or if they have just been briefed by a search firm or out-placement counseling firm.

These basic beginning questions, or one-step probes, have been selected out of a larger universe of possible questions because they meet the following criteria: They're easy to ask, they're easy to answer, they're seemingly casual, they don't telegraph what you're looking for, and they're easy to follow up. Questions that meet these criteria are wonderfully helpful, and you should have them available to you. These questions do not claim to be magic questions or ones that you've never heard of before—there are no such questions; however, they're good, solid, fundamental questions, to which you'll naturally add very specific technical questions and knowledge questions related to the particular job you have in mind.

PROBING AND LISTENING TECHNIQUES

But you still have a problem. If, during the course of the interview, I were to ask Mark one of my well-researched questions, and he gave me an answer, my next problem would be: How do I know whether he's told me the truth? How do I know that what he said is an accurate representation of what he's really like?

Penetrating the facade of a bold-faced liar is relatively easy; that isn't the most critical issue. The greatest danger for interviewers lies in the fact that candidates are often not very accurate judges of themselves. They may honestly and truly, deep in their hearts, believe that they're systematic, orderly, and logical in their decision-making processes—but as it turns out they're wrong—the fact might be that they have always felt most comfortable operating in a mode of intuition, impulse, and chaos. They may really believe that they don't mind checking with six people before making a decision—or that they can work in an environment where they are expected to take direction from more than one person at the same time—but it's a problem for them once they come on board.

Beyond a candidate's self-report, or his or her own self-perception, it's the job of the interviewer to make independent judgments regarding whether the candidate has the qualities necessary for success, because the individual's honest self-appraisal often includes a perception that is inaccurate. This is one reason why when the "help wanted" ads are written, it's really a waste of time to say, "In addition to experience and technical skills, you also must be meticulous, organized, systematic, cooperative . . . ." No one will decide not to respond because those qualities are required; all job seekers naturally believe they possess them. Maybe they do, in a way—but they may not have them in the form that you need; that's the problem.

Probing and listening techniques are the mechanisms by which you can test and validate the basic information candidates supply for you in their answers to the key questions. These techniques also allow you to probe beneath the surface, ultimately enabling you to make sophisticated judgments. Finally, I'll show you ways of using these techniques without interrupting the conversational flow as you proceed step-by-step through the interview.

PRESENTING INFORMATION EFFECTIVELY AND CLOSING PROPERLY

Obviously, when the time comes to influence a talented candidate, presenting information in the most persuasive way possible is a very important skill. Even if yours is just a screening interview, or if for some other reason the "influence" aspect is handled by another interviewer in your organization, you will still want to make sure that you never have anyone coming on board and saying, "Nobody ever told me that," or that the interviewer has missed covering some important administrative procedure.

Except for the preparation phase, everything else we have discussed so far has had to do with what you do "live" with the candidate, face to face. The issues that remain to be covered involve other facets of the selection process that interact with the interview.

NOTE-TAKING TECHNIQUES

Having an accurate record of what occurred during the interview is a very important piece in the puzzle. However, most interviewers don't take notes. The reasons they give are usually that they anticipate that taking notes will interfere with the flow of the interview, or that they have tried it and it absolutely has interfered. However, those are problems of technique. I can show you ways of avoiding these obstacles, and how you can have an accurate record of the interview without interfering with the process.

REPORT WRITING AND DOCUMENTATION

Wait, what happened to our key element—"Organizing and Interpreting Information"? Well, the fact is most interviewers jump from an interview—or maybe, if they're unusually thorough, after scanning their notes—to write their report or documentation. Or they may even pick up the phone and call somebody with their decision. Alternatively, if they're delivering a report in a written form, the result may be a creative writing exercise where the idea is apparently to write a composition on each candidate, with each composition being different.

ORGANIZING AND INTERPRETING INFORMATION

But if you back up a step, and spend even five minutes organizing what you've learned against the original criteria decided on in the preparation phase, then your report can easily spring out of that. Your writeup (or your oral report) summarizes the key job-relevant assets of the candidate, as well as his or her limitations for the job. You will weigh and balance them one against another and come up with a rational judgment that has a sturdy foundation in fact. The organizing principle that I'll introduce will enable you to make a decision not only more quickly, but much more accurately than if you had proceeded in the ordinary way. Any writeups you have to do will involve matching what you've learned during the interview against the job criteria arrived at earlier and will be both easier and less subjective than a creative writing exercise.

MANAGING SEQUENTIAL INTERVIEWING—WHEN SEVERAL INTERVIEWERS WILL SEE A CANDIDATE

Up until this point I have been talking as though it were up to you alone to do everything that needs to be done regarding the selection of the new employee—that is, as if you were the only one conducting the interview, analyzing the job, taking notes, organizing the information, and making the final decision. As you know, however, except for a screening or campus interview, there are usually several interviewers involved. You might decide on the criteria together, you might parcel up the interview in some ways, you certainly may coordinate the decision with others and try to make a joint decision with several interviewers involved. The sequential interviewing process, where the candidate is interviewed by several people in the course of a day or a week or more, can make for a much more effective judgment, provided that all the interviewers are using the same criteria and a similar or at least comparably organized approach. But, if they're all using different criteria or approaches that are not comparable, the net result may be a less effective judgment. I will show how to manage every basic variation of that circumstance, and review five different models for coordinating activities between interviewers to make that work effectively.

CONDUCTING FAIR AND LEGAL INTERVIEWS

Finally, every interviewer (not just someone from Human Resources, Employment, or Personnel) is responsible for conducting a legal, as well as a complete and thorough interview.

All too often in my experience, this is an issue that is covered exclusively from a legalistic point of view. If I were to include a copy of Title VII in the Appendix and advise you to memorize it I doubt that it would change anyone's behavior very much (although, I've seen some interviewers drop their voices in the interview, and say, "Well, I'm not supposed to ask you this, but . . . ." and they ask anyway!).

I will give you a way to get all the job-related information you need, without ever asking a personal question, an insensitive question, or a patently illegal one. Not a clever loophole or way to circumvent the rules, but a way to do your job as an interviewer within the spirit as well as the letter of the law.

≡2≡COMMON ERRORS MADE BY INTERVIEWERS

The common errors I'm about to review are not necessarily things you do, but you may have encountered them when you yourself were interviewed for a job—or perhaps you have noticed them being done by peers or subordinates. They're mistakes that are typically made by many interviewers, even those with lots of experience; in some cases, interviewers know they're prone to making these mistakes, but nevertheless have been unable to avoid them.

Some of the information presented in the list below was culled from interviewers' reports about themselves, and some of it comes from their observations of other interviewers. By far the biggest source of the following list of errors was candidates reporting what they feel interviewers do that reduces the effectiveness of the process.

TALKING TOO MUCH

Most interviewers talk half the time or more during the interview. Think about it. If you're talking 50 percent of the time or more, you're not learning very much. The candidate should be talking 80 or 90 percent of the time; you should be talking 10 or 20 percent, at least for that portion of the interview during which you're collecting information. But to make that happen requires the application of structure, probing skills, and a variety of other techniques.

TELEGRAPHING DESIRED RESPONSE

Mark is sitting in my office and I tell him: "In addition to your technical competence, experience, and skills, it's also critical that anybody in this position be able to work on a small project team and coordinate with other people effectively. Tell me about your experience and interest in working in such a setting."

Well, Mark wants the job or he wouldn't be here. It won't take long for him to figure out that for the next 20 minutes every chance he gets he should find an opportunity to mention how much he likes working on a small project team ("Let me give you three examples"), even if it's not particularly true. The candidate now knows what I'm looking for.

You might not be as obvious about giving the candidate such an advantage as I was in the example above, but here's what many interviewers do: In the beginning of the interview, intending to relax candidates, to make them comfortable, and to set the stage for the interview, they dump a lot of details about "what our organization is all about" ... some special circumstances of the job ... challenges to face ... what a typical day is like—and then turn to reviewing the candidate's background. Later we'll see that this doesn't accomplish its intended goal of relaxing the candidate. But beyond that, there's the additional liability of telegraphing your punches and contaminating the interview.

Now the candidate knows what to highlight, what to down-play, what to include and exclude. This seems obvious, and yet many interviewers give the candidate a lot of data up front and then wonder why all the candidates are so targeted for that job. And, of course, if you are also interested in influencing a candidate, you will be missing the opportunity to tailor or adapt your presentation to their needs and interests.

JUMPING TO CONCLUSIONS

Often interviewers do what most of us do in other human interactions—they make judgments about people relatively quickly. In fact, studies clearly indicate that interviewers usually reach a decision during the first six to eight minutes. It is not necessarily the correct decision, but it is very difficult to change that judgment once formed.

Now, I don't mean to say that you should ignore your momentary hunches and guesses. The more experience you have managing people, the more relevant your hunches and guesses become. Pay close attention to them. You should then use them as hypotheses or clues and then test and validate them in the course of the interview! It's impossible to eliminate hunches anyway, and it really isn't necessary—your job is to make them function rationally within a larger context. The point is not to make a decision based on them alone: the firmness of a handshake, the steadiness of a voice, or that certain yet indefinable air of maturity should not weigh too heavily in your decision. They're relevant, but get past them to the facts that may or may not corroborate your first guess.

Initial Impressions Get in the Way of the Facts

You may have noticed that what I've just mentioned are things that might influence your initial impression in a positive vein. Of course, it could work in reverse. You might notice that the candidate doesn't maintain good eye contact with you, or seems uncomfortable, or makes you uncomfortable. Or the candidate might casually say something that turns you off, or perhaps light up a cigarette in your presence without saying, "Do you mind if I smoke?" or something else that will momentarily make you uncomfortable or provide—you think—some clues as to what kind of person the candidate is. Again, I do not advise you to ignore those things; there will be a place for them in your final evaluation of the candidate. But you mustn't allow the subtle bias they evoke to hinder your search for other relevant information.

FAILING TO KNOW THE JOB REQUIREMENTS

When it comes to this crucial area the most common error isn't walking into an interview ignorant of the basic job requirements, but rather it is not knowing the requirements in a way that is helpful in the interview. If all I have is a general sense of the job—"Oh, I want somebody who's technically skilled, bright, lots of energy"—then chances are that the interview will take the following form: I'll chat with the candidate for half an hour or 45 minutes. Then she'll walk out the door, and a few moments after the door has closed behind her I'll sit down and say: "Let me see now, what do I think? Well . . . she seems to be a pleasant person, and she seems to be kind of organized in her thinking with me in the interview, and her background and experience doesn't look too bad, and she seems to be the kind of person who might work well with people on a team—I think she's okay. We'll give her an offer." Or, on the other hand, I could sit for a few moments at the end and say, "Well, I don't know, she seems a little fumbling in her thinking through certain concepts, and she didn't seem to be immediately able to answer certain questions right away, and, Oh, I don't know! She might be a little, well, indecisive."

This kind of global judgment made at the end of the

interview isn't irrational; but it is generally low in accuracy, especially when compared with a decision made at the end of the interview in which you've been able to test and validate the information moment by moment as the candidate speaks. The problem is to connect the little things candidates say off the top of their heads—things the significance of which they themselves might not even be aware—with the specific qualities you're looking for. That's not going to happen simply by chatting with the person. You need a sharp and clear understanding of what qualities are needed on the job, and you need some kind of logical, orderly plan. This brings us to our next point.

NOT USING AN ORGANIZED APPROACH

Suppose I am about to interview four candidates for a job. I may not have a scientifically based, systematic, organized approach, but that doesn't mean that I don't have any way of proceeding. I can talk to people and ask questions about their backgrounds. I sit down with Mark and I say casually, "Well, Mark, I've read through your background here,"—at this point I give the résumé an offhand rap with my knuckles—"You're really a talented person, with a lot of rich experience, and I'm glad to have the opportunity to talk with you today. But,"—now I clear my throat—"you know, I'll never be the expert on you that you are just by reading a piece of paper, so, uh, tell me about yourself."

Well, Mark can handle that. He gives me information. His statements trigger off questions and I ask them. I throw in my pet questions. I give him the opportunity to ask me questions and I answer those. I give him additional information about the job opportunity, and that's the first interview; on to Karen, the next candidate. In the meantime, I have glanced at the clock. "Well, I've read through your background, you're obviously a very talented person . . . but I must say that we're running a little short of time, it's not really your fault, but we can catch up easily—just hit the highlights of your background, give me those things you think most important and we'll focus on those."

This is another version of "tell me about yourself." And Karen can handle that. And in fact she gives me lots of information, I ask questions, I give her information about the job, that's the end of that interview, on to the next.

Without an Organized Approach It's Hard to Make Comparisions Between Candidates

This goes on. At last I've finished four or five interviews—or if the interviews are being held on a college campus, perhaps 14 interviews. All I have to do is pick the best and the brightest out of this group. After all, the reason I interviewed several people is that I wanted to be able to make rational comparisons between them. The problem I am facing now is that I don't have comparable data on these candidates. I have randomly collected information. I have— if you like—different data bases on each candidate and it's really going to be hard to measure one person against another. To compare candidates validly we need some kind of organized approach—nothing so mechanical as taking a survey, but a flexible, sensitive way to collect information that permits meaningful comparisions.

Without an Organized Approach Each Individual Interview May Be Invalid

It certainly isn't easy to compare one candidate with three others if I have different data bases for all of them. But let's turn the tables for the moment and suppose I was the one being interviewed by four interviewers, each one using a different approach off the top of their head each time. What do you think it would be like if they all got together afterwards, when the day was over, and decided to compare notes—using their different data bases as their criteria of judgment? I can hear Mark saying, "Boy, that guy Swan, lots of energy, motivation, initiative, he's really great—just what we're looking for, let's make him an offer!" And Karen, managing to look bored and startled at the same time, says: "What? Really? I mean, what are you talking about—Energy? Motivation? Where on earth did you get that from?" Totally different perceptions of me, not because I was different in each interview, but because they had different data bases—and perhaps none of the interviewers has an accurate reading of me, since they each randomly collected information.

It's More Difficult to Conduct Interviews Without An Organized Approach

Another point about not having an organized approach—a small point, but one that on a human level I think is quite important—many people hate to interview. One of the reasons they hate to interview is that every time they sit down with somebody they have to decide on the spot what they're going to do and how they're going to do it. Well, that's awkward. If, however, at the outset of the interview you have an idea of the topics you are going to cover, the order of those topics to be covered, and a sense of sequencing and timing, the interview will become just another business activity for which you are organized and prepared. It never has to seem like an ordeal again.

II ≡≡≡ HOW TO PREPARE FOR THE INTERVIEW

Suppose Bob, a new manager in the communications depart-
ment I head, knocks on my door first thing Monday morning
to tell me that he has scheduled a series of candidates to be
interviewed for a programmer/analyst position that has re-
cently become available. "I've never interviewed anyone before
and I need some help on how I should go about preparing for
it," he explains. Bob, a very methodical and conscientious
fellow, continues: "Before I even sit down with the first
candidate on the schedule I want to know what I should do
between now and then to be as organized and systematic and
prepared as I can possibly be." My task, then, is to provide
Bob with a list of everything he should do before the interview
that would increase his chances of selecting the best candi-
date. What exactly do I tell him?

To get him started I would give him an overview of the
tasks that lie before him. "First of all, you've got to determine
the job requirements," I'd tell him, "and organize them in a
way that's useful for the interview."

The basic fundamentals of what I'd tell Bob concerning
these important first two steps can be found in Chapter 3,
which is entitled "Where to Learn the Job Requirements—
and Determining the Knowledge and Skills the Job Calls

For." I would go on and show him how he can break his job requirements down into three categories—"Knowledge, Skills, and Abilities" (covered at the end of Chapter 3); "How to Determine the Required Job Behaviors" (Chapter 4); and "How to Determine the Job Environment" (Chapter 5).

Next I'd give Bob some tips on how to get the best use out of résumés and applications, I'd make some points about the often taken-for-granted subject of what location and physical arrangements get the best results from an interview, and I'd provide Bob with the checklist of things to bring to the interview. My advice on these many disparate but nonetheless important topics is covered in the appropriately titled Chapter 6—"Everything Else You Need to Do to Be Prepared for the Interview."

≡≡3≡ WHERE TO LEARN THE JOB REQUIREMENTS— AND DETERMINING THE KNOWLEDGE AND SKILLS NEEDED ON THE JOB

No component of the selection process is as critical as getting, at the outset, a precise idea of what you're looking for—it's what gives focus to the interview, it's the reason behind every question you're going to ask the candidate, and it's what will give meaning to the answers. You may recall that not knowing the job requirements in a way that gives focus to the interview is one of the most common interview errors.

WHERE TO GET INFORMATION ABOUT JOB REQUIREMENTS

The sources of information about the job requirements can be divided into two basic categories: paper, or document sources, and people. You will not need to review all of these sources before every interview, but you should do an exhaustive job once, and then periodically update your understanding of the position requirements.

Paper Sources of Job Requirements

The Job Description—and Its Limitations.   The first, most obvious document to review to understand the job requirements is the job description. This document is often prepared by human resources or personnel with the help of the managers or supervisors knowledgeable about the position. Reading it is, of course, a good place for anyone to start collecting information about the position criteria. However, it is important to point out that the job description is designed for wage and salary administration purposes—not for selection purposes—and is therefore usually an incomplete depiction of the full range of qualities and skills needed for the job. Review it, certainly. It is one of your sources of information. But it is not enough.

Performance Reviews.   Performance reviews of incumbents or former incumbents of the job are another source of information that will help familiarize you with the job requirements before the interview. Look for patterns of qualities that make people successful and qualities you want to avoid in your next hire.

People to Ask About Job Requirements

Although documentation such as job descriptions and performance reviews, if available, can be very useful, you will probably find that people—not paper—are essential sources of the kind of information about the job requirements that will be useful during the interview. After all, the job you are interviewing for does not exist in a vacuum. It is surrounded by other functions in the organization. There are those in roles above or below it, those who have virtually the same job. Each of these people has a different, and possibly useful perspective on the job that they could share with you.

Yourself.   First of all, you talk to yourself. What do you know about the job, from your own direct experience or perhaps having done it at one time, or what would you assume the requirements to be by imagining yourself in that role?

Thinking about the organization or department's goals and objectives for the next year, or what new or different projects the new hire will be asked to handle may give additional insight into specific qualities you will need or aspects of the job a new hire will have to deal with.

Direct Superiors.   If the person being hired is not going to report to you directly, you should talk to the person to whom he or she will report. They will have definite ideas about what's needed in a subordinate.

Incumbents and Peers.   It would also be useful to talk to the people who are actually doing the job now, or former incumbents; or talk to peers, or co-workers—here again, as in the performance reviews, you'd be looking for a refinement and more subtle picture of the qualities that make for success on that job. But by discussing it with others now, instead of just taking what's handed to you on a piece of paper, you will be able to target questions for the particular kind of information you need.

Subordinates, People in Other Departments, Outside Vendors, Clients, Customers.   By now you may have more information than you can handle! But if you don't, and you would like to further refine your picture of the job requirements, you might, in addition, talk to subordinates, if the role has subordinates; people in other departments who would interface with the person performing the particular job; to outside vendors who might interface with the person who currently has the job you'll be interviewing for or to customers.

You would not necessarily have to contact those last several sources before every interview; however, over the course of time, especially if this is a role you have to fill again and again, you should find out from all these people what qualities are related to superior performance.

HOW TO ORGANIZE THE JOB INFORMATION IN A FORM THAT WILL BE USEFUL IN THE INTERVIEW

Collecting the information in the manner I've just described was merely the first part of a two-part process. The second part involves digesting the information that you acquire and organizing it into a form that will be useful during the interview.

You'll probably notice a pattern to the sorts of things you learn about the job requirements from these various sources. There are items that are pretty cut and dried: perhaps the candidate has to have an MBA or a college degree in some other specific subject area. On the other hand, it is very likely that you will also hear about qualities that are harded to identify, like "motivation" or "initiative." Then there will probably be a third kind of item that may have more to do with what kind of environment the job will fit into—you may be asked to find a "team player" or someone who can tolerate stress or a lot of weekend work.

In fact, if you sorted a typical "wish list" gleaned from the information-collection phase described above into three columns under these heads, here's how they'd look:

JOB REQUIREMENTS

Knowledge, Skills, and Abilities	Behaviors	Environmental Issues
Work experience	Motivation	Team orientation
Education	Interests	Independence
Technical skills	Goals	Socal effectiveness
Communication skills	Drive/Energy	Interpersonal style
Specialized training	Reliability	Stress tolerance
Analytical skills	Initiative	Limitations
		—Travel
		—Overtime
		—Relocation
		—Weekend work

These three columns amount to a comprehensive array of job requirements. As we'll see in Part III, when we turn from understanding the job to our search for the right person for the job, this same analysis will yield three related columns. The Knowledge, Skills, and Abilities required by the job will be refocused as Can This Candidate Do the Job. The Behaviors required on the job will be refocused to Will the Candidate Behave in the Way We Need; the Environmental Issues will translate into Will This Person Fit into Our Unique Environment?

USING THE JOB ANALYSIS WORKSHEET

Figure 1 shows a form called the Job Analysis Worksheet. This form divides job requirements into the categories I've just shown you; consider it a tool to help you keep track of the data you collect about the job and to guide you as you continue to determine job requirements. The front of the form provides questions for you to ask yourself or others while you go about collecting the information you need.

The back of the form is used to translate this information about job requirements into the qualities to look for in the candidate.

Figure 2 helps explain the logic behind the Job Analysis Worksheet.

INTERPRETING WHAT YOU LEARN FROM YOUR SOURCES

Many of the requirements listed on the back of the form in the section headed "Knowledge, Skills, and Abilities" are clear and unambiguous. They're the easier things to define, they're what the job description focuses on, and they're the first thing interviewers usually think of when it comes to job requirements.

When Bob speaks to the person who would be supervising the programmer/analyst, the manager tells him: "Well, for this job, we need somebody who's technically competent: a good knowledge base, these kinds of courses, this kind of very specific experience, a person who can think quickly, be analytical and logical in problem solving, and program in COBOL." If the job was in manufacturing instead of systems, the requirements might include familiarity with quality control procedures; if the job were in sales, product knowledge or experience developing a marketing strategy might be required.

The Knowledge, Skills, and Abilities category includes but is not limited to technical competence. It includes all the intellectual, experiential, and educational requirements necessary for effectiveness. These are critical issues. A candidate who does not measure up in these areas can be eliminated as a contender. Most interviewers can define these issues and feel reasonably confident in evaluating a candidate on their knowledge, skills, and technical competencies.

The other areas present special difficulties and that's why we'll be devoting more effort to them in the next two chapters.

JOB ANALYSIS WORKSHEET

Job Title _____

Grade/Salary Level _____

Position Reports To (Title) _____

This form is designed to help define the qualities and talents needed for a particular job. The questions are designed to give data useful not only to determine technical requirements (can do), but also the motivational factors (will do) and the interpersonal/environmental factors (fit).

Use this form to analyze a job prior to an interview by completing it yourself or use it as a guide when gathering job information from others.

I. JOB INFORMATION

List the most important duties and responsibilities. (Typically 5 or 6)

_____
_____
_____
_____
_____

Describe key involvement with others: superiors, subordinates, peers, vendors, customers, or other contacts. _____

_____
_____
_____
_____

What are the potential sources of satisfaction? (List up to 5)

_____
_____
_____
_____
_____

What are the potential sources of dissatisfaction? (List up to 5)

_____
_____
_____
_____
_____

What jobs or career opportunities might be available? (Indicate even if limited)

_____
_____
_____
_____
_____

Fig. 1. Job Analysis Worksheet (continued on p. 34).

II. PUTTING JOB INFORMATION TO USE *(Defining "Can Do", "Will Do", and "Fit")*

Can Do Factors

Can they do the job — what specific experiences, skills, equipment knowledge, abilities, prior training or education, physical requirements etc., are required or desired for successful job performance?

_____
_____
_____
_____
_____
_____
_____

Will Do Factors

Will they do the job — what specific behaviors are required or desired in order to be sure that individuals will apply themselves and behave in ways that are associated with success on the job?

_____
_____
_____
_____
_____
_____

Fit Factors

Will the person fit into the specific environmental circumstances of the job? Include information about the type of industry or business, atmosphere of your organization, circumstances of work at department or area level and the circumstances of the specific job.

    a) Environmental circumstances

_____
_____
_____
_____
_____

    b) Knockout items (what specific situational factors such as long hours, overtime, shiftwork, weekend work, travel, relocation, physical demands etc., are required on this job) What circumstances would eliminate the person from consideration?

_____
_____
_____
_____
_____
_____

Fig. 1. (continued).

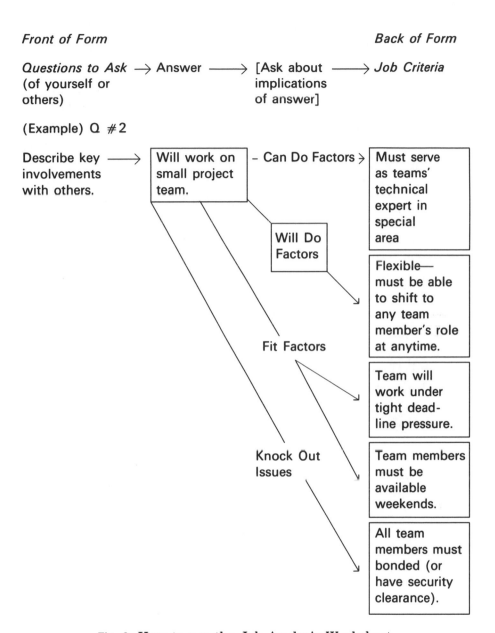

Front of Form   *Back of Form*

Questions to Ask → Answer ⟶ [Ask about ⟶ *Job Criteria*
(of yourself or   implications
others)   of answer]

(Example) Q #2

Describe key ⟶   Will work on   – Can Do Factors ›   Must serve
involvements   small project   as teams'
with others.   team.   technical
                                                        expert in
                                    Will Do   special
                                    Factors   area

                                                        Flexible—
                                                        must be able
                                                        to shift to
                                                        any team
                                                        member's role
                                    Fit Factors   at anytime.

                                                        Team will
                                                        work under
                                                        tight dead-
                                                        line pressure.

                                    Knock Out   Team members
                                    Issues   must be
                                                        available
                                                        weekends.

                                                        All team
                                                        members must
                                                        bonded (or
                                                        have security
                                                        clearance).

Fig. 2. How to use the Job Analysis Worksheet.

These Behaviors and Environmental Issues are clearly important factors for success on the job. However, how in the world are you going to find out if someone's got them? You don't get a diploma for motivation or initiative or career-mindedness. You may not even be absolutely certain what those words mean, and if you don't know that, how can you tell whether a candidate has them?

Every interviewer recognizes the importance of these qualities, but because of their ambiguity they are sometimes called the "subjective" factors—subjective is what they are if you don't know anything more about them. Subjective is what we cannot allow them to remain if they're going to be any use to us in the interview.

In the next two chapters I'm going to take a closer look at these other categories, and I'll show you how to interpret these seeming abstractions—in a way that will be useful to you in the interview. I'll show you how you can probe beyond the generalities people hurl at you when they're asked about job requirements, and translate them into concrete, verifiable behaviors that can guide you in your search for the ideal candidate.

4 HOW TO DETERMINE THE REQUIRED JOB BEHAVIORS

WHAT ARE JOB BEHAVIORS?

When you ask about the job requirements, in addition to simply rattling off a list of the technical skills and knowledge that are required, people will say things like this, "We also need somebody in this job who's motivated, ambitious, energetic, career-minded." They might add, "flexible, adaptable, a self-starter, and has initiative. Otherwise we have no criteria!" This is usually the kind of thing that you will hear from the direct superior. The incumbent might be more likely to say something like this, "In this job you need confidence." A peer might say, "I need someone I can count on, someone who will do things on time so I can get my job done."

These other qualities, which fall into the two basic categories of behavioral and environmental factors, are not as cut and dried as the skills and abilities needed. If Jeanne can draw scale diagrams, for example, is simply a lot easier for the interviewer to determine than whether she has the interest to learn new things, or whether she would be able to withstand the pressures put on her by tight deadlines.

WHY "QUALITIES" MUST BE TRANSLATED INTO "BEHAVIORS"

Motivation ... Adaptability ... Flexibility ... Ambition ... Energy ... Career-mindedness ... Initiative ... Confidence ... Decisiveness ... Maturity ... and so on. These words are not meaningless. We know instinctively that they refer to realities that actually do count in the workplace. The problem is that different interviewers mean different things by them, and therefore as words—whose meanings are neither job-specific nor behavioral—they are useless in the interview.

First, they tend to be universal qualities that are desirable for any job. Let's take the word "motivation." Would you ever expect to hear somebody say, "Well for this job, we definitely need somebody who's de-motivated; that's really critical!" Sure, we always want people who are motivated—for all jobs at every level. Except what we mean by motivation is different in those different circumstances. Yet we use the same word.

Second, if you ask several interviewers, "What does motivation mean?" you'll get totally different definitions, or definitions with different shades of meaning. If each of these people interviewed you for a job, each would come to a different conclusion as to whether you were motivated, or your degree of motivation, even though you presented the same information in every case. Furthermore, it very well might turn out that none of their individual personalized definitions had all that much to do with what was really called for by "motivation" on that particular job.

HOW TO TRANSLATE "WORDS" INTO REAL JOB-RELEVANT BEHAVIORS

When you ask yourself—or others—"What qualities does this job require?" and a quality like motivation comes up, here is the critical question to ask, "If you already had somebody on the job who was motivated, how would he or she behave to show us that?" Remember we're not talking about a candidate now, but attempting to visualize an ideal, highly "motivated" employee—so we can understand what that job requires.

I don't know what the answers to those questions would be for all the jobs for which you interview, but I can give you some examples, to show you how to go about translating ambiguous attributes into concrete and specific job-relevant behaviors.

Look at the Behavior Itself

A manager once said to me: "What I mean by motivated is this: Suppose I'm handling a problem, a pretty complex one, but this ideal employee is not directly involved. Nevertheless, if this person was motivated they would come to me when I'm through and ask me lots of questions in order to find out how they should handle it in case they ever had to face it on their own without me around. If, in fact, they were to do that—to come and ask me lots of questions—I would know that they were motivated."

Is that a good dictionary definition of motivation? No. You and I might label that behavior differently. You might call it "initiative." I might call it "planning ahead." But none of these labels matters—including "motivation." Because we've taken those words, "motivation," "planning ahead," and "initiative" and nudged them all down to the level of the specific job-relevant behavior. Armed with that piece of behavior you can now search into a candidate's background to see if they've ever behaved that way. If I can demonstrate they've behaved that way, especially that they've exhibited this behavior repeatedly over the course of time, then I can predict with some confidence that they're likely to behave that way again.

But let's suppose Joe has never behaved that way. Or worse yet, he's behaved in the opposite way. I would then be on pretty shaky ground to say: "Well, Joe's a bright guy, he's got lots of technical skills and experience, and I'm sure he can develop. He seems flexible, and around here we give people opportunities to grow and all that—what the heck, let's bring him on board and he'll grow into those other qualities." That's a noble statement, but wait around for, or try to develop within someone, qualities like initiative, dependability, reliability, conscientiousness, a high energy level . . . you've got a long wait ahead of you. Even if you are truly a molder of human beings, it would be a tough job—and speaking for myself, I don't want that job. I'd rather get somebody who has the two or three absolutely critical job behaviors in their repertoire, and then develop them further.

For another example of how an attribute might be translated into a specific job behavior, let's take a look at "energy level." Nowadays when the management in almost any organization is asked what they need in their new employees, they say, "We need somebody with a high energy level: we have fewer people doing more work, and therefore need employees who have lots of drive, energy, and stamina," or they say, "Energy is critical around here—no deadheads, no bumps on the log, nobody who's going to burn out at three o'clock and coast the rest of the day, or burn out on Thursday and coast through Friday."

How Candidates Behave in the Interview Is Not an Accurate Predictor

That may seem like a clear mandate. "I'll search in the interview for people with high energy." I submit to you that if that's all you know, your understanding of that job requirement is inadequate. You may not agree with me. You may think that you can spot a high energy level in a person. But then the first candidate, Chris, comes in. He walks kind of slow, and doesn't volunteer a lot of information. He answers all of your questions, has detailed, specific information to give you, and obviously has all the knowledge and skills and abilities necessary for the job. The only problem is that while you're talking with him it's kind of hard to keep awake! And once Chris leaves, you say, "Well I may not be a nuclear physicist, but it's pretty clear to me that this person is no human dynamo."

Ah, but the next candidate, Morganna, what a difference! Morganna comes in and walks fast, talks fast, sits in the front third of the chair, doesn't even lean back; she's animated; she gestures as she speaks, her voice moves, it's modulated, she's certainly dynamic and outgoing, and in fact she displays right in the interview a high energy level.

For the sake of discussion let's assume these two candidates are exactly the same in all other ways, including knowledge, skills, experience, and training. If they are equal in all these areas and the only difference between them was this piece of behavior you noted during the interview—and on top of that you knew that the job required a very high energy level, most interviewers would prefer the second candidate—and I would understand why. However, as you have probably guessed, while you could also be absolutely correct about these two candidates, you also could be absolutely wrong.

Somebody's behavior in front of you, while not irrelevant, is very low in accuracy as a predictor of how they will behave in the future on the job. Yet that's what most interviewers do. They observe behavior in the interview; based on that notoriously unreliable index of future behavior they make a judgment about candidates. Two or three weeks or a month later, when the person is a disappointment, they say: "I don't understand that, they seemed so mature, they seemed so logical, they seemed so cooperative, they seemed so interested. Why aren't they now? How can that be?''

The answer is that a candidate's behavior during the interview is contaminated by an incalculable number of other things. Some candidates have been coached and prepped and powder-puffed and as a consequence come across smoother than they really are—or than they will be when they get the job. On the other hand, another candidate may have been told by his search firm just prior to his interview with you that it would be pointless to send him on any more interviews. "You keep on coming off as pushy and aggressive. Knock it off if you want to get a job!" So now this person may overcompensate and come across as hesitant and quiet or reserved. But you, of course, won't know the reason why. Someone else may appear to be very energetic—or very nervous—and the hidden explanation is three cups of strong coffee that on an average day she would never drink, but this isn't an average day: She arrived very early and stopped off nearby for coffee to kill time before this interview. And that worried look may have more to do with the fact that the candidate's car is parked in a tow-away zone than anything that's really relevant to his job performance, for all you know. The point is that you don't know, and you can't possibly know all of the random factors that might affect the candidate's behavior at this particular moment in time. Even if the interview were not in itself an unusual and exceptional event in the life of the candidate, the 30–45 minutes that you'll have to observe them add up to much too small a sample of their behavior to be valid, and if you base your conclusions on it, you're liable to be surprised later. Finally, even if their behavior in the interview was an accurate representation of the candidate's "motor activity level," this may not be the behavior meant by "high energy" for a specific job. I'll show you an example of this below.

The "Second Date" Effect

By the way, perhaps you're already familiar with this phenomenon of erroneous judgment from initial behaviors. It's called the "second date" effect. You go out with someone socially for the first time and everything is perfect; then you go out a second time. You say to yourself, "Uh oh, is this the twin brother or twin sister of the person I went out with last week? They're so different! What's going on?" Well, of course, they were on their best behavior the first time. Now the real personality is starting to emerge. Now they're arguing with the waiter, they're reaching into your plate with their fork—that's the real them. In any event, you certainly don't want a total surprise when somebody comes on board as a new employee. In order to prevent this from happening, what you have to do is get a clear idea what specific behaviors are needed on the job so that you can search for them in a candidate during the interview.

Refining Your Definitions

Let's go back, for the moment, to the issue of energy level. You still want to find out how you can determine whether the candidate possesses the "high energy" that is required for the job. If you can't judge this by how he or she behaves in the interview, what can you do? You can follow the same steps I have already described. Before any interview, when you're thinking about the criteria, talking to yourself or others, ask, "If a successful employee in that job had the quality we mean by high energy, how would that person behave on the job to tell us that?"

This question will be answered in different ways depending on the job. Here are two completely different examples. "Well," one manager once told me, "by high energy I mean I need somebody who can juggle four or five things in the air at the same time—complex things—and shift back and forth from one to the other all day long without resisting it, resenting it, or being exhausted by it, because that's the job." Now if that's what you mean by high energy, then you can search into a candidate's background during the interview to see if they've ever behaved that way, and you are no longer fooled by how they behaved momentarily in front of you.

Another manager gave me this definition: "Well, by high energy I mean I need someone who is just as detail-minded, just as systematic, and just as focused at 7:30 at night as they were at 7:30 in the morning. What they're working on then is just as important and there's no room for error. So I need a person who, after a long hard day, can be accurate, follow procedures precisely, be detail-minded, and able to concentrate."

Now I have a completely different definition: not perhaps what I would have meant by the word, and maybe not what the dictionary would have said, but that doesn't matter. All that matters is that now you know what to look for. Now you can search candidates' background to see if they have behaved in the way required by this manager's definition of the word "energy."

Now we need to discuss the last of the three categories of job requirements—the environment they have to function in.

≡≡≡5≡HOW TO DETERMINE THE JOB ENVIRONMENT

$\mathbf{W}$e have come two-thirds of the way through the process of organizing the job requirements in preparation for the interview. To recapitulate: Identify and think through the requisite skills and abilities and technical competence that will be needed; identify and think through those behaviors that would be needed for success on the job.

Remember, the interview hasn't begun yet. You're thinking the job through, talking to others, talking to yourself, and assembling the information into three categories.

We've talked about how to distinguish between the relatively straightforward Knowledge, Skills, and Abilities required by a particular job and other, supposedly more "subjective" qualities—and I've shown you how to translate some of those qualities into specific, job-relevant Behaviors.

WHAT IS THE JOB ENVIRONMENT?

But there are still other issues that crop up again and again in your preliminary investigations into job requirements. These issues will have less to do with what a person in the job has to do than with the person's ability to adapt to the peculiar conditions of this particular business and workplace. People will say things like, "Whoever is in this position should have lots of political savvy, know how to deal tactfully with different user groups, be able to work on evenings and weekends." Whoever has it must wear a beeper on weekends. There might be an unusual amount of deadline pressure. One of the people you're asking about job requirements might remind you of the fact that yours is an industry in which recent deregulation is having a considerable effect and whoever works here will have to be able to cope with change. It might be that in your organization, a high value is placed on a strong sense of ethics. Or, take something less grand, but perhaps just as important in its effect on whether a given individual might stay on the job. It might be that until enough office space can be acquired in this building (maybe next year), whoever is hired for this position will have to work in the building across the street and make a couple of trips between here and there every day for meetings.

Like Behaviors, a discussion of Environmental Issues is not likely to be found in the job description or in the performance reviews. Nevertheless, they are, as I will ademonstrate in the next several pages, very important factors for you to consider when determining how someone is likely to perform on a job, and how long they might stay.

Many interviewers hope to determine if a candidate will "fit in around here." But unless we have thought through the environment into which they fit, such judgments remain subjective.

HOW TO THINK THROUGH THE JOB ENVIRONMENT

When it comes to the job environment most interviewers think about the things like who potential employees might report to or what kind of pressures they'll be under, and they often stop there. While these factors are important, and I'm going to discuss them, they are not the only issues pertaining to the environment that need to be considered, or even the most important. Let's look at everything you need to think about, starting from the most general and working our way down to the most specific.

What Type of Business or Industry Are You in?

Your business or industry is unique and special. It has its own set of circumstances. There are certain attitudes and values that will get in the way and there are certain attitudes and values that will enable an employee to make a commitment, to work with full effort, and to stay for a reasonable period of time. What is special about your industry? What kind of changes is it going through? What are the popular opinions about it? How will someone feel telling other people they're working in your business?

Take the issue of glamour. At one end of the glamour scale are advertising agencies, the travel and airline industry, fashion, publishing, the entertainment and television industy ... at the other end of the glamour spectrum is no, not insurance, but the pest control industry. Having had the opportunity to work with the world's largest pest control company, I can tell you that they are quite organized and sophisticated. They employ programmers, salespersons, engineers, auditors, and secretaries—people whose tasks, at first sight, might not seem to be industry-specific. These roles also exist in the insurance and airline industry. From the standpoint of required Behaviors and Knowledge, Skills, and Abilities, perhaps a programmer analyst for a pest control company and a programmer analyst for a major airline are doing virtually the same tasks. Objectively they're the same—but try and get them to switch jobs. There may not be any practical difference, but there's a difference in image, and that matters to people.

Some people would rather you didn't know that they work for a pest control company. There are others who would be proud of it. Some people couldn't relate to working for a tobacco company or a defense contractor. Companies in these businesses are quite aware that individuals who are able to accept and commit to that type of business will stay longer and be more productive employees.

In any event, people who have taken jobs in industries where because of basic attitudes and values they don't feel they belong will probably move somewhere else pretty quickly. They are also potentially underproductive or disruptive while they're there.

Your Specific Organization

Narrowing our view even further, your particular organization within your business or industry has its own unique and special environment. This level of the job environment is currently called the "corporate culture." Perhaps it's a warm, supportive, benevolent, caring organization where everybody feels part of the whole and every division feels that Corporate Headquarters is always thinking about them. Perhaps there is clear communication and well-established systems and procedures, and all the support services are available, and all the things necessary to do your job on an everyday basis are right there within easy reach. Or . . . on the other hand . . . it just might be that this idealized portrait bears no resemblance at all to the place you go to work to every day. But whatever the truth is, it's not good or bad—it's just a reality. If it takes six people to sign off on a simple decision in your organization, then this is a fact that you as an interviewer should take careful note of, not as a flaw to hide from a talented candidate, but as one basis for selection. Someone who can't work in a bureaucratic structure is going to have a problem surviving even though he or she might be technically skilled and bright and have lots of energy and motivation. You must take the particular realities of your organization into account, whatever they may be.

Two Different Environments

To illustrate, I will tell you a story about two premier financial institutions whose hiring practices I happen to be personally familiar with, having worked with each of them as a consultant.

In Company A they purposely hire three times as many people as they need for any given position, whether it's an entry level position in the systems area, a training position in the audit area, or the credit training program. They say, in effect, to the three individuals hired for a particular position, "Only one of you will be here in a year. Good luck," and then they let these new employees fight it out. They believe that through this kind of highly charged competition the best talent will rise to the challenge.

Company B, on the other hand, has a completely different approach. Once they hire someone, they do everything they can to help that person succeed. Each new employee is given a mentor, a human resources department contact, and a feedback session after every engagement or assignment. And, if necessary, assistance in correcting deficiencies. They do everything possible to ensure the success of whoever they hire—because they want that person, as an individual, to succeed.

There are some candidates who would thrive and contribute more and be around longer in the first environment. That happens to be the kind of place that is best suited for them: They work better in a highly competitive atmosphere. And then, there are other candidates who would be better off in the second, more supportive environment, and therefore that's the kind of place they belong.

If somebody is mismatched to an organization, it doesn't mean that they will fail on day one. But you can be sure that they're not going to be around as long: There will be productivity problems, morale problems, attitude problems, and then finally the turnover problem—problems that you can avoid or reduce if you are able to determine ahead of time what kind of place your organization is and what kind of person is going to fit in best.

Division/Department/Function Area

But you're not hiring someone merely for your organization as a whole. You are hiring for a particular division, or department, or program, or subgroup, or unit. Well, each one of these has its own unique environment. Within a given organization there are some areas that have tremendous time pressure or deadline pressure and other areas that don't. There are different management styles in different departments and divisions, and even different geographical locations present employees with different challenges they will have to cope with and live with. You need to identify the realities of the subgrouping.

The Specific Job: Frustrations and Satisfiers

Finally, at the most specific, most nitty-gritty environment level, there is the specific job. Beyond the obvious realities that you and the candidate need to consider (issues like work schedules, extensive travel, last-minute overtime, weekend work), two other subtleties should not be overlooked. First, you will have to consider and evaluate the everyday frustrations that are an inevitable part of the job. Is this a job for which secretarial or word processing resources have to be shared and are therefore sometimes unavailable? Do a lot of people have to sign off on every decision no matter how trivial? Will whoever is lucky enough to get this job spend the first eight months in a tiny cubical amid falling plaster and workmen with drills and ladders while the shiny new offices on the 38th floor are being readied for human habitation? Are there changes in equipment or procedures that will require a lot of flexibility from this employee? Or is there a big project coming up that will call for a lot of weekend work?

Second, you should weigh and consider some of the satisfiers that the job has to offer as well—the everyday satisfiers that make the everyday frustrations tolerable. The sense of pride that comes from working on something that's really important, or seeing the results of what you do put to use; being told by other departments or user groups that you've made a real contribution. For some people, intellectual stimulation is a satisfier—they enjoy solving complex problems. Other people just like to have a lot to do and like to be kept busy. Undoubtedly in certain cases what one person defines as a frustration another will call a satisfier, and vice versa. But if anything at all connected with this job is a potential satisfier, be sure and find out what it is. Because if you find somebody with all the energy, motivation, initiative, and the personal qualities that fit every other aspect of the job, but the everyday satisfiers are meaningless to them, there will be nothing to build a fire under them and there will be no glue to hold them.

And, of course, this level would include the person to whom the prospective employee would report (presuming that information is available to you). What kind of management style does this manager or supervisor have? Supportive and encouraging? Sink or swim? If hired, would the candidate be working for someone who has had a lot of difficulty with subordinates in the past? This is also a facet of the job environment.

THE PRACTICAL VALUE OF CAREFULLY ORGANIZING JOB REQUIREMENTS

Now that I've walked you through the Knowledge, Skills and Abilities, Behaviors, and Environmental Issues and how to go about defining and evaluating them, I'd like to give you an example that pulls it all together. Let me see if I can show you the practical value of bothering to research and organize job requirements in the systematic way and with the kind of depth that I'm advising.

Let's suppose I'm interviewing Nick for a particular job. Nick is telling me about a project he worked on two years ago. After he has finished telling me about it I ask him the following seemingly casual question, "Tell me Nick, what are some of the things you liked best about that job?"

There's nothing very amazing or startling or fascinating about that question, and it may not impress you very much—nonetheless it is a potentially useful one—and one that can put things in perspective for you. It meets the five criteria of a well-designed interview question we'll discuss later in this book: It's easy to ask, it's easy to answer, it's seemingly casual, it doesn't telegraph what we're looking for, and it's easy to follow up. Its innocuousness is one of its values.

Since it's easy to answer, Nick responds by saying: "Well I must say, it was a pretty demanding job. I had a lot to do, a time frame to do it in, and a quality level to achieve, but how I did it was completely up to me. The order in which I did things, the sequencing, the formatting, whether I worked at one thing at a time or three things at once, who I checked with, if I focused on something for three days and something else for the next two—none of that mattered, as long as I got things done on time at the appropriate quality level. And I really loved the autonomy and freedom that that gave me; I think I was more productive because of it and I certainly loved it."

Well, that's interesting; but I submit to you, "So what?" We really don't know what this story means. We can guess at the qualities it implies, and ask him more about it, but it's only an interesting story for now. In the course of a half hour or 45 minutes I might pick up a dozen or more of these little stories from the candidate. By the end of the interview, what do they tell me about him? Well, he seems like a bright guy, and I get the impression he's mature. He's a pleasant person, has solid experience and a good technical background, and he seems to be levelheaded. I could get along with him and he seems to get along well with people. He seems really interested in the things I'll ask him to do around here . . . I have all sorts of impressions. Not necessarily incorrect, but subjective, and difficult to measure. That's the way most interviews are conducted. The interviewer chats with the candidate and gets impressions. When the candidate walks out the door, the interviewer weighs and balances the overall impressions and makes a judgment. This way of proceeding isn't irrational, but it's not as accurate as if we had understood the real job requirements in advance.

Back in the Preparation Stage

To demonstrate, let's back up. It happens that before I interviewed Nick or anybody else, back in my preparation for the interview, I spent time finding out about the job requirements. One of the things I learned in the course of my preinterview investigations was this: The environment of this job includes working on a small project team where everyone's individual activity needs to be coordinated carefully so that their efforts all come out at the same time. Another group will take that information to the next level. This could be a systems project, an audit team engagement, a marketing team strategy plan, or any other complex task requiring the coordination of individual efforts.

What does that really mean? That means that on an individual day, if I had that job, I might be told by my boss: "Bill, this is what I'd like you to work on today. As you know, Ken and Cliff and Karen and Kate are working on these other facets, here's the part I want you to work on. Now, here's the order in which I need you to do it, here's the formatting it has to be in, and here are some of the resources to get you started. Now I'm going to be out of the building most of the morning, but I'd like you to work on these items on your own—I'll call in about 10:30 to see if you're on target and make sure there are no dilemmas because of my not being around, and after lunch, if you can get to lunch, I'd like to meet with you to see how you're doing. And before you leave today you must check with me so that we can coordinate your activities with the others and so I can plan your agenda for tomorrow."

Now you may not want that job, but what I've learned about the environment of the job isn't good or bad, it's just a reality. This job happens to include that. I know about the job environment before I begin my interview. And I interview Chuck and Susan and Sandy, and I finally get to Nick. I walk him through his background step by step and I reach a particular job, the very job I referred to earlier. Now presume this is my first interview with Nick. He tells me about that project two years ago and I ask the same question at this point, "Tell me, Nick, what were some of the things you liked about that job?"

And, of course, he answers in the same way he did in my previous example: "Well I must say, it was a pretty demanding job. I had a lot to do, a time frame to do it in, a quality level to achieve, but how I did it was completely up to me. The order in which I did things, the sequencing, the formatting, whether I worked at one thing at a time or three things at once, who I checked with, if I focused on something for three days and something else for the next two—none of that mattered, as long as I got things done on time at the appropriate quality level. And I really loved the autonomy and freedom that that gave me; I think I was more productive because of it and I certainly loved it."

Now it's not just an interesting little story anymore. It is in fact going to cause a red flag to go up in my head. Given the circumstances of the job, with the close, over-the-shoulder direction and supervision, if he's right about himself being more productive working without much outside control, then here's a potential problem. The point of all this is that without an understanding of the job environment in detail, the information was just an "interesting story." Its significance was unclear. Now its relevance jumps out at me.

Notice I'm not going to jump to any conclusions (one of our common errors mentioned earlier). But now that I am alerted to this potential problem, I know I must search carefully throughout the rest of the interview (with techniques this book has yet to unveil) to see if this is a real problem. As I poke around, suppose I discover that Nick has experienced structure in a lot of settings. And he's stayed reasonable periods of time. He was productive and successful. Well then, my concern diminishes. I've found a preponderance of evidence to support the conclusion that while he may not prefer close supervision, he can handle it.

But suppose as I poke around in Nick's background, I find that he's never experienced a lot of structure. Or, worse yet, that when he has experienced it he's resisted, he's resented it, he's bucked against it, he still has negative things to say about supervisors, managers, co-workers ... professors, teachers, coaches ... anywhere in his life where someone tries to give him direction, he's fought it tooth and nail. Of course, he always blames them. He doesn't consider it a problem for himself. He always talks about himself in a positive light. He doesn't know he's revealing anything that might be a problem, but I recognize a pattern here that tells me there is a potential problem. At the end of the interview my red flag is still up. And so now I take all the facts and weigh and balance them to make a decision about Nick for this job or compare him with other candidates. I may still offer him the job. Nobody's perfect, and he has many other qualities that I want. So I still take him, knowing full well what I'm getting into, and I plan to supervise around it.

Or I say. "Well, I don't know, Bob and Nick, they're equally skilled, actually Nick has more skills than Bob, although Bob has the basics—but Bob matches the environment better and has more of the behaviors we need: Overall, Bob's the best of these two very talented candidates."

There is yet another angle from which I could assess this situation. I could say, "Nick is a pretty talented person, but, well, let's see, I think the best thing for us to do would be to shunt him down the path with that particular manager or supervisor, who gives a few more degrees of freedom, and let's give him more autonomy on special projects occasionally. . . . " I see a way to maximize his effectiveness by placing him in circumstances that will make the most effective use of his talents. And so I make placement recommendations for this talented person that will increase the likelihood of us being able to hold on to him the longest, and that will see to it he is as productive as he can be.

The lesson to be learned from the example of Nick is that if you make an effort to think through the Knowledge, Skills and Abilities, Behaviors, and Environmental Issues surrounding the job, you will have a context in which to place any information you collect, and the meaning of what candidates say will jump out at you. Without this, we are just chatting and getting impressions.

≡≡≡6≡EVERYTHING ELSE YOU NEED TO DO TO BE PREPARED FOR THE INTERVIEW

While ascertaining the job requirements is the single most important component of preparation, your task is by no means complete when you've accomplished that. The other items are little things, but there are a lot of them: How can you get the best use out of résumés and applications? Where do you conduct the interview? What do you bring to the interview? What do you tell the receptionist to do when the candidate arrives? What information should you have at your fingertips? These miscellaneous but important issues are covered very thoroughly in the following pages, from which you should be able to compile a checklist of steps that apply to your particular circumstances.

HOW TO USE RÉSUMÉS AND APPLICATIONS

Résumés and applications can be useful as screening tools. They can provide assurance that job candidates will meet the minimum requirements for Knowledge, Skills, and Abilities before interviewers commit themselves to putting in all the time and effort an interview can entail. They also can be employed prior to the interview as sources of clues for questions to ask. Résumés highlight the information that candidates consider important, the specifics of their backgrounds, and perhaps a description of a particular experience that might help to round out your understanding of them—however, useful as these documents can be, I advise against relying too heavily on them.

If Possible, Obtain Application Beforehand

I have never been able to understand why it is that after interviewing and, in some cases, even making a decision to hire, the last thing many organizations do is to send the candidate down to personnel to fill out the application. The résumé is the candidate's public relations sheet—and the interviewer will find it useful—but it's also helpful to have the completed application.

What is the application for? First, it's a legal document which candidates must sign, acknowledging the truthfulness of the information they give. Second, while résumés have all kinds of formats, the application is a document specific to your organization. You are familar with this form, its layout, and how it is organized. It can help you to become focused more quickly before and during the interview. Finally, it requires the applicant to respond clearly and in detail. For example, the application asks for the month and year of the beginning and end of a given job. This can be much more revealing than the "1987–1988" you might find on a résumé. The answers to the questions "Why you left" and "Salary desired," which are required on some applications, can be very helpful as well.

In short, the application is a useful device, and if your

company's procedures would allow you to obtain this document before the interview, it would be a good idea to do so. You might mail it to the candidates ahead of time, or have them fill it out in the reception area when they first come in. Ask the candidates to come to the office a little earlier than scheduled so that they will have time for the paperwork. Don't allow candidates to say "see attached résumé" on the application in lieu of filling it out. Some interviewers are reluctant to ask for a completed application for senior or professional positions, thinking the request may put candidates off. Of course, no one wants to fill out an application, but if you simply explain that it is part of your regular procedure and is necessary for legal reasons, candidates usually respond without hesitation. While no one piece of behavior should be the basis for a hiring decision, the active refusal to complete an application would not be on the positive side of the ledger.

Get Résumés Ahead of Time

While theoretically someone should have arranged to send you a copy of the candidate's résumé in advance in order to give you the time to study it, you can't always depend on that happening; so whether you are an employment professional or a line manager, you should do what you can to avoid finding yourself in the uncomfortable position of saying, "I'm interviewing somebody in five mintues—I never got the application!" or "I never got the résumé!"

Since you are the person to whom the résumé will make the most difference, be sure you get it. Do something! Make phone calls, have someone send it to you. If necessary, leave your office, walk down the hall, and get it yourself.

Take Notes

Now you have the résumé before you, with ample time to spare before the interview. At this point, most interviewers—at least those who don't interview for a living—proceed as follows: They glance at the résumé, they say, "Oh, okay, I'll ask about that, that seems interesting . . . uh, I wonder why she took those courses . . . ah, that experience looks extensive, but what training could she have received . . . ?" and so on. Then they put down the candidate's paperwork, go to the reception area and get the candidate, and conduct the interview. They have written nothing down—why should they when they will be seeing the candidate only a matter of minutes after reading the résumé and formulating their questions?

If you follow this procedure, however, there is a strong possibility you will never get around to asking several of the questions you had planned to ask based on your review of the résumé. You will get caught up in the candidate's background, you will get sidetracked, and you won't remember those questions. Certainly, in those circumstances when you might be conducting a great number of interviews in a day—on campus, or in a new facility, or in the human resources department of a large organization—you can't be certain of remembering every question that went through your mind when you glanced at that piece of paper earlier.

If you are going to review somebody's paperwork, whether you have an application or a résumé or—on campus—a data sheet, make a note of questions as they occur to you. Then, with that list on your desk, you can be sure all those questions you thought of before the interview will actually get asked during the interview. As elementary and mechanical as it might seem, that little step can be useful. It is the professional thing to do, and it will safeguard against you ever finding yourself right after the applicant has left snapping your fingers and saying, "I meant to ask about X, but I forgot." By the way, the résumé and application are legal documents; do not write on them. Use a separate piece of paper for your questions.

What if You Get the Materials at the Last Minute?

But then again, despite all your efforts you still might not receive the résumé or application ahead of time. You might get it the moment the candidate walks in the door. These things happen. The candidate walks in, sits down, and hands you the résumé. If that's the case, to make the best out of a bad situation, say to the candidate: "Well, Maria, I appreciate the opportunity to talk to you, but obviously I've just received your résumé this moment. I'm going to take a minute or so just to quickly review it. So just relax a minute, and let me take a quick scan."

If you spend more than two or three minutes reading it, it may become awkward, but if the process takes only a minute or two, the candidate can look around the room and relax while you take a quick scan. Get an idea of the range of their experience, education, training, and the special issues that might be important to them. It is not the ideal situation but it's better to do that than to try to read the résumé for the first time while you're conducting the interview.

What if You Don't Get the Résumé or Application?

Suppose you can't get any paperwork ahead of time and the candidate doesn't bring any at the time of the interview. It certainly doesn't mean you can't conduct an effective interview. But under those circumstances it would be even more critical for you to walk through the candidate's background step-by-step to make sure that nothing is left out and that the information you get is not left entirely to the candidate's discretion. Without the paperwork, you may not be able of focus the discussion as quickly and efficiently. But at least with the structure and probing techniques I'll introduce in subsequent chapters, you're going to have a systematic way of proceeding.

WHERE SHOULD YOU CONDUCT THE INTERVIEW?

Privacy is the Goal

When it comes to deciding on where to conduct an interview, your most important consideration should be privacy:

That means a room with a door that shuts and walls that go to the ceiling. If your personal space does not happen to possess these desired features—if you're in a cubical or open space—then you should try to obtain temporary access to some other area in which to conduct the interview.

A conference room is one common alternative. However, this kind of space often presents problems that should be dealt with carefully. For one thing, such a room may be enormous. If that's the case, set up a little corner to be your interviewing area and, to avoid interruptions, consider putting a note on the door saying, "Interviewing, please do not disturb." This will be more private than an area which, to the eye, might seem quite compact and perhaps intimate, but where candidates can hear the conversations in the next cubical and realize that your conversation with them can be overheard as well.

Remember, privacy isn't just a place, it's a state of mind. Even if you are conducting the interview in a quiet office, complete with lots of polished dark woods and original oil paintings on the walls, the effect of all that mellowness will be lost and both your concentration and that of the candidate disrupted if every five minutes there is someone standing in the doorway waving a spreadsheet at you, or the phone keeps ringing and you keep having to interrupt the interview to answer it. To avoid interruptions, alert the secretary to pick up on the first ring, turn off your phone if possible, or call forward it. If you are likely to be periodically interrupted, you might want to warn the candidate ahead of time.

What if You Can't Get Privacy?

Privacy may not always be obtainable. Still, even if you have no other options and you are forced to interview in a cubical or some place where the conversation may be overheard, there are a couple of things you can do to make the best of the situation.

First, alert the people around you that you're interviewing, so maybe they'll disappear for a while or at least keep their voices down. Then you might actually say to the candidate, "Well, Bob, I wish we had an alternate place to interview, but with your cooperation we'll make the best of it."

If you acknowledge that you realize it's not ideal, you put the candidate in the same boat with you. You're working together to make the best of it. Ignoring it causes candidates to say to us during debriefings after interviews, "Oh, I guess they didn't care, I guess it didn't matter to them, they had no sensitivity to the issue," even though the interviewer probably did.

Interviewing in Public Places

Again, this is not recommended, but there are circumstances where you may have to interview in public places—if you are interviewing people around the country, or you have traveled to a different city to conduct the interview because that's where the candidates happen to be, or you are a regional manager interviewing out of your own particular geographical location. In such cases, you may be forced to interview in, say, a restaurant. First, try not to do it at the height of the lunch rush hour if it can be helped. Schedule the interview for earlier than the busiest time or later. If you must interview over lunch, then I recommend that you have lunch quickly, finish lunch, and over coffee start the interview, thereby reducing distractions and interruptions. Try and find a table at the far end of the restaurant and position the candidate's chair to face the wall, so that there will be fewer distractions. Again, you're making the best out of an awkward situation.

Are you interviewing in the lobby of a hotel? The lobby of your own facility? The employee dining room? The basic rule to follow for all public places is to try to conduct the interview during a time during which it is likely to be least crowded and to move yourselves to the far end of the facility or wherever distractions can be minimized.

WHAT TO BRING TO THE INTERVIEW

With the possible exception of pen and paper all of the items covered here are optional. Since I am assuming for the moment that you are responsible for every facet of the information-collecting and information-giving phases of the interview, these are things you may need to have on hand during the interview. Consider this an annotated checklist, and select those items relevant to your role in the interview process. Remember that the most obvious items are routinely overlooked by interviewers. Good preparation can help avoid awkwardness during an interview.

The Basics

You should be slightly embarrassed to have to ask the candidate, "Can I borrow your pen?" Yet candidates repeatedly remark on how interviewers are so ill-prepared they have nothing to write with, or ask: "What was your name again? I can't seem to find your résumé." Make certain you have a few pens or pencils as well as something to write on. You should also have with you the candidate's résumé, the application if the candidate has filled out one, and your evaluation form if your organization has one.

Optional

Paperwork on Other Candidates. If you have interviewed other candidates for this job, reviewing the previous paperwork on other candidates that you've seen either in the recent or the distant past would help add to your understanding of the candidates and would better enable you to "calibrate" your judgment of the qualities required.

Job-Related Information to Give the Candidate. In some cases it may be useful for you to have at your fingertips an organization chart, an outline of a training program the candidate might experience, work samples, a description the candidate might experience, work samples, a description of your services, or maybe even actual samples of the products the company may offer. Please note, however, that you may not want to show all of these things to the candidate, but you now have them in case they would be useful to you. You should also be particularly careful when to show them so as not to telegraph what you're looking for or reveal confidential information.

Geographical Information. In cases where the job might require the candidate to relocate, it could be important to have some information on hand about the area: about schools, housing, and recreation. You might want to have this kind of information available for the information-giving phase of the interview either to show or to use to answer questions. This type of information heads the list of "information I wish the interviewer had given me during the interview."

Benefits Information. Of course, you may not be the one responsible for giving benefits information, but it might help if you could answer some questions or be generally knowledgeable. Suppose the candidate asks, "I heard about the great tuition reimbursement plan your company has, but I also heard from the last interviewer that there is so much overtime and weekend work that I might not be able to take advantage of it—is that true?" Would you know the answer to this question?

Your Business Card. If you have a business card you should bring it. But consider: Are you the person that the candidate should contact after the interview is over? If you give candidates your business card, it might be construed that you are giving them the message to call you, or even to write you a note afterward. (It used to be that it was extra special if, after an interview, the applicants wrote a note to their interviewers. Now, if they don't do it it's noticeable.)

In any event, if you give a candidate your business card, you should expect a call. If you do not want that person to call you, then you should say, "Here is my card as a reminder of our conversation, but here is the person you should be contacting after the interview process." Take a pen and cross out your phone number and write in the name and phone number of the person the candidate should call for information on the progress of their application.

Certainly, in situations like the campus interview, where candidates talk to one another, you should make sure not to give your card out selectively. Either give the card to everybody or to no one. Otherwise, the third student will say, "Uh oh, I obviously didn't do well, I didn't get a business card."

Company Literature

Annual Report. For most managers and superiors the annual report is not a document that is referred to on an everyday basis. But if you are going to hand the candidate your annual report, it would be wise to read it first. That way you won't find yourself in the position of hearing a candidate saying to you, "Oh, by the way, I noticed in your annual report that . . .", and have no idea what they're referring to. Of course, as a general rule, it makes sense to be reasonably familiar with any information you give candidates so that you can appear to be articulate and knowledgeable.

Product Descriptions, Brochures, Newsletters. Perhaps more useful than annual reports are product descriptions, division brochures, or operations summaries. Newsletters are a nice touch—candidates report that they read them with interest.

What to Bring When Interviewing on Site

If you interview occasionally in a location other than your office, you should maintain a folder containing all the standard things that you bring to every interview. A month or two later, at the time of an interview, you can stick a particular candidate's résumé and application in that folder and go to the site of the interview with the assurance that you have everything you need.

Have a Record of the Candidate's Schedule

One last note: Assuming that, as is usually the case, the candidate is seeing more than one interviewer at your organization on a given day, at least find out who is before you and who is after you on the schedule. If you know who is before you and the candidate hasn't arrived in your office, you know who to call to find out if they're just late or if they haven't come in that day. If you know who to hand the candidate to afterward, there's no awkwardness if the candidate says, "Well, where do I go next?"

III ≡≡≡THE INTERVIEW

Building on the ideas introduced in Parts I and II, Chapters 7–17 lay out on the table, for leisurely examination, the skills that you'll be deploying during the 30–45 minutes of your actual face-to-face encounter with a candidate.

In Chapter 7, "Building the Proper Atmosphere," you'll learn very specifically how to generate the kind of relaxed, spontaneous atmosphere that gets the best results in the interview. Chapter 8, "Translating the Job Requirements into a Form that Applies to a Candidate: Can Do, Will Do, and Fit Factors," takes the job-related categories introduced earlier (see Chapter 3) and translates them into terms that apply to the candidate you're interviewing.

In Chapter 9, "How to Organize the Interview: Interview Guide—Part 1" and Chapter 10, "The Logic Behind Structure: Interview Guide—Part 2," I'll explain the intentions and values built into the Interview Guide (see Chapter 9, Fig. 6). This Interview Guide is the very heart of this book. It presents the structure that will obtain the best and most reliable data and serves as as springboard for all the other tactics you will be using.

Having covered the overall structure of the interview, we'll hone in on the techniques that are needed to make that structure work. The actual, nitty-gritty conversational elements in Chapter 11, "The Art of Asking Good Questions"; Chapter 12, "What Questions You Should Ask: One-Step Probes"; Chapter 14, "How to Make the Interview Seem Conversational—and Still Maintain Control"; Chapter 15, "How to Phrase Your Questions: Avoiding Closed-Ended

Questions"; Chapter 16, and "How to Probe for Details and Test for Truthfulness."

On the way I'll make the case for the optimum time frame for an effective interview in Chapter 13, "How Much Time Should You Spend in the Interview?"

Finally, since the best interview in the world isn't much use if the candidate whose best for the job won't accept your offer, Chapter 17, "Presenting Information Persuasively and Closing the Interview Properly," shows a way of presenting information that sells the candidate on the job and on your organization. Then it shows you how to wrap up the interview in a way that's efficient and leaves all candidates feeling good about the process.

≡≡≡7≡BUILDING THE PROPER ATMOSPHERE

Fill in the blank. "Admiral Rickover is the father of the
_____ ."

The nuclear navy? The atomic sub-
marine? Very good. You may then also know that he is, in
addition, the father of the Stress Interview. Admiral Rickover is the person who perfected it. On a day he was feeling
particularly warm and benevolent, he would nail a chair to
the floor and say to the candidate, "Pull up a chair, Captain,"
and wait to see what the candidate would do when the chair
wouldn't move from the corner of the room where it had been
nailed. How would you like to be ushered to a closet by the
interviewer? Would you enter? If you did and the door was
shut behind you, would you knock to get out? How hard?

Putting candidates under pressure or stress in the interview, in order to gauge how they're going to handle the

identifiable pressures or stresses of the job, is a flawed and inadequate technique. If it worked, it would be my responsibility to tell you how it worked and show you how to make it work. However, it doesn't work. All the research on interviewing makes it clear that putting candidates under pressure or stress in the interview is only successful in predicting they're going to be able to handle pressures or stresses in an interview. The results cannot be generalized back to the job itself. This doesn't mean, however, that the goal of predicting how a candidate will react under pressure isn't a valid one—after all, if the job has identifiable pressures and stresses, there ought to be a way of finding out whether the candidate will be able to deal with them. This can be accomplished best, however, without having to resort to extreme—and ineffective—techniques like those described above.

What kind of overall tone or atmosphere is most productive, then? To begin with, not only an atmosphere of tension, but even a stiff, formal, mechanical, or constricted atmosphere should be avoided. We want

☐   A conversational tone
☐   A relatively informal atmosphere
☐   Reduced tension and anxiety
☐   A sense of mutual trust and respect

Since it takes at least some effort to create this tone, I'd better explain why it's worth doing, before I discuss how to do it.

THE BUSINESS VALUE OF BOTHERING TO BUILD THE RIGHT ATMOSPHERE

Why do we want to bother with creating the right atmosphere? How does it benefit the interview process? Well, to cite a few reasons, building the proper atmosphere:

- ☐ Gets more and better data
- ☐ Gets a more natural response
- ☐ Gives a positive impression of your organization
- ☐ Increases the "accept rate" of talented candidates

The importance of the first two items—getting more and better data and eliciting a more natural response—might have piqued your interest. After all, if I can show you a way to get more, better quality data and a more natural picture of the person, independent of the particular questions you asked, I'm sure you'd be interested. The other items, however, may not be immediate "grabbers." These benefits of building the proper tone are often passed over by interviewers, and there is clear evidence that they are quite significant issues. So I'll start with those.

Goodwill and Positive Impression of Your Organization

Developing and promoting goodwill serves an important business purpose. When you conduct an interview you are bringing a stranger into a brief, but very memorable contact with your organization. Whether you interview 10 people for every one you hire or only three, the fact remains that the vast majority of candidates don't come on board as employees. Where do they go, all those people who were interviewed but not hired? They don't go to cracks in the earth. They go to competitors. They go to clients. They go to other employers in your industry, they go to related industries or government agencies. They are potential users of your products or services. And they all carry with them an attitude about your organization based on their one human contact with it—the interview. This may not be a fair way to evaluate a complex organization, but that's what people do. If they experience the interview as one in which they were not fully heard or fairly treated, they carry a negative attitude and message wherever they go.

You could be very tough-minded and say, "I'm not interested in hiring them, so what do I care what they think?" But you may be interested in them three years from now once they gain some experience, knowledge, or some expertise that would be useful to you. And even if that never happens, someday they might be sitting next to someone who you desperately want to hire, and the last thing you want is for them to turn to that person and say: "Oh, I was interviewed there only a year ago myself. What a horrible place. They don't care about people there, they're disorganized, they're mechanical . . . ." And don't forget that these same candidates you didn't hire are potential users of your products or services.

Talented people with choices are often influenced by what they hear about your organization from others. After a campus interview, when a student goes back to the dormitory, the cafeteria, or class, what's the first question they're asked? "How did it go? What happened?" If the interview was cut short, and with good reason, what's the reply? Maybe it would be, "Well, um, we left after about fifteen minutes because it was quite apparent that my background didn't match at all with the job requirements, and I was actually wasting the time of the interviewer and that's why we ended early!" I don't think so. No, what they say is: "I was there for about fifteen minutes and the interviewer threw me out! He didn't even give me a chance to explain myself!"

You may know that some campus interviewers find that some students don't show up for their appointment at the end of the day. Occasionally, that's because of what that student has been hearing about the interviewer. Every candidate should leave with the feeling that he or she has been fully heard and fairly treated. Think of the number of people you personally interview a year. Multiply that by everyone else in your organization who interviews. Multiply that number by five years—we may be talking about thousands and thousands of people—we have the equivalent of a major public relations campaign!

More and Better Data and a More Natural Response

Having pointed out how what you do during the course of the interview can affect the goodwill and reputation of your organization, I'd like to turn your attention to the following point: If you create a conversational tone and a relatively informal atmosphere, you'll get more information, better quality information, and a more natural picture of the person.

If the candidate feels comfortable, he or she is more likely to answer your questions and add information. This spontaneous information is highly predictive data—it goes beyond the candidate's prepared presentation, beyond an intellectual answer to the original question. In some respects you could say that creating the conditions for spontaneous responses gets the results interviewers are groping for when they start off the interview with, "Just by reading this résumé I'll never be the expert on you that you are, so tell me about yourself." But it does it in a way that works, without the interviewer relinquishing control of the interview.

Compare the following two interviews. In interview A:

- ☐ I ask Jeanne a question.
- ☐ She answers me.
- ☐ I ask another question.
- ☐ She answers.
- ☐ Another question.
- ☐ Another answer.

I continue this for 40 minutes. Well, that can work. It's a bit impersonal and not conversational, but she gives me lots of information and it seemed pretty efficient to me; I seem to have covered a lot in a short period of time.

But let's compare that interview with interview B. Now you interview Jeanne, and ask all the same questions I did. But suppose you also do something to create the kind of tone or mood in the interview that makes it seem conversational. You're still asking all the same questions I asked in the first interview and you'll get the same information I got, but with you she'll feel comfortable enough and conversational enough to occasionally throw in an aside. This time she'll feel comfortable enough to add: "Well, of course, that's the way it was supposed to work, but, I must say, the bureaucratic structure there drove me crazy. As a matter of fact, one of the reasons why I got out of that place was," or "One of the ways I got around it was," or "One of the things that really frustrated me was ...." Subtleties about her. Things she hadn't prepared to talk about in advance. She begins to emerge as a person. What really bothered her. How she dealt with issues. You couldn't even think of the questions to ask to get at these subtleties, which emerge more of their own accord if you create the proper tone or mood.

Positive rapport gives you the opportunity to get details not ordinarily available, things you would never think to ask about. And, though I call them "details," they may be of key importance in distinguishing one candidate from another or in signaling the areas that will call for further probing later in the interview.

HOW TO BUILD THE PROPER ATMOSPHERE

You may have your own ideas about what you can do to put a candidate in the right frame of mind for the interview. Obviously, there's no need to be tied to the particular items I'm about to mention. But you're a lot more likely to be successful if you know what the proper atmosphere is and also know of a logical way to achieve it.

The process of building the proper atmosphere can be defined by three distinct phases. Each has a unique purpose. Don't be deceived by the fact that they seem similar to social courtesies. They are steps designed to help you get more and better information from the candidate. You should be in command of these simple but powerful phases of the process.

☐ The greeting
☐ Small talk
☐ Maintaining rapport

The Greeting

By focusing on something as commonsensical as the greeting, I may seem to be looking at things a little too closely, dicing things a little too small. Next, I'll be telling you how to breathe! And indeed, most people can be forgiven for taking "Hello" for granted. "Hello" seems to be a word without content; and, "How are you?" as everyone except a crashing bore recognizes, usually isn't a real question. That's because the things we say at those moments aren't about what they claim to be about. They have an unspoken subtext; they are the ways we have of tacitly orienting a new person coming into our orbit—and that is precisely why, effortless as they may seem, they have an impact on this issue of building the proper atmosphere.

We're talking about what happens during the initial contact with the candidate, the first 30 seconds, 60 seconds, or so. The interview has not yet officially begun, but you are already working. It's your job at this point to overcome and diffuse the tension and awkwardness that every candidate will inevitably feel as they approach the interview. Remember, they're coming into a new and unfamiliar territory and are therefore not totally at ease to begin with, and in addition, they're coming in to be evaluated. No matter how confident somebody is as a human being, how mature they are, how self-assured they are, or even how self-assured they appear to you in the interview, no one is their natural, charming, witty, clever, completely open self when they know they're being evaluated.

Whether you're going on a first date, meeting your in-laws for the first (or hundredth) time, or you're shaking hands with a politician or celebrity, you want to be your most clever and most charming self, but under those circumstances, too often, you end up acting quite differently. You spill coffee, you say silly things, you can't talk, you say, "Uh huh, uh huh," rather than anything of substance. Why is that? It's because you're trying hard and feel too self-conscious to behave as your most open self.

Inevitably, the candidate is experiencing reactions like this. What we want to do is take some steps during the greeting that will diffuse the initial awkwardness. You engage in these behaviors already in your everyday social interactions. Say you're giving a dinner party. You're talking to two of the more interesting guests 10 or 15 minutes before you're going to have everyone sit down for dinner. The doorbell rings. A guest near the door opens it, and two more guests arrive. Chances are that you wouldn't stay at the far end of the living room, and look at your guests framed in the doorway and shout, "Come on in—join the fun!" No, you'd say, "Excuse me," to the people you're talking to. You'd hurry to the door, give the new guests a handshake (or a hug if you know them well enough), take their coats or show them where to put their coats, lead them to the bar, maybe mix them a drink, introduce them to a few people . . . and then back off.

If I were to ask you, "Why do you bother doing that?," your first reaction would probably be, "Well, that's the job of the host." But when you think about it, you'll realize you're actually trying to influence the tone or atmosphere of your get-together. When everyone finally sits down for dinner, the last thing you want is for your guests to be staring at one another in silence. Maybe you know about those parties; that's where you can hear everybody's fork hitting their plates. That's the party during which the host or hostess coughs nervously and says, "Well, why don't we all go around the table and talk about our last vacation?! And we'll start with you, Robert." How contrived. You don't want that. What you want is for Jerry to start talking to Robert, and while they're talking, David's been busy talking to Betsy. But when Betsy hears something that Jerry said and she turns to him and says, "Oh, I didn't realize you were involved in that. I myself . . . ." Meanwhile, Robert joins a conversation across from him. They have cross-conversations. People are interrupting one another as one idea triggers another. You have spontaneity. That means everybody is having a good time. It's not stiff and formal.

You want to create that atmosphere of spontaneity in an interview. The initial greeting uses the same logic you might use in any social situation.

There are three things that the research on interviewing indicates you should always do in the course of greeting a candidate. These are the most powerful means of affecting people right in the beginning, as well as the things candidates remember after the interview as affecting them. What's the magical formula? It is important to follow the sequence:

1. Call them by name.

2. Introduce yourself.

3. Thank them for coming.

Three simple things. Altogether they take about 30 seconds to do, but they have a payoff. Let's take them point by point.

Call Them by Name

People's names are quite important to them. You should use the candidate's full name when you first make contact. Calling people by name makes it clear that you know who they are. Candidates, students, and highly experienced professionals alike have told me in debriefings: "With that interviewer, I wasn't sure if they had the right résumé in front of them. I don't think they're going to remember me after this interview; they never called me by name at the beginning or any time during the interview."

On college campuses, with the considerable number of candidates you have to go through, it is quite possible that you may actually have the wrong résumé in front of you. By the middle of the interview you may find yourself calling the candidate by the wrong name. "No, that's not me," they'll tell you. And, "Oh, sorry, you're the next résumé, aren't you?" you'll respond. If you call somebody by name during the initial contact, and periodically during the interview, you'll be certain to avoid that embarrassment and you'll also reduce the uncertainty on the part of the candidate.

Should you use their first name? In an American context, calling people by their first name after the initial contact usually works well. However, if the candidate is significantly older than you or if they seem rather formal, it might be better to use last name. After all, you don't want to create tension, you want to reduce it. Calling candidates by name is the important thing. If they're from another culture—the Far East, the Middle East, Latin America—but have gone to school in the United States, I might still be tempted to call them by their first name. But if they went to school in those other cultures, you should call them by their last name, recognizing that in those cultures, people tend to be more formal.

Should you ask for help in pronouncing a name? If you are uncertain about how to pronounce a name, you certainly could ask. But here's what happens all too often. The interviewer asks how to pronounce a name, but never uses it during the interview for fear of mispronouncing it. Or they proceed to say it grossly incorrectly throughout the interview. The candidate may wince inside each time it happens.

So, if you are going to bother in the interview to ask how to pronounce a last name, I advise you to hold that part off until you actually sit down with the candidate in your office or in the interviewing area. At that point, write the pronunciation phonetically so that periodically during the interview you can say it correctly. Sometimes even a first name can pose difficulties. It may be that one particular Matthew prefers to be called Matt, and another one hates it. Some Richards like to be called Dick and some don't. There are Patricias who do, and others who do not, like the nickname Pat. Again, go ahead and ask if you like, but do it when you're in a position to make a note of the answer.

Introduce Yourself

Telling candidates your name and title may not be sufficient to properly introduce yourself to them. Remember what you're trying to do—you're building the proper atmosphere by orienting the candidates—and think of their problem. They're wondering: "Who in the world is this person? Is this a person I might work for, or is it someone on my own level I would work with? Does this person know anything about my technical background?"

The candidates' ability to relax and be spontaneous, even their particular way of expressing themselves and characterizing things will be affected to some degree by their understanding of who you are. In some circumstances, it may be patently obvious to them who you are. Perhaps they have had a previous contact with you. Maybe they've been briefed carefully, so they know who you are. But if they don't—or you have no reason to suspect they do—then your job is to say in a sentence or two something that immediately positions you in the organization.

Thank Them for Coming

When candidates are debriefed, one of the things that they say is: "With that interviewer, right from the beginning, I felt as though they were glad to talk with me. I didn't feel as though I was interrupting their day. It seemed as if they had actually been looking forward to talking with me. It was clear to me that they had done their homework about me—it really made me feel a lot more comfortable to have that happen in the beginning."

What sophisticated device did the interviewer use to communicate that complex message? The interviewer said: "Well, Matthew, I appreciate the opportunity to talk with you today. I've read through your résumé. There are a lot of interesting things I saw there, and I've been looking forward to the opportunity of going over your background with you. Come on in."

That's it. That's all it takes. In your own words make it clear that you've read through the candidate's material, that you're glad to see them, and that you're looking forward to the interview. Something like that defuses the awkwardness a candidate often feels. Perhaps as a candidate you yourself have encountered an interviewer who seemed distracted or rushed, and you realized you were a big interruption. The last thing that person really wanted to do at that moment was to interview you. That's not the kind of tone you want to communicate. It doesn't encourage openness on the part of the candidate.

The three items in the order given—Call them by name, Introduce yourself, Thank them for coming—are the critical ones, but of course there are other possibilities that may occur to you. Some interviewers offer coffee if it is readily available. Do whatever makes sense to you to help candidates feel welcome and comfortable when they first sit down.

Small Talk

You've gone through the initial greeting, you've brought the candidate in, you've sat them down, now we're at stage two: small talk. Many people look on this phase of the interview as the awkward, mechanical little process that convention forces them to engage in just before the real task begins. If you interpret it that way, you might as well skip it, because it will not serve you well. But if you recognize its intention, you might be able to get it to work for you, because it's more subtle than it might seem. The purpose of this phase is to "lubricate" candidates verbally.

To get them rolling and establish a pattern in which they, and not you, do most of the talking.

Many interviewers think it relaxes people to talk at them. Perhaps tell them about yourself in detail or describe the job. That's a mistake. Not only is it not effective to give data up front because it telegraphs your punches, but it also does not relax people. Let me explain why. Perhaps at one time or another you've been called on to stand up and make a few announcements at a professional association, or to do a presentation, for example, in a training program. I'm sure that at some time in your career, faced with a challenge like that, you have found yourself getting a little nervous, at least during the first few seconds. Maybe no one else in the room noticed, but your hands were shaking a little, your voice wasn't as strong as you wanted it to be—but a few seconds later you were fine. Imagine getting up in front of the group and waiting for that nervousness to pass before you begin your presentation. Big mistake. That would make you more nervous! In fact, what defuses the tension a person inevitably feels in those circumstances is talking, and thus ending the suspense. Actors standing in the wings are notoriously nervous, but as soon as they take one step onto the stage and start speaking their lines, the agony ends. They're into their role and the jitters are gone.

The purpose of the small talk stage is to start candidates talking and get them loosened up. It's a process that should take about one or two minutes. Now, how do you do it?

Ask a Procedural Question About an Outside Interest. If you can manage it, the perfect method is to come prepared with a question about some hobby, some outside interest mentioned in their résumé or application. If it's possible— for a handy fact like that may not always be available—find something of that sort, a neutral, a nonevaluative item, and ask about it procedurally (this is a subtle but important point). That means don't look at Beth's background and say: "Beth, before we go into the details of your professional background, I notice that you're a golfer. As a matter of fact, you've been in some tournaments it seems. What connection do you see between tournament play in golf and being an employee in our organization?" That's not the question to ask. This isn't the interview yet. You'd have a much better chance of loosening Beth up if you said: "Beth, before we go into the details of your professional background, I notice that you're a golfer. As a matter of fact, I see you've been in some tournaments. Now, I know about basic golf, but I've never been in tournament play....? Since players keep their own score, how do the officials know it's correct? How does that work?"

Or, say the candidate enjoys outdoor activities—camping or fishing. You might ask: "Phil, I haven't had a chance to do much fishing. By the way, I never understood why people get into those big hip boots and climb into the water—why don't they just stand on the shore and throw in the line?"

It may seem contrived in this context, but when you actually do this in an interview, in the right tone, you'll be amazed at what happens. The effect is instantaneous. As people start to answer your question, they lean back in the chair and say, "Well, it's really kind of simple, there are three reasons...." You can see them relax right in front of you, because it's something they know a lot about and they also know they're not being rated on their answer.

How to Ask About the Weather. However, you may not have the necessary information for the examples given above. When forced to use other things because there is nothing specific to the candidate to go on, interviewers usually retreat to the weather, the trip to the office, and all that. I prefer to avoid that kind of small talk, because it usually goes nowhere. "Isn't it a beautiful day out? Spring is finally here." To which the candidate loquaciously responds, "Yes, it is a beautiful day." And then you say, "Well, I see you used to work at Honeywell. Tell me about it." That isn't small talk. It doesn't get them loosened up.

If you are forced to use items like the weather or the

traffic, at least recognize the necessity of asking about them in an open-ended way. Your goal is to get the candidate to speak, not to get the answer to the question. And so I'd say: "Well, Mike, before we go into the details of your professional background, I just want to let you know that I've been cooped up in this office since early this morning, and I'm kind of curious what's it like out there. It was a little threatening when I first came in. What's it like out there now?" Or, "I notice you live up north, what route did you come in on? I know there's some construction out there. How was your trip in?" Rather than, "Did you have a good trip in?" or, "Isn't it nice out?" We're more likely to get a sentence or two or three out of them by phrasing it as an open question.

Maintaining Rapport

Maintaining rapport is something you'll work at throughout the interview. Right now I'm going to cover the things you can do in the interview to assist in maintaining good rapport.

Seating Arrangements (see Fig. 3). Interviewing across a desk is interviewing across a barrier. Any human relations expert will tell you that barriers decrease communication. The problem is that if you take that concept to its logical extreme, wouldn't that mean that the best way to interview would be in a barren room with only you, the applicant and two chairs, so you can really relate? Somehow it seems pretty clear that wouldn't be effective either. It would be too intense. This is not an encounter group.

If you have no choice, if you are on campus, and you have an airless cubical with a card table, and you are forced to interview across it, you can adapt to these circumstances. Even a big desk in your office can be made to work. Be sure to turn over confidential information, neaten it up, and move the in/out box so you and the candidate are not staring at each other around it. What you say and how you

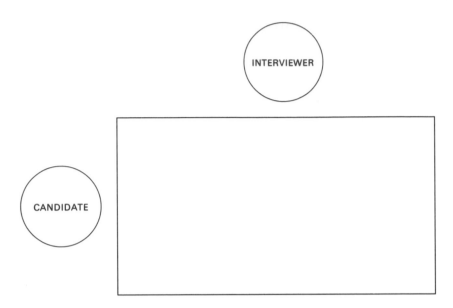

Fig. 3. Seating arrangements.

organize the interview are more powerful than the seating arrangements. But if you have a choice, research tells us that there is a better seating arrangement for the interview. Interview around the corner of the desk: place the candidate's chair on the right side of the desk—or put your chair on the side and the candidate's chair in front of the desk.

Interviewing around the corner of the desk gives the candidate choices. It allows them to get closer to the desk, if necessary, or move back a couple of inches. The surface of the desk is a practical place to put a cup of coffee, an ashtray, a purse, or any of the materials that need to be brought in or carried out. If you hand the candidate a brochure, they don't have to put it on the floor. This arrangement gives you the practicality of the desk or table and a certain amount of openness around the edge of it. And by the way, it's no accident that most of us have L-shaped conversational areas in our living rooms. A couch and a chair or two at a right angle, or two chairs practically at a right angle. That's not some decorator's nightmare imposed on you. It's been determined that sitting at a right angle from somebody actually facilitates conversation. Two chairs in front of the desk can work, but that's a seating arrangement more suitable for two people who are about to review documents together, as in a performance appraisal or other business meetings.

Should You Go Get the Candidate Yourself? It is slightly preferable for you to go to the receptionist's area and get the candidate yourself. However, if it's not practical (if they have to through security, for example, or for any other reason it is too complicated), then you would let the secretary or receptionist bring them to you. Get out from behind your desk, greet them in your office just as if you had brought them in from the reception area. Call them by name, introduce yourself, thank them for coming. You don't want to be sitting behind your desk, writing away, when they come in, and say, "Have a seat—Oh, move those printouts, I'll be with you in a second."

It's also a good idea to let the receptionist know the expected time of arrival and name of candidate so that they can be appropriately received. It's so much nicer to be greeted by a receptionist who says, "Oh yes, we're expecting you," than with a curt, "Do you have an appointment?"

OTHER TIPS FOR BUILDING THE PROPER ATMOSPHERE

At this point in my seminar, to generate discussion, I usually ask the participants for other suggestions for building the proper atmosphere. Since some of the suggestions are quite useful, I thought I'd share them with you here. For example:

Move and speak at a relatively moderate speed so candidates don't seem to be rushed.

Show them where to put their coat. You may not personally feel comfortable taking somebody's coat, or you may feel very comfortable with it; in any case, you can certainly tell them where the closet is.

Offer them coffee. Let's suppose I bring the candidate in and say, "Well, Cliff, before we get started, it's kind of a cold day, maybe you'd like a cup of coffee or tea?" and Cliff says, "I'd love to have one, that would be great," and I'm forced to say, "Okay, fine, then I'll go get one, I'll be back in about ten minutes, I'll have to go down to the cafeteria." Of course, that would be silly. Offer the candidate coffee if you want to—and if it's convenient. If you're going to walk past a coffee machine, you might have some quarters in your pocket to throw in and get a cup of coffee for the candidate. You might in fact get one if you're passing the cafeteria, but there's no reason to go out of your way.

On the other hand, if it's a cold, wintry day, and candidates are coming in with icicles on their eyebrows ... and you have this warm cup of coffee that you're sipping and they have nothing ... well, that would be rude. You might want to avoid that.

Dress appropriately. That means don't be dressed in any way that would be a distraction for the candidate. You should dress in a way the candidate would consider appropriate for the occasion. How you dress specifically is not important: However, your appearance should be such that it is not a distraction, and it is not an issue for the candidate.

≡≡≡8≡TRANSLATING THE JOB REQUIREMENTS INTO A FORM THAT APPLIES TO A CANDIDATE: CAN DO, WILL DO, AND FIT FACTORS

O̲ur purpose in organizing job require-
ments into the categories of Knowledge, Skills, and Abilities
and Behaviors and Environmental Issues (see Chapters 3–5)
was to provide a conceptual framework for all the information you discovered as you researched the job requirements.
As you recall, I demonstrated how keeping these categories
in mind can greatly enhance the interviewer's ability to ask
focused and relevant questions.

As we get ready to move from the preparation stage to the
interview itself, the task that lies before us is to show how
the same categories we developed to understand what the
job requires are also used to determine a candidate's suitability for the job. Our focus now is on the candidate in
relation to the job—rather than just the job in and of

CAN DO	WILL DO	FIT
Work Experience	Motivation	Team Orientation
Education	Interests	Independence
Technical Skills	Goals	Social Effectiveness
Communication Skills	Drive/Energy	Interpersonal Style
Specialized Training	Reliability	Stress Tolerance
Analytical Skills		Limitations: —Travel —Overtime —Relocation —Weekend Work

Fig. 4. Can Do, Will Do, and Fit.

itself—and for this shift in focus, we will require a new terminology.

This new terminology has as its reference point the same categories—Knowledge, Skills, and Abilities and Behaviors and Environmental Issues. Essentially, all that changes is how we look at the categories. We are now talking about a candidate. The job-analysis questions were: "What knowledge, skills, and abilities, what behaviors and what environmental demands make up the total requirements for this job?" When we are interviewing a candidate for that job, the questions become: Can they do the job? Will they behave in the ways necessary? and Will they fit into our special environment?

Figure 4 shows a chart of these Can Do, Will Do, and Fit factors with a sample listing under each heading. Let me explain how you can make these concepts work for you. These three broad questions are ultimately the questions the interviewer has to be able to answer. Ultimately, the whole interview process boils down to this: Can this person do the job? Will they do this job?, and Will they fit into our very special set of circumstances?

CAN DO FACTORS

Can the candidate do the job, in terms of relevant Knowledge, Skills, and Abilities? Do they have the relevant prior work experiences, technical skills, formal educational background, specialized training, intelligence, communications skills, leadership abilities, ability to prioritize, or organizational skills? Can they operate a Wang? Can they program in COBOL? Are they familiar with our marketing approach? Do they have an analytical approach to problem solving?

If we determine that a candidate "CAN NOT DO the job," meaning they lack the necessary Knowledge, Skills, and Abilities, and we cannot train them, then nothing clsc matters: that eliminates them. This is a critical set of issues.

WILL DO FACTORS

I'll bet you realize that just because someone is technically competent and has solid previous work experience and everything else that indicates they "Can Do" the job, there is still no assurance that that candidate will behave in the ways that you need. If he or she is not mature enough or is not flexible, or isn't dependable or doesn't have the perseverance you need, or isn't interested in what needs to be done—or if the candidate doesn't have an accurate self-perception or rational goals in the short run or doesn't stick to commitments or doesn't respond well to direction and authority—then that candidate is not going to be successful no matter what technical assets or skills he or she might possess. We want to know if the candidate will behave in the ways required on our job. Remember in Chapter 4 we spent a lot of time talking about how to make qualities such as these jobs relevant and behavioral—so we could spot these qualities in a candidate.

FIT FACTORS

We considered several levels of Environmental Issues when we were formulating the job requirements. Now, you want to know if a candidate is going to "Fit" into your particular set of environmental circumstances. Do they have the values and attitudes needed to work within your industry and your specific company? Do they have the teamwork ability or the ability to work independently, requirements needed in order to function in that department or division? Can the candidate deal with the everyday tensions, pressures, and ambiguities of the job?

Knockout Issues

And there's a subcategory of Fit factors, those job criteria that are not subject to evaluative judgment—the Knockout Issues. Is the candidate able to travel extensively, to relocate to your area? Can they work evenings and weekends, can they stay beyond the standard day if that's required? Can they work a second shift? Whatever the realities of the job, you have to know whether the candidate will fit into it. I call Knockout Issues those job criteria that need no interpretation. Either candidates can meet them or they can't. Either they have the legal right to work in the United States, or they don't. If your job requires the candidates to have an accident-free driving record for three years in order to be able to drive a company vehicle under your insurance coverage, that's a Knockout Issue. Either they are willing and able to commit themselves to working weekends, to extensive travel, and relocation, or they are not.

I'm not using the phrase Knockout Issue colloquially. For example, "Well, I think not having enough prior experience knocks them out." That is a minimum critical level, requiring an evaluation of the candidate's experience. I'm talking about those job criteria that are immutable. The candidate must be able to work weekends; must be available for extensive travel; must be bondable; must have a security clearance or be eligible for one. Those are absolutes.

Ideally, these criteria should be used first in the screening process. You could say, even in a telephone screen: "By the way, this job would absolutely require you to be available for work on Saturdays. This is an absolute requirement of the job. Therefore let me ask you: "Is there anything that will prevent you from meeting this absolute requirement?" Why bother bringing in candidates for a series of in-depth interviews if they can't meet the requirements of the job?

HOW AN ORGANIZED INTERVIEW PLAN CAN HELP YOU DETERMINE IF THE CANDIDATE MATCHES THE CAN DO, WILL DO, AND FIT FACTORS

So the task is simple. All you have to do is find out: Can the candidate do the job? Will they do it?, and Will they fit in? Well, perhaps not that simple. The challenge you are faced with is that you can't ask any of those questions directly— at least, not directly and profitably. Go ahead and say to a candidate, "Well, Cindy, can you do this job, and will you do it, and will you fit into our very special set of circumstances?" Surely, barring cases of an overprepared MBA student who thinks you are applying a double-ganger ploy on them, the answers will be: "Yes," "Yes" and, perhaps for the sake of variety, "Certainly!" "And how!" and "You bet!"

And even if you were to get a bit more specific and ask directly for the qualities listed under each of the headings, the results would be just as predictable and of just as little use. You can't say, "Ken, can you work on a small project team?" or "Susan, are you the kind of person with the proper values and attitudes for this organization?" or, "Tell me, Steve, are you really going to be interested in what we ask you to do?" or "Marion, we need someone here who can stick to commitments once they make them. Are you that kind of person?" or, "Carol, we need a person who really has a logical approach to problem solving—does that describe you?"

These are not questions to ask, but judgments you hope to make. These questions about motivation, interests, and goals are the ones that you, and not the candidate, will answer. You'll arrive at those judgments about the candidate based on their answers to questions that, if you are

skillful enough, will have had no obvious relation to particular traits. That's the goal: Somehow without tipping your
hand you need to find out if Ken has the technical skills, the
leadership abilities, the rational goals, the ability to work
independently, run a team, and so on.

You need an organized plan or a way to collect information that is so comprehensive that if there is no evidence
that the candidate has ever displayed the quality that you
mean by "maturity," you can say with some degree of
confidence that they haven't got it.

Now if you just chitchat with the candidate, of course,
you might miss the evidence. But if you use the comprehensive plan you will be following, and they have the qualities
you need, it will come up in six different places. If they
haven't got it, it will be patently obvious. That's the value
of having a structure or a plan for collecting information in
a comprehensive way.

Most interviewers concentrate almost all their attention
on the Can Do factors. It's not that they don't know that
those other issues exist (otherwise "motivation" and "energy" wouldn't be the clichés that they are). But most
interviewers concentrate by default on the Can Do qualities,
because they're qualities that can be more easily assessed,
tested, and measured. They're more "objective," easier to
talk about. We concentrate our attention on these Can Do
qualities and give up those other two columns, because . . .
we don't even know how to define them, much less search
for them. So I want a person with a positive attitude. What
does that mean? How do I find that out? I want a person
who's dependable; what does that mean—that they came to
the interview on time? Someone who can handle ambiguity?
How do I find that out in an interview?

Sometimes these are referred to as the "subjective" issues.
They are subjective unless you develop behavioral examples
of environmental features out of them. Then they are not
just intangible matters of opinion. They are specific job
requirements. Then, after a comprehensive interview and
with the facts available, two interviewers looking at the

same candidate would be able to evaluate these qualities with the same accuracy and unanimity they might exhibit if they were making a judgment about the relevance of a candidate's prior work experience.

To make these issues more tangible, redefine them in the same way we did in Chapters 4 and 5 when we were calling them Behaviors and Environmental Issues. You need to find the most job-specific, objective definition of a given trait. It's not enough to say we need somebody who is mature. The question to ask yourself is: If we had the ideal employee on the job now, how would they behave to demonstrate they have the quality we mean by maturity?

Once I know what exactly it is that I mean by mature or any number of other qualities that I feel this particular job requires, then I can search into Marion's background to see if she has ever behaved that way, and can find a consistent pattern of that valuable behavior.

THE PLAN

To be able to collect the data necessary to answer the three critical questions (Can they do the job, Will they behave in the ways necessary, and Will they fit into our special circumstances), we need some kind of plan. We need to know what topics to cover, have an order in which to cover them, and have a command of sequencing and timing. Figure 5 shows the basic structure we're going to use. Across the top are the questions you're hoping to answer as a result of the interview. On one side are the areas of a candidate's background you will cover in the interview. We're going to look into the candidate's (1) work experience in its entirety, (2) educational background, (3) outside interests and activities, and (4) self-assessment. Four building blocks.

I'm sure you're not surprised by any of these categories. If you were a candidate, you wouldn't be surprised if they were covered. You as an interviewer might not have chosen them all, or put them in that particular order, but there's

		CAN DO	WILL DO	FIT
WORK EXPERIENCE	Early ↓ Recent			
EDUCATION	Early ↓ Recent			
ACTIVITIES AND INTERESTS				
SELF ASSESSMENT				

Fig. 5. The plan.

nothing intrinsically shocking about any of this; if any-thing, it seems kind of obvious. It should be. For one thing, it wouldn't be useful to give you a plan that would "blow the candidate away." By the same token, if I were to give you a plan that was so awkward or cumbersome or different from what you would anticipate doing, chances are you wouldn't use it. Any workable approach to this subject must be elegant: simple and easy to use, yet profound in its effect. (Simple will be immediately apparent, profundity will become apparent as we get more exposure to this process!)

The Plan Helps You Move Beyond a Narrow Range of Information

Look at the shaded bands that run across Fig. 5. They represent the very narrow range of information usually covered by the typical interviewer in the typical interview. They review the candidate's most recent, full-time, professionally and/or technically relevant work experience, and the most recent educational experience or specialized training—and that's it. After those two topics are covered, the interviewer then says, "All right, what questions do you have for me?" and shifts into the information-giving phase.

Are those narrow bands of information relevant to the interview? Of course they are. Not only are they relevant, they're quite important; they should be emphasized. The problem is not with covering them; the problem is with only covering them, and stopping there.

The "Swan Poll"

Suppose I told you that I did a national public opinion poll and I discovered that 87 percent of the American population were in favor of armed intervention in Nicaragua by American troops today. You'd be a little surprised. You might scratch your head and say, "Well, I never would have expected that." You might go so far as to challenge me a bit. I've heard of the Nielsen Poll and the Gallup Poll, but the Swan Poll doesn't ring a bell. You might say, "Tell me something about your sampling methods."

Suppose I told you this: "I know what I'm doing. I'm an expert. I was in California a few weeks ago, and I talked to a few people out there; on the plane back to New York I sat next to someone from Chicago, so I got my Midwest sample; I know people from Connecticut and New Jersey, and I asked them a few questions; and my cousin who lives in Houston asked a few of his friends the question, and reported the results back to me. And I took all those numbers, added them up and came up with my projection of 87 percent."

You probably wouldn't be very impressed with my sampling methods. You'd probably say to yourself—how can he pretend to draw any rational conclusions about the nation's opinions from that limited sample? He didn't talk to enough people. If that's your complaint I can still argue with you. I didn't talk to enough people? I suppose you think Neilson and Gallup talk to 225 million people? Well, they don't. They only talk to three to four thousand people and you believe them. Okay, I'll talk to 10 thousand people.

Even under those circumstances, with that many people, it would be a mistake to believe my poll. It's true that

Neilson and Gallup don't talk to 225 million, but they don't have to. They can talk to two or three thousand people because they talk to a statistically adequate sample. They talk to people who represent a range and cross section of public opinion all over America, and therefore their conclusions about the nation's opinions are accurate. Their sample is a microcosm of the country—and it is valid to predict from that sample.

Look again at the shaded bands in Fig. 5. All the research on interviewing makes it pretty clear that these two narrow bands are an inadequate sample of the candidate's past behavior. And, therefore, predictions and projections drawn from them about how candidates will behave in the future are notoriously inaccurate.

I have heard interviewers say: "Well it may be true that if I were to interview those two narrow bands covering two things (which we both agree are the most obviously relevant aspects of the person's background), I might be a little off, but if all the evidence points to 'yes,' how wrong could I be? A little off, okay, but I'm still likely to be reasonably correct in my perception." That would be the same as if I walked down the street, stopped 10 people, asked the key question from my survey, and all 10 gave the same answer. Would it be reasonable for me to say under those circumstances: "Well, I might be a little off when I asked 10 people about invading Nicaragua. But all 10 were willing and eager. What the heck, I'll just reduce the 100 percent to 85 percent to allow for 15 percent error." This would not be a reliable methodology.

The same thing is true in the interview. Those narrow bands are deceptive. All the evidence can point to yes, but when the candidates come on board they turn out to be complete "duds," or in some other respect dramatically different from what you need. And rarely are they different in a positive way—usually the surprises are unpleasant.

It's bad enough when you interview in those two narrow bands, hire somebody, and ultimately discover them to be inappropriate or less than totally effective in the way you'd like; but at least you find out about those errors, the false positives. What about all those people you interviewed in those narrow bands and, as a result, didn't learn enough about to really feel they were going to make a real contribution; they were not such superstars that their virtues were plain, but if you had hired them they would have turned out to be really good performers. Those are the false negatives. You never find out about those and that's a great loss.

Our more comprehensive plan for those four categories will still emphasize the items in those narrow bands. But we'll go back to a little earlier in their work experience, a little earlier in their educational background, and we'll consider those other categories—activities and interests and self-assessment as well. Those four categories in combination will enable you to make the most accurate possible judgments because they will give you a more valid sample of the candidate's history.

I'm not asking you to spend more time on the interview. The idea is to spread whatever time you have out among those categories. In effect, what I'm asking you to do is to take a series of snapshots from several different angles of a candidate's background. When all the evidence has been collected in that way, you can make a much more accurate decision. Let's examine the four categories in more detail.

The Four Categories

Work Experience. First, you take a picture of them from the perspective of their job history. You'll concentrate on their more recent jobs, but you'll take the history from the beginning, looking for a consistent pattern of the qualities you want: the maturity, positive attitudes, how they deal with tension and pressure, flexibilty, dependability, prioritization ability, organizational skills, relative work experience, if they can handle ambiguity, if they're the kind of person willing to commit to traveling extensively, if they're willing to learn technical skills—anything about them from that vantage point of earlier jobs to the present.

Education. Then you're going to shift the camera and take a picture from another vantage point—their educational background. Don't be fooled into thinking that mere academic achievement is enough here. Grades, while not irrelevant, are a notoriously inaccurate predictor of future success on the job. There is no evidence to support the conclusion that one candidate is better than another just because the first has a 3.2 and the second a 2.8 grade point average. We may ask about grades, but as a topic they comprise just one small piece of the puzzle: They're a factor, but not the only factor, within the category of education.

We have to find out what's behind those grades to make judgments. Use the candidate's educational background as an excuse to learn about them as a person . . . another perspective on the same candidate. From that vantage point we're looking for evidence regarding all the factors that we've determined are most important to the job: motivation, how they work with others, how they respond to authority or deadlines, or logical thinking ability.

Activities and Interests. Then shift your camera and look at them from a third direction. How do they choose to spend their time outside of work? Don't poke around in their personal lives, but give them an opportunity to mention those aspects of their background that transcend formal work and formal education and would help add a dimension to your understanding of them. Often subtleties in a candidate's outside interests can help correct or corroborate insights that have been gained earlier. They have demonstrated their capacity to get things done through other people without formal authority. That might tell you something about their leadership skills that you may have been concerned about earlier. Maybe they demonstrated that they do six things at once and love it—the fact that this pattern shows up here indicates that even when they have a choice they do it. In any event, since this category might tell you something about them, you should touch on it.

Self-Assessment: How Candidates See Themselves.
Finally you should shift the camera in a fourth direction:
You take a snapshot of how they see themselves. What do
they perceive to be their strengths and what areas would
they like to improve or develop?

Those are the four categories. From those multiple vantage points, you're going to be able to form a kind of
hologram of a candidate, a picture that will be dramatically
more accurate at predicting how somebody's going to behave in the future on a job than what usually passes for
"structure."

Structure in the conventional interview means being con-
trolled or limited by the candidate's résumé or the things
they rehearsed in front of the mirror the night before, or the
things they happen to think are important or just happen to
remember. The interviewer says, "All right, I see you used
to work as so-and-so, tell me about that," and the person
does. "I see, and you were also involved in these duties, tell
me about that," and the candidate does. "And I see that
before that you had a job with so-and-so, tell me about
that," and they do. "All right, and I see you majored in this
particular course area while you were in school, and then
you had these particular courses here," and ask about that.
And, finally, after looking over the rest of the sheet and
finding nothing more of consequence, you say: "All right,
Mark, I guess that's about it, what questions do you have
for me?"

Is the material on the résumé important? Of course it is.
We might even emphasize it in terms of time investment.
But it is crucial not to be limited to this information. You
need a more comprehensive picture of the candidate than
the résumé will give you.

All of what I have discussed here is my way of giving you
the intellectual background of the Interview Guide (see
Chapter 9, Fig. 6), which I'm going to dissect and explain
piece by piece in the chapters ahead.

≡≡≡9≡HOW TO ORGANIZE THE INTERVIEW: INTERVIEW GUIDE—PART 1

Now I'm going to introduce the Interview Guide, an invaluable tool for giving organization and structure to the interview. In this chapter I'll walk you step-by-step through its various features. Then, in Chapter 10 I'll explain the way it works a little more thoroughly and answer the questions that are most frequently asked about the Interview Guide. Together, these two chapters comprise an in-depth treatment of a plan for organizing and structuring the interview. If you are not particularly interested in explanations but would like a proven systematic way of conducting the interview and just want to execute it, you can turn directly to the Interview Guide (see Fig. 6, located in the back of this chapter). You can then begin reading again at Chapter 11. On the other hand, if you think it would help you to know why things are done the way they are on the Interview Guide, why things are separated the way they are, the order of the items, and the logic out of which the structure has sprung, then you might want to continue reading through the next two chapters. If you understand why you're doing certain things, you can make them more natural and be more flexible during the interview. Whatever your choice, I hope you'll at least scan the next several pages so you can have a clear understanding of the "logic" behind the plan.

The Interview Guide is the practical application of all the issues that make up the basic plan of a good interview. It contains a lot of subtle information packed into a very condensed form, and the chances are that the rationale for everything will not be immediately apparent. In the next few chapters I'm going to take the Interview Guide apart and put it together again, explore the overall strategy, and examine the part each individual section plays within that strategy.

Keep in mind that the Interview Guide is just a training device. I don't expect you to have it in front of you when you conduct an interview. I certainly don't want you to read the form to the candidate. The Interview Guide should serve as a tool through which you learn the logic of the interview. Eventually, you'll put it into your own words, using my form as a reminder and reference. In addition, I will be adding specific questions in each category for your use. First, though, the overall plan needs to be reviewed.

In order to get an idea of what the Interview Guide is about, let's first take a quick scan of the entire form. You notice on the top it has a reminder about the Greeting and Small Talk Phases, some suggested Transition Questions, and an Overview Statement. You then introduce the topic of Work Experience. After you've covered the candidate's complete Work Experiences, it allows you to introduce the educational aspects of the candidate's background; the categories of Activities and Interests come next, followed by the candidate's Self-Assessment. There is then another Transition Question to bring you to the information-giving phase, after which you close the interview.

What you have in front of you, then, is the skeletal outline of the interview: the topics to cover, the order to cover them in, sequencing, and later even the timing of the interview is incorporated. I'd like you to view it as a road map for the interview; and I'm going to begin by describing the basic stages of the journey.

THE TRANSITION QUESTION

Suppose you have gotten through the Greeting Phase, and now, according to plan, are engaged in Small Talk. You and the candidate are discussing some nonevaluative issue such as fishing or golf or (if necessary) traffic or the weather. Small Talk may be going well, but you don't want to spend 20 minutes at it. You need some way to shift to the information-collecting phase of the interview. To do so you will make use of a Transition Question.

GREETING

SMALL TALK
   (*Hobbies, interests, travel, city of residence, etc.*)

TRANSITION QUESTION (*Select One*)

   How did you happen to become interested in our organization?

   How did you hear of the opening?

   What has been your contact with us in the past?

   What is your understanding of the position you're applying for?

As you can see, there are a couple of optional transition questions on the form. You can pick any one you like—or you can make one up.

The Transition Question is not a substantive question. It is not meant to get information but to act as a signal to the candidate that it's time to get down to business. Perhaps Susan is explaining the intricacies of stamp collecting. You've drawn her out a little to talk about her hobby, but now you're ready to move on. To get her attention you say: "Well, I appreciate your mentioning that, Susan, but tell me how did you hear about the opportunity we're talking about today?" or, "What previous contact have you had with us?" or one of the other Transition Questions listed in the Interview Guide.

The intention of the Transition Question is to signal to Susan that you're shifting gears, getting down to business; therefore, no matter what she says in answer to one of those questions, use the Overview Statement (eventually in your own words) to set the stage for the interview and introduce the Work Experience section:

OVERVIEW STATEMENT

OVERVIEW

Before we start, let me give you some idea of what I'd like to cover today. I want to review your background and experience so that we can decide whether we have the opportunities in our organization suited to your talents and interests. So, I'd like to hear about your jobs, education, interests, outside activities and anything else you'd like to tell me. And after we have covered your background, I want to give you information about our organization and the job, and answer any questions you might have. (*continue below*)

WORK EXPERIENCE

A good place to start would be your work experience.

I'm interested in the jobs you've held, what your duties and responsibilities were, your likes and dislikes, and what you felt you may have gained from them.

Let's start with a brief review of your first work experiences, those you might have had part-time during school or during summer, and then we'll concentrate on your more recent jobs in more detail. What do you remember about your very first job?

I know what you're thinking: "Well, that's a mouthful! Do I have to say all that? That's pretty time-consuming, I only have 30 to 40 minutes, after all. And do I have to use those words? Those aren't my words. And why go back to the first jobs, anyway? How relevant can that be?" These are some of the momentary objections my seminar participants have voiced on first hearing the Overview Statement. Even if no such battery of objections leaps into your mind, I'm sure it will help clarify the process if I give you reasons why you should consider this approach.

While it is true that this way of starting an interview is longer than the typical interviewer's introductory remarks to the candidate, it is not objectively long. If you actually timed it, it's about 45 seconds. In 45 seconds, notice what you've accomplished. You've told Susan:

One: "I know what I'm doing. I have a plan, and by implication I'm in charge of the interview"—but you've done it nicely.

Two: you've told her: "There aren't going to be any tricks or surprises in this interview; it's going to be a rational logical interview—perhaps more comprehensive than you'd anticipated, but still, a pretty logical approach. I'm not going to ask ridiculous questions or do something to make you uncomfortable."

Three: "I've built in time to give you information and answer your questions. Don't worry, that will happen once we're through reviewing your background."

Unspoken are the implications of positioning the information-giving phase carefully: "But frankly, Susan, I'm not going to give you a lot of details up front because I don't want to contaminate the interview and telegraph my punch."

And on top of that: "If it turns out I'm not that interested in you I don't want to waste my time giving you too many details up front, because once I know something about you I may regret it. Or if it turns out you're a star performer, I want to be able to influence your decision about us, and knowing something about you first will enable me to tailor and adapt my presentation to your specific interests and goals."

And finally, I've let her know: "These are the topics we're going to cover, here's the one we'll start with, here's the way we're going to go through it, and here's the place to start."

All done in 45 seconds or so. Compare that with starting off the interview by saying: "Well, Susan, thanks for the opportunity to talk with you, I've read through your background here, but I'll never be the expert on you that you are, so why don't you tell me about yourself?" or, "Give me the highlights of your background." Or, "Oh, let's see, you've got a lot of interesting jobs, here, hmm, this one is interesting, why don't you tell me about it?"

None of those ways of starting an interview accomplishes any of our purposes. So, while you will eventually put it in your own words, you ought to make sure your introduction to the interview process contains the elements that are needed to accomplish all the things I've just listed—and even if it takes a minute, in the long run it will result in a much more effective interview.

When Introducing Work Experience and Education, Why Start with Earlier Experiences and Move Forward Chronologically?

WORK EXPERIENCE

A good place to start would be your work experience.

I'm interested in the jobs you've held, what your duties and responsibilities were, your likes and dislikes, and what you felt you may have gained from them.

Let's start with a brief review of your first work experiences, those you might have had part-time during school or during summer, and then we'll concentrate on your more recent jobs in more detail. What do you remember about your very first job?

(Select specific FOLLOW-UP QUESTIONS for each job and move forward chronologically.)

EDUCATION

You've given me a good review of your work experience—now let's talk about your education. Why don't we start with high school briefly and then cover more recent schooling and any specialized on the job training you may have had. I'm interested in the subjects you preferred, your grades, extracurricular activities, and anything else of importance. What was high school like for you?

(Select specific FOLLOW-UP QUESTIONS for each educational experience and move forward chronologically.)

After the statement from the Interview Guide introducing Work Experience or Education to the candidate, the Interview Guide instructs you to "Select specific FOLLOW-UP QUESTIONS for each job (or educational experience) and move forward chronologically."

The words FOLLOW-UP QUESTIONS are capitalized because they refer to the key, well-researched questions, or "One-Step Probes" provided in the Complete Interview Guide (see Fig. 6), which we will eventually incorporate into the structure.

But what about "move forward chronologically?" I would not be surprised if you were hesitant to follow this instruction, or at least wanted to know the reason for it. Every interview you've done, probably every interview you've experienced as a candidate, and certainly, every application and résumé you've seen, have all proceeded from the current job backward. Why are we suggesting going the other way?

It is important that you understand that it is not a casual choice. It's not simply my favorite way of interviewing; I am not asking you to please do it my way because it's the Swan Technique, nor is it "the current fashion." This procedure, in particular, has been carefully researched and thoroughly field-tested. So before you make any changes, at least consider the logic behind this approach, and try it out a couple of times so you can see that logic in action; once you try it out, its value is immediately apparent.

Most interviewers, of course, do go backward in time, but is that because they have made a conscious, rational decision to do so? No, of course not; they're just following the person's résumé. Résumés and job applications do go backward in time. I don't mean to imply that résumés and applications are designed incorrectly. It's just that they're intended for a somewhat different purpose than the interview. Consider the role of the résumé or application. Of the three categories—Can Do, Will Do, and Fit—the Can

Do factors are the category that résumés and applications are designed to help you assess. While résumés and applications aren't the sole basis for your final judgment about a candidate's technical competence or knowledge base, these documents should give you some indication of the relevance of a candidate's work experiences, formal education or training, and technical skills. They should also provide some clues about those issues that you'd explore further during the interview. Therefore, résumés and applications are designed to emphasize recent experiences. For screening purposes, this approach is quite sufficient.

But you wouldn't hope to get any clues from résumés and applications about a candidate's teamwork ability, values and attitudes, response to direction and authority, dependability, interest, reaction to ambiguity. Those are things you hope to learn from the interview, and to see them you need a degree of richness and subtlety that doesn't come by going backward in time. To learn about the whole person, you have to approach the candidate's history from the angle that yields a full, comprehensive picture, which shows the patterns of a person's behavior as they grow and develop over time.

Going backward in time gets you an annotated version of the candidate's résumé. You see the tips of many icebergs—you learn what happened—but the candidate is less likely to recall or mention the choices made or the transitions that occurred. Events lose their connection to one another when you view them in reverse chronological order. Run a movie backward in your video tape recorder and attempt to reconstruct the story: You'll see enough to know which characters are present in which scene, you'll see their meetings with one another, but what these people are like, why they're behaving this way, how one thing led to another will be difficult to tell.

For the interview, the forward in time, chronological process is dramatically more revealing and effective. Try it—it works.

Look for Patterns

Am I suggesting that you hire someone based on a quality they displayed 15 or 10 or 5 years ago? Of course not. It is true that recent experiences are more relevant, and your time investment in the interview should be weighted to reflect their greater importance. You're not going to dwell on the past, but touch on it briefly and move on. "Where'd you go to after that? What was your next job? What happened next?" Moving forward in time, you'll devote the bulk of your attention to the most recent, and one or two other relevant experiences.

On the other hand, it would also be inaccurate to base your decision on a behavior, positive or negative, that the candidate displayed yesterday. Only patterns are accurate. People say the best predictor of future behavior is past behavior, and that's true—so long as you've defined the behavior carefully, and if you can determine that the person has behaved that way with consistency.

Let's suppose that in his most recent job, only a week ago, Jordan has displayed the very behavior I mean by "flexibility." I could put a big check mark in my mind next to that item, saying, "Well, at least he's got flexibility." But I would be jumping to a conclusion. While it is of course more encouraging to find one occurrence of the desired behavior than not to find any occurrences of it at all, just one or two examples in his most recent experience is not enough to justify my conviction that he's going to behave that way in the future. But what if I saw an instance of that behavior in an earlier job. A later job. An earlier educational experience. A later educational experience. In his outside interests. Everywhere he goes, whichever way you look at him, he displays that quality: Then I'm on pretty firm ground to predict that he's likely to behave that way again because it's part of him.

ACTIVITIES AND INTERESTS AND SELF-ASSESSMENT SECTION

ACTIVITIES AND INTERESTS

Turning to the present, I'd like to give you the opportunity to mention some of your interests and activities outside of work—hobbies, what you do for fun and relaxation, and any community activities. How do you spend your spare time?

(Select specific FOLLOW-UP QUESTIONS)

SELF-ASSESSMENT

Assets

Now let's try to summarize our conversation. Thinking about all we're covered today, what would you say are some of your strengths—qualities both personal and professional that make you a good prospect for any employer?

(Select specific FOLLOW-UP QUESTIONS as needed)

Developmental Needs

You've given me some real assets, and now I'd like to hear about areas you'd like to develop further—all of us have qualities that we'd like to change or improve. What are some of yours?

To get back to our walk-through of the Interview Guide: After Work Experience and Education topics are covered, you should now give candidates the opportunity to share their outside interests and activities. You can help them summarize the full picture of themselves with the Self-Assessment category.

TRANSITION TO INFORMATION-GIVING PHASE

> **TRANSITION QUESTION** (*To Information-Giving Phase*)
>
> You've given me a good review of your background and experience, and I have enjoyed talking with you. Before we turn to my review of our organization, and the job, is there anything else about your background you would like to cover? (Get answer before continuing.)
>
> Do you have any <u>specific</u> questions or concerns before I give you information about the job and the opportunities here?

The information-collecting phase ends, as it began, with a transition question—in fact, with two questions. You might at first think it odd to end on a question, but it makes sense when you consider what the transition question is for and how it accomplishes these goals. First, it's a means of controlling the interview. You want to keep the information-getting phase separate from the information-giving phase in order to seal off the information-collecting phase, and to be able to get the candidate's full attention when you turn to giving information.

You also want to make sure that the candidate has had the opportunity to add any additional information they think is important. The first question, "Is there anything else about your background you would like to cover?" accomplishes this. It is purposely a closed-ended question so that the candidate doesn't feel required to add more information. Get an answer before continuing.

The second question is, "Do you have any specific questions or concerns before I give information about the job and the opportunities here?" The word "specific" is underlined because you don't want to encourage questions.

PRESENTING INFORMATION AND ANSWERING QUESTIONS

> **PRESENTING INFORMATION AND ANSWERING QUESTIONS**
>
> All right, now I have some information I'd like to give you.
>
> *(Review organization, the job, benefits, location, etc.)*
>
> *(Tailor your presentation as appropriate to your interest in candidate)*

This topic, especially the part that says "Tailor your presentation as appropriate to your interest in candidate" is complex enough and important enough to merit a chapter by itself (Chapter 17, "Presenting Information Persuasively and Closing the Interview Properly").

CLOSING

> **CLOSING**
>
> Do you have any other questions about us, the job, or anything else?
>
> What is your level of interest in us at this point? (Explore any doubts or reservations.)
>
> Let me review what the next steps are.
>
> (End the interview) I want to thank you for coming today...

The way you close an interview should vary depending on your level of interest in a candidate. For now I'll briefly review the basic purposes of the various components of the Closing section.

Do You Have Any Other Questions...?

You ask this to tie up any loose ends, to make sure, as you did earlier with the Transition Question, that candidates won't be kicking themselves afterward because of what they forgot to ask.

What is Your Level of Interest in Us at This Point?
(Explore Any Doubts or Reservations)

The phrase in parentheses is the reason behind the question. Not always, not even most of the time, but often enough to make it well worth asking, a question about "level of interest" will encourage the candidate to express a specific doubt or reservation about the job, which you can then directly address, and perhaps remove. Often, clarifying some issues that are still troubling candidates at this point is vital in having top candidates accept a position.

Let Me Review What the Next Steps Are

Of course, for you the next step may be to simply pass the candidate on to the next interviewer. But if you are responsible for explaining what will happen after the candidate leaves, it is also very important to explain what the remainder of the selection process will be like. Include the number of subsequent interviews, if any, when and how the applicant will be informed of a decision (e.g. phone, letter), and any other relevant information. Don't assume that candidates are aware of how your organization operates. Maybe in your organization it's typical for candidates to be notified of a second interview weeks after an initial interview. It that's how things are, and you don't explain it, candidates might assume long before the time has elapsed that they've been rejected and accepted another position. You can avoid misunderstandings by making a special effort to clarify the procedure.

(End the Interview) I Want To Thank You for Coming Today

The interview is now at an end. You can make that clear to the candidate by standing up and shaking hands. By taking the initiative you can avoid putting the candidate in the position of trying to figure out what to do next or what will happen next. Don't glance at your watch and say, "Oh, we have another minute or two, what other questions do you have?" After having gone through all the previous steps the candidate doesn't have any questions. Also, some candidates will think they're supposed to figure out what you want them to ask about. They'll think that you're testing them.

This ends our tour of the Interview Guide (Fig. 6). Of course, there's a lot more to be said about this form and the structure it codifies. In the next chapter I'll explain the reasons behind this structure, show how it works in practice, and address some commonly asked questions about it.

INTERVIEW GUIDE and FOLLOW-UP QUESTIONS

GREETING

SMALL TALK

Probe with: What . . .
Tell me . . .
Review . . .
Explain . . .
Describe . . .
Give me an example . . .

(Hobbies, interests, travel, city of residence, etc.)

TRANSITION QUESTION *(Select One)*

How did you happen to become interested in our organization?

How did you hear of the opening?

What has been your contact with us in the past?

What is your understanding of the position you're applying for?

OVERVIEW

Before we start, let me give you some idea of what I'd like to cover today. I want to review your background and experience so that we can decide whether we have the opportunities in our organization suited to your talents and interests. So, I'd like to hear about your jobs, education, interests, outside activities and anything else you'd like to tell me. And after we have covered your background, I want to give you information about our organization and the job, and answer any questions you might have. *(continue below)*

WORK EXPERIENCE

A good place to start would be your work experience.

I'm interested in the jobs you've held, what your duties and responsibilities were, your likes and dislikes, and what you felt you may have gained from them.

Let's start with a brief review of your first work experiences, those you might have had part-time during school or during summers, and then we'll concentrate on your more recent jobs in detail. **What do you remember about your very first job?**

Cover earliest jobs first, including part-time, plus full-time positions, military assignments and volunteer work. End with future career directions.

ASK:
- **Things liked best**
- **Things liked less well**
- **Accomplishments**
  — how achieved
- **What learned from job**
- **Difficult problems faced**
  — how handled

- **Opportunities for promotion and advancement**
- **Ways most effective with people**
- **Type of challenges**
  — how met them

- **Reasons for changing job**
- **Frustrations on job**
  — how resolved
- **Preferred job environment**
- **What looking for in job**
  — in a career

EDUCATION

You've given me a good review of your work experience—now let's talk about your education. Why don't we start with high school briefly and then cover more recent schooling and any specialized on the job training you may have had. I'm interested in the subjects you preferred, your grades, extracurricular activities, and anything else of importance. **What was high school like for you?**

Start with high school and then review college and any further education. Also review specialized on-the-job training, recent courses and future educational plans.

ASK:
- **Subjects liked best**
- **Those liked less well**
  — why?
- **Reactions to teachers**
- **Level of grades**
  — effort required

- **Why chose college**
- **How chose major**
- **Toughest courses**
- **Major achievements**
  — how attained?
- **Extracurricular activities**

- **Relation of education to career**
- **Satisfaction with education**
- **Specialized training (on-the-job)**
- **Recent courses**
- **Future educational plans**

Fig. 6. Interview Guide and Follow-up Questions (continued on p. 118).

ACTIVITIES AND INTERESTS

Turning to the present, I'd like to give you the opportunity to mention some of your interests and activities outside of work—hobbies, what you do for fun and relaxation, and any community activities. **How do you spend your spare time?**

Give opportunity for discussion of interests, hobbies, civic and community involvements, geographical preferences and any personal limitations which may prevent them from meeting specific job requirements. Be sure that line of inquiry is job relevant. Avoid personal discussions.

ASK:	• Spare time activities	• What activities desired but not engaged in	—travel
	• Hobbies and interests		—relocation
	• Community involvement	• Given these commitments, availability for specific job requirements such as:	—overtime
	• What learned from activities		—weekend work
			—evening assignments

SELF ASSESSMENT

Assets

Now let's try to summarize our conversation. Thinking about all we've covered today, what would you say are some of your strengths—qualities both personal and professional that make you a good prospect **for any employer?**

ASK:	• What contributions made	• Best qualities as seen by others
	• Specific talents or abilities	• Assets in working with others
	• Recent performance review (positive)	• Relevant interests

Developmental Needs

You've given me some real assets, and now I'd like to hear about areas you'd like to develop further. All of us have qualities we'd like to change or improve. **What are some of yours?**

ASK:	• Areas of improvement	• Areas for improvement in working with others
	• Qualities wish to develop further	• Further training or experience needed
	• Advice received from others	• Recent performance review (things to improve)

TRANSITION QUESTION *(To Information Giving Phase)*

You've given me a good review of your background and experience, and I have enjoyed talking with you. Before we turn to my review of our organization, and the job, **is there anything else about your background you would like to cover?**

Do you have any <u>specific</u> questions or concerns before I give you some information about the job and the opportunities here?

PRESENTING INFORMATION AND ANSWERING QUESTIONS

All right, now I have some information I'd like to give you.

(Review organization, the job, benefits, location, etc.)

(Tailor your presentation as appropriate to your interest in candidate)

TELL ABOUT:	• Career Opportunities	• Training
	• Mobility	• Salary
	• Location	• Benefits

CLOSING

Do you have any other questions about us, the job, or anything else?

What is your level of interest in us at this point? (Explore any doubts or reservations.)

Let me review what the next steps are.

(End the interview) I want to thank you for coming today . . .

Fig. 6. (continued).

≡≡≡10≡THE LOGIC BEHIND
THE STRUCTURE:
INTERVIEW GUIDE—
PART 2

Authorities on the selection interview are unanimous in advising the use of a structure similar to the one presented in our Interview Guide (see Chapter 9, Fig. 6) because all the research shows that it is easy to use and that it gets the best results. Yet despite its proven effectiveness, many people when they first encounter the Interview Guide perceive it to be potentially mechanistic, or believe that the sequencing and order are arbitrary. In the next several pages I will address these concerns and hopefully succeed in showing you how the Interview Guide can be a very effective—and completely unobtrusive—tool in the interview.

THE INTERVIEW STRUCTURE ASSURES CANDIDATES OF A FAIR INTERVIEW—AND HELPS YOU WIN THEIR COOPERATION

As soon as candidates sense that you have a structure and a system that is the same for every candidate, they'll know that they're going to get a fair shake in the interview. One of the things candidates say in response to this process is: "Well, I couldn't control the interview. I wasn't able to limit the interviewer to certain parts of my background. But the whole thing actually flowed pretty smoothly and naturally and I really got a chance to explain myself. The interviewer really was interested in me, a lot of data came out, I gave a fair picture of myself. And I think I'm on a level playing field with other candidates. Nobody's going to come in and look a lot better than me just because they gave a better theatrical performance."

THE INTERVIEW GUIDE KEEPS YOU FROM GOING OFF ON TANGENTS

In Chapter 9 I suggested you regard the Interview Guide as a road map. It furnishes you with a basic structure, an itinerary for covering the major categories—Work Experience, Education, Outside Interests and Activities, and Self-Assessment—which you need to examine during the course of the interview. Those of you who are experienced interviewers may already plan to touch on these topics—but without an organized plan you might not get to them with every candidate. Inevitably, some candidates will take you off on tangents. In the middle of talking about work experience they might mention an education experience. You may accompany them on these side trips because you lack an alternate plan; in the meantime, you'll lose track of what you wanted to ask them and you may never get back to it.

For example, while reviewing the candidate's various work experience, you ask, "What were some of the things that you liked about that job?" The candidate says: "Well, I liked many aspects of it. I liked the fact that I had the opportunity to work at my own pace and had a certain amount of freedom and autonomy—but frankly the most important thing for me was that while I was at school I was studying economics and I was planning to major in that and it seemed to me that this type of activity would be very useful for me, and that's why I got this job in the first place. So I must say that aside from the task itself I liked that kind of activity because of its connection with my intended major."

At that point many interviewers then shift immediately to: "Oh, and what other majors did you consider? And why were you settling on economics? Was the professor instrumental in your making that decision?..." and now they're on a completely different subject ... education, majors, other issues ... will they get back to the work experience? They might. But the focus is lost when you jump around from one category to the next. This loss of focus has important consequences.

The Interview Guide Helps You Monitor and Control the Amount of Time Devoted to Each Topic

By blending categories of a candidate's background, there's no way of telling how much time is being devoted to each of them, so it's hard to maintain the appropriate balance between topics.

The extensive research on the interview has not only revealed the four topics that are worth covering, but it's given us a pretty good idea of how long, proportionately, it's best to spend on each topic. In a 35-minute interview, to get the best results, you'd spend roughly 10–15 minutes on Work Experience, 6–8 minutes on Education, 5 minutes on Activities and Interests, and 5 minutes on Self-Assessment. The remaining time is spent giving information and wrapping up the interview.

By using the Interview Guide you will be sure to cover each area with the degree of thoroughness it requires.

REVIEWING THE CATEGORIES OF A CANDIDATE'S BACKGROUND SEPARATELY HELPS YOU MAKE MORE ACCURATE JUDGMENTS

Suppose you ask questions relating to Work Experience, Education, Activities and Interests, and Self-Assessment, merely as they occur to you and to the candidate, not in the order suggested by the Interview Guide. Even if by some lucky accident you do end up spending about the right amount of time on each category, the quality of the data you collect will be diminished because there will be no separation of the categories; it will be there in one big mush. If you see the same behavior in different categories of a candidate's background, you have the more powerful evidence. If you use "free association" to guide you through the interview, you won't get the "holographic" or "different camera-angle" effect. By using the Interview Guide you can be sure of getting to all of the categories in the right order and sequence and of covering them all in a consistent way with every candidate. Comparisons between candidates are then more valid.

If You Maintain Separation Between Categories You Will Be Able to Make the Best Use of the Key Questions

Finally, you are going to come to the interview equipped with a special set of key, well-researched questions called "one-step probes." Each set is specifically designed for each category. There will be a set for Work Experience, another set for Education, and so on. Each set is designed to work with a particular category to give you a different angle on the candidate. Obviously, if you scramble the categories you won't be able to get the most out of these tools.

USING THE "OVERVIEW" STATEMENT SETS UP THE INTERVIEW—IT RELAXES THE CANDIDATE AND KEEPS YOU ORGANIZED

The logic of the Interview Guide is what's important, not the exact words. Once you are able to present the Overview statement in your own words, the effects are immediate. Watch the candidates as you explain the process, and you will actually see them lean back in their chairs, thinking, "Okay, this makes sense." You can see them getting a sense that the interview is going to work, and realizing that the burden of guiding the interview is no longer all on them—they will also realize that they won't have to worry about what's ahead, because you've told them. There's no need for them to sit nervously on the edge of their chairs, waiting, wondering, trying to anticipate, asking questions, and making whatever points occur to them at random to make sure you do not overlook a particular interest of theirs. Now they know they will have the chance to have their say, and they will now be able to give their full attention to your questions.

But the Overview statement does more than that: By putting the process in perspective, it keeps you on track as well as the candidate. It gives you a reference point to reflect back on later in the interview; whether the candidate gets you off track, or you let yourself get off track, you can refer back to the plan. In addition, it can be very useful to refer to this opening statement as a rationale for bringing the candidate back on track. You say: "That's very interesting. I really enjoyed talking with you about this, but as I said in the beginning, I will be covering your educational background in detail in a separate topic. Let's just finish our review of your work experiences and we'll get to that. What was your next job?"

WHY NOT COMBINE WORK EXPERIENCE WITH EDUCATION? OR COVER EDUCATION FIRST?

Common sense might suggest combining Education and Work Experience, since, for many people early work experience and early education occurred at the same time. The empirical evidence, however, the accumulated research on all the optional ways to organize an interview, clearly point to separating them. In short, it works this way. Usually, interviewers are simply used to reviewing education first or blending the topics. It is no problem for the candidate to separate them with a little guidance from you.

In addition, the categories are not of equal time weight, as I've already mentioned. You will spend most of your time on Work Experience, less on Education, and even less on the remaining topics. They are arranged in order of decreasing time investment.

Finally, it's quite critical to keep these categories separate if you want to benefit from the extra added emphasis and value, the "holographic" or "different-camera-angle" effect that you get from comparing information about the candidate's behavior in different contexts. We're interested in finding out about the candidate's Can Do, Will Do, and Fit factors, which only the interview can disclose for us, and so we want to examine each category—Work Experience, Education, Activities and Interests—as a separate theater for the possible display of the qualities or behaviors required by the job. To accomplish this we're going to take the same time frame and examine it from different directions, to look for evidence of the same behaviors coming up in different facets of the candidate's life.

Why Not Cover Education First?

It is no accident that Work Experience is placed before Education. To some of you it might seem to make more sense to start with Education, especially if Education came first in the candidate's career. Nevertheless, with every candidate you should start with Work Experience. When it comes to those cases in which you would be most tempted to start with Education, as in the case of a student or someone recently out of school, for example—especially with these candidates, you should start with Work Experience. It gently steers them away from their prepared presentation and encourages them to reveal more of themselves.

In the middle of talking about their Work Experience candidates might start drifting into a discussion of their Education. I wouldn't cut them off if they are just making a casual statement or reference, but if it looks like this casual aside is about to turn into a full-fledged digression, I would say something like: "Well, as I said in my overview, we're going to get to that in a few moments, but let's first complete our review of your Work Experience. What was your next job?" Keep them on track—gently.

Categories Are Arranged in Decreasing Order of Their Contribution to the Decision

Another reason I advise against covering Education first is that the categories in the Interview Guide are presented in decreasing order of their contribution and therefore of time investment. Activities and Interests or Self-Assessment should be covered more briefly than Work Experience and Education. The bulk of your time should be spent in Work Experience, a little less in Education, and a lot less in Activities and Interests and Self-Assessment. While I would advise you against running past the optimum length for any of these areas at the expense of the others, taking them in this order assures that you will give adequate coverage to the most important ones.

This is not a pure chronological interview, it is chronological by category. Remember that the interview is designed to give a number of distinct views of the same candidate, views from different perspectives, the same life story told from four different points of view.

Beginning with Work Experience Hinders "Coached"
Candidates from Taking Control of the Interview

Candidates fresh out of college or technical or professional
school usually receive some sort of preparation for the job
interview, whether it be a two-week course on the interview,
an hour videotape, or reading a book on the subject. Which
facets of their background do you think they focus on when
they prepare for their interviews? Naturally, their educational background, their specialized courses, the projects
they worked on. Perhaps they'll include their experience
working for a food co-op while they were in school or during
the summers. But what they mostly prepare for is a discussion of their education. It's been the most important thing in
their lives for a long time. Their principal concern is how
they are going to explain why they took those particular
courses, how much it's helped them, and how it's going to
help you.

They have also heard that interviewers have no idea what
they're doing, and that when the interviewer says, "Tell me
about yourself," all it means is that the interviewer doesn't
have a plan and this is the opportunity to implement their
plan. That plan consists of inserting into the conversation
five or six accomplishments they've thought about in detail,
then getting the interviewer to tell them what they're looking for and saying to the interviewer, more or less, "What a
coincidence, that's exactly the kind of person I am!"

Covering their work experiences first gently guides them
away from this plan. Candidates who have had formal
preparation for the interview say to us in debriefings: "Well,
when I sat down with that interviewer, it was clear she had
a plan. I hadn't anticipated that. I knew I wasn't going to
get by just giving my three or four prepared accomplishments. And we started out with Work Experience first. I
really hadn't thought much about that. And my earliest
work experiences on top of that. I hadn't thought about
them at all. And so with that interviewer I basically said,
"Okay, what do you want to know about me?' and gave up

trying to control the flow of material." The realization that Work Experience is going to be covered first, and covered in depth, doesn't knock candidates off their stride to the point where they can't continue. However, it does make it more difficult for them to control the process or limit the interview to certain areas . . . and it encourages them to present their real selves.

Is it magic to start with Work Experience? No. But it's better, especially if you do it in every interview, interview after interview. All the various options have been carefully researched, and this approach works best. Would it be the end of the world if you started with Education? Of course not. But if you were to do it first, at least separate the two categories. You will find that covering Work Experience first not only works well, but it also doesn't seem awkward or illogical for the candidate. The fact that you're used to covering Education first isn't a reason to continue doing so when it's so easy to start with Work Experience and it works so well.

WHY COVER VERY EARLY WORK EXPERIENCE?

Indeed, something a candidate did while still in high school, for example, would seem to have little or no relation to what he or she is doing now. How could it have any significance? It is certainly true that early work experience is probably not going to unearth a lot of technical skills. But Can Do factors like intelligence, prioritization ability, organizational skills, common sense, or communications skills might come up. Even if they don't, the beginnings of patterns of the Will Do and Fit factors are present to some degree. If candidates have demonstrated maturity, or a positive response to direction and authority, or the ability to work well with people on a team, or perserverance, you can bet they're going to bring those qualities with them—if they've displayed the opposite of those qualities, you shouldn't expect them to change their stripes now just because you're going to give them a new title and put them in a job with other responsibilities or even new training. So, even if you don't dwell at great length on early work experiences—and I don't advise you to—you should touch on them.

Here's a real example from the many candidates I have interviewed personally. Interviewing for the same position, I asked three people in three different interviews, "What was your first job ever?" and all three answered, "Well, I used to mow lawns while I was in school." You might be tempted to say: "So what? Let's move on past that." But then I probed it one step deeper—I spent another 60 seconds on it. In one instance it turned out that Candidate A never physically touched a lawn mower. He hired other students, rented the equipment, got the customers, collected the money, paid off the students, paid off the equipment, and at the end of the year filled out and filed the tax forms, virtually running a business without ever touching a lawn mower.

Candidate B is one of those who pushed a lawn mower. This candidate was proud of getting more lawns done on any Saturday than anybody else. Boy, what a whiz—if there was an award given out for speed and volume of work done, Candidate B would have gotten it. However, there were some complaints. He nicked a few trees, and never mowed under the bushes. "Nobody sees under the bushes anyway, so what difference did that make?" There were a few complaints, but a lot of lawns got done and Candidate B felt proud of that.

Candidate C also pushed a lawn mower, although without getting nearly as many lawns done as Candidate B. But this candidate felt that mowing under the bushes was part of the job, and she always did so even though nobody might ever notice. There were never any complaints, and the job was always done with the degree of meticulousness that she thought was appropriate.

These are the beginnings of three different people. I

wouldn't accept this one little example as being decisive in any of these interviews, but what if I see an entrepreneurial streak in the first candidate as a pattern over time? Or perhaps Candidate B's story supplies the first example in a pattern of getting things done quickly but superficially, with more concern for volume than quality. That might tell me something about that candidate which may or may not fit my job. If I want somebody to be meticulous and pay attention to detail, somebody who may not get as much done but will do it right every time, then Candidate C—assuming the pattern holds up—might be the one for me.

WHAT ABOUT MILITARY EXPERIENCE?

The time a candidate spent in any of the armed forces should be considered as a part of the candidate's work experience. It will come up in the chronology as you ask, "And where did you go after that?" The same questions asked about a work experience apply to military experience. Specialized training received during that period might be covered later under Education.

WHAT IF THE CANDIDATE NEVER WORKED?

It may turn out that a candidate fresh out of school has never done any kind of a job for pay in his or her life. Obviously, you can't cover a job if there's no job to cover, so if this is the case, there is nothing else to do but divide the remaining time among the other categories. Or course, if there has been no job since the candidate mowed lawns that summer, you'd be ill-advised to spend 20 minutes talking about mowing lawns—instead, you would spend a few minutes on it and again divide up the remaining time between the other categories. But let me emphasize that any work the candidate did for money should be covered.

BUT HOW DO YOU FIND OUT WHAT THE CANDIDATE'S ANSWER MEANS?

The Interview Guide as I've presented it so far has organized logic and comprehensiveness, but has no depth. All it does is introduce a category (i.e., Work Experience) and then, in effect, it drops you off a cliff. However, as a flip forward to Chapter 11 will show, there's more to using the Interview Guide than what I've explained so far. In this chapter, I'll supply you with the sets of key, well-researched questions, or "one-step probes" specifically designed for each category. Then I'll introduce the second set of questions, the "two-step (and three- and four- and five-step) probes", which will enable you to test and validate the candidate's answers to your initial questions.

But without going into detail now, let me point out that candidates will reveal a lot when you ask seemingly casual questions like: "What do you feel you have accomplished?" "What are the things that you liked the best?" "What are the things that you could have done a little differently?" "What kind of feedback did you get from others?"

Let's take Candidate C, the worker who was meticulous and mowed under the bushes. She seems to feel that that aspect of her work was a real positive. But you may know that that kind of behavior will never work for the particular job that you have in mind. That job requires somebody who moves quickly. It won't be necessary to get absolutely everything done, but there's a lot of time pressure, and it would be better to leave the mop-ups undone and get on to the next task—that's the job. So, while in the candidate's personal value system, and perhaps in our own, we might regard this kind of behavior as positive, in fact it might be a negative for a particular job. The candidate who says: "Well, frankly, the thing I think I did the best was getting so many lawns done. I found a way to cut some corners. I didn't do things that weren't necessary, and other people were just doing things because they were supposed to be done a certain way. But I found a way to get more work done and to make more money in any single day...." This candidate took pride in the way he increased volume. But the way he increased volume was by cutting corners, which in some jobs may be a plus and in others a minus. In cases such as these, the candidates are not conscious of revealing anything negative about themselves, they're just talking about themselves—they have no idea of the connection, because that is specific to the very detailed job requirements that only you know about. Indeed, information of this sort is neither negative nor positive in itself. It only acquires a value in the context of the job.

THE TRANSITION QUESTIONS ON THE INTERVIEW GUIDE SET UP EACH MAJOR TOPIC—THEY'RE NOT MEANT TO BE A BATTERY OF QUESTIONS

I bring up this point just in case you're thinking: "Boy you're firing a lot of questions at once. How can anyone be expected to remember all that? Isn't that putting too much pressure on the candidate?" I can see how it might look that way. It seems that you're saying: "Tell me about your work experiences—describe your duties and responsibilities, what you liked, disliked, and learned from each of your jobs, start with your first job—GO!"

Perceived as a list of questions for the candidate to remember and answer, the Transition Questions might look burdensome—but fortunately that's not how the Transistion Questions are intended. All the candidate has to remember is the last thing you asked. These introductory sentences are just intended to give them a sense of what's going to happen next in that topic. Just as the Overview statement introduces the plan for the entire interview, each of these topic lead-ins sets the stage for that area of discussion. Of course, once you're in a topic alike Work Experience, you will ask specific questions to probe each individual job in detail. You'll be asking these questions throughout the interview, guiding the candidate through each topic.

When you make the Transition Questions that leads into Work Experience or Education or Activities and Interests, you can demonstrate with your tone—casual up until the last sentence—that everything up until that final question is an overview, and that now you're giving them a place to start. Do that, and it will not be perceived as a series of specific questions. It should be clear to candidates that the only part they need to address themselves to immediately is, "What do you remember about your first job?" And then, even if you haven't managed to convey that message solely through your tone of voice, it will be very clear when you follow their first answer with your next question.

IF YOU MENTION THAT YOU WILL BE COVERING AN ASPECT OF THEIR BACKGROUND IN ONE OF THE TRANSITION QUESTIONS, BE SURE TO GET TO IT

Remember the intention of a plan is to organize the candidates and you. Follow through on whatever you say you want to cover. For example, in the introduction to Education you mention that you're going to cover "any specialized, on-the-job training you might have had after your formal education." As you walk through their educational background and complete your review of their formal education, say: "All right, I did say we were going to talk about any specialized on-the-job training. What training have you had on the job or anything beyond formal education that you'd like to share with me?" If you mentioned you were going to get to a subject you should get to it.

ISN'T IT INTRUSIVE TO ASK ABOUT ACTIVITIES AND INTERESTS?

ACTIVITIES AND INTERESTS

Turning to the present, I'd like to give you the opportunity to mention some of your interests and activites outside of work—hobbies, what you do for fun and relaxation, and any community activities. How do you spend your spare time?

You might legitimately wonder if it's worth asking candidates questions about their activities and interests. Won't candidates object to personal questions? What are we going to learn from them anyway? What does it really mean, and why bother?

Activities and Interests Are Not Covered at Great Length—
But They're Worth Some Attention

We're not going to dwell on Activities and Interests as a subject. If you spend 15 or 20 minutes on Work Experience, you may spend only 5 minutes on this category. On the other hand, while it is not worth the same investment of time as Work Experience, it should play its role in refining your understanding of a candidate. All the research on interviewing has focused us on four categories: (1) Work Experience (where you spend most of your time), (2) Education, (3) Activities and Interests, and (4) Self-Assessment. These four categories contribute the most to accurate decisions.

Activities and Interests Are Not Meant to Be Personal or Intrusive

We want to be sure that during the Activities and Interests phase we do not intrusively ask people about their personal background. We want to give them the *opportunity* to share with us whatever they think relevant and appropriate to the interview about things they do outside of formal work or formal education. It's not our intention (and it would not serve our purpose) to turn up embarrassing or merely personal aspects of their private lives. In fact, what we're exploring here isn't their private lives at all—it's just that part of their public lives that happens not to fall within either the area of Work Experience or Education. And their response is entirely up to them. It's important to bear that in mind when it comes to tone.

Activities and Interest Can Confirm Patterns You've Seen in the Other Categories

Beyond that, you might still be asking, "Well, so they play golf a lot, suppose they build model ships, suppose they play tennis, so what?" You would have a point if we were to go no further than merely labeling an activity. Just as in the case of the lawn-mowing service, it was necessary to probe to get all the subtle data. To get anywhere with the Activities and Interests section it is important to probe below the surface. You must take each experience and ask the candidate: "What have you learned from it? How often do you do it? What do you like about it? How do you get started?" With a series of seemingly innocuous questions, you can find out what the activity means to them.

You might find out that Allen, who says, "I play golf," has a set of golf clubs in the trunk of his car that haven't been touched for five years. In which case it means nothing. On the other hand, you might find out that he does play frequently, and with further probing you might discover that what he really enjoys is the precision of it. It turns out he doesn't particularly care how many strokes it takes to get the ball on the green, but, when he's out there he's fascinated by the way wind resistance, the slope of the green, which way the grass is growing, and every other conceivable factor contributes to getting that ball into that little hole. So it appears that patience and a love of precision may be a component of his personality—and we would be more confident that this indication is valid if we had seen indications of the same qualities when we explored the candidate's Work Experience and Education.

On the other hand, it might be that Allen really plays golf to compete with his friends; he likes to be friends with very competitive people; that's the kind of dynamism and those are the kinds of relationships he prefers. Or it could mean something else again. You won't know what it might mean for your purposes unless you probe and find out what it means to him. With the probing questions I'm going to show you later, you'll be able to do just that.

Activities and Interests Can Reveal Qualities NOT Shown in Other Categories

Another point is that sometimes, in activities and interests outside of work, people display qualities that they are not able to exhibit any place else. It might be that only in the context of the Parent-Teacher Association does Mark have the opportunity to show he can get things through others even when he has no authority over them. Or maybe it shows that he does six things at once even when he has choices. Or maybe it demonstrates that he really enjoys being given big problems of a global nature. In his everyday job he's only handled little things of a specific nature, but he really likes the global approach, and that may be important to you.

Activities and Interests is Useful to Generate a Practical Discussion of Special Circumstances of the Job

Finally, some of the time you're going to spend on this category can be devoted to one or two issues about your job that are quite critical. Suppose you're interviewing for a job that has a lot of last-minute overtime, or weekend work, or project work that will require the employee to stay late. In response to what Beth has told you, you might say: "Well, Beth, it seems to me that you're very involved in that community group committee, and you're making a real contribution. But this job you're being considered for will include last-minute work into the evening without a lot of notice. How would you go about meeting this absolute job requirement, given your commitment to your committee? And how have you handled such conflicting demands in the past?" You can sometimes get a healthy discussion going about the reality of these conflicting demands more readily than just mentioning them at the end of the interview— "Well, the job requires occasional evening assignments. Any problem with overtime?"

Aren't There Equal Employment Opportunity Issues Raised by Activities and Interests?

The legal aspects of effective interviewing will be covered in greater depth later (Chapter 21), but in case you have any concern on this score in connection with Activities and Interests, let me deal with this problem briefly now. You should not probe areas that are likely to reveal candidates' affiliation with certain groups, whether religious, political, or ethnic. However, one could also argue that it is not fair to deny candidates the opportunity to talk about things they've done outside of work or formal education that might reflect favorably on their suitability for the job.

When candidates say, "Well, I'm pretty active in my local church," your job is to say, "Religious affiliation aside, what are some of the things you learned from that experience that you would like me to know?" Or, "What were some of the benefits of that experience?" Or, "What qualities did you develop while you were there that you think you'd like to share with me that might be applicable to the job?" Or, as the case may be, "What were some of the things you learned from your involvement in that political group, political affiliation aside, that might be applicable to this job?"

The answer might be, "Well, I did a lot of public speaking," or you might discover that a candidate had to motivate people to action, or had to organize things or to handle funds. You might uncover all kinds of subtleties about a person in this way. The point is that you explore the experience—not the label. If you make your intentions clear, people will appreciate the fact that you're not poking around in their personal background but, rather, want to give them a chance to show you something you haven't yet learned about them that is relevant to the job. Remember, the phrase to use here is, "To the extent that there's any aspect of that you'd like to share." Then move them on.

If in the course of talking about some outside activity or interest candidates happen to raise personal issues that are not job-related, you should change the subject. Don't ask anything more about it, don't write it down, and don't pass that information on to anybody else. It's important not to probe into areas of a personal nature, such as family background, even if candidates volunteer the data.

In conclusion, recognize that Activities and Interests occupies only about five minutes of your time. Also, note that by probing you can find out what the particular activity or interest means to the candidate. If you proceed according to these guidelines, it will be reasonable and very useful for you to cover this area, briefly. To neglect it will reduce the accuracy of the interview by a small but measurable amount. Of course you could omit it, but as you keep lopping off things, the effectiveness of the interview keeps diminishing. I urge you to try it even if you have reservations. In the next three interviews you do, if you find that even once the person looks at you and says: "What? My outside interests? How ridiculous! Why do you ask me that?", then never ask it again. I'm confident that if you phrase your inquiry the way I've suggested, that will never happen, and in two out of three instances you'll actually get valuable information that will give you subtle insights into the candidates and help you refine your understanding of them.

SELF-ASSESSMENT

In the collective unconscious of interviewers, over the years, there are themes that reoccur, and one of them is the question, "What are your strengths and weaknesses?" Interviewers usually see it as a single question rather than as a topic category. Interviewers ask it routinely and candidates can answer it in their sleep. The results are generally not very rewarding.

The Self-Assessment category I refer to is not the same thing. In the context of the Interview Guide, there is a substantive difference between exploring the category of "Assets and Developmental Needs" and asking, "What are your strengths and weaknesses?" I won't argue that calling strengths "assets" is a great distinction. But notice how we lead into the topic: "All right, now let's try and summarize our conversation. Thinking about all that we've covered up to this point, work experiences, education, outside interests and activities, what are some of the qualities, both personal and professional, that make you a good prospect for any employer?"

When you rephrase that in your own words the key components of your message are:

> We're going to summarize . . .

(so this is not a request for new information or novel insights on their part, it's a summary)

> the personal or professional qualities that you'd like to share that would make you a good prospect for any employer.

However you ultimately rephrase the statement into your own words, those points should be made. Each of them plays its role in making this little section work. I don't want you to ask, "What are the strengths that make you a good prospect for this particular job with us?" Sure, you'd like to know that, but candidates don't really know the answer to that question. They can guess at it, they can narrow their thinking down to what they suppose is appropriate, but they don't know the job the way you do, and, in any case, that's not their task, it's yours. Let them talk about their assets in a broader context, and you'll connect what they tell you to what you know about the job.

"Weaknesses" Versus "Development Needs"

When it comes to discussing the second half of the Self-Assessment category, there will certainly be more awkwardness if you use the word "weaknesses" instead of "developmental needs." Weakness is an emotionally charged word. I'm not, however, recommending for merely cosmetic reasons that you substitute a neutral phrase for one with unpleasant connotations. "Developmental needs" is not just a euphemism for "weaknesses." I would want you not only to avoid using the word "weaknesses," but avoid them even thinking in those terms.

When candidates are debriefed after being asked about their "weaknesses" what they say is, "Well, I may not be perfect, but I don't have any weaknesses, and if I did I wouldn't tell an interviewer about them anyway." But if you've asked them the question they have to say something. I don't have to tell you how candidates respond to this kind of question. You've done it yourself: "Well, I feel that one of my most devastating weaknesses is my total inability to accept irresponsibility. Wherever I experience it, I reject it, I rail against it. . . . " Or, the more common one is: "Well, I feel that—and I've got a lot of negative feedback about this—I'm just too hard a worker. People have told me, 'Go to lunch, go to lunch,' and, 'Go home, will you? You can't stay past ten o'clock at night!' I'm sorry, I just can't help it. I'd rather work than eat."

The interview is a game now. We don't want it to be a game. I'd rather say: "Well, Cliff, you've shown me some real assets and I appreciate that. You're obviously a very talented person, but all of us have areas in which we'd like to improve or develop: What are some of yours?"

The specific follow-up questions for this area will give you a clearer idea of the tone of the inquiry. Clearly you aren't trying to get them to admit any "weaknesses." These are reasonable follow-up questions that candidates can respond to in a meaningful way: "What additional training could you benefit from?" "What qualities would you like to develop that you haven't had a chance to develop yet?" "What were some of the things you'd like to do even better than you're doing now?" "What additional experience do you think would round you out and make you more valuable?" "What have you learned about yourself in a recent performance review that you're working on or would like to work on?" "What advice have you gotten from your friends or peers or co-workers or employees in the past?"

Questions like these should make it clear to the candidate that you're not looking for an admission of anything horrible. The candidate will also be clear on the importance of this phase of the interview by the proportion of time you devote to it. And again, if we spend 20 minutes on Work Experience, we spend about five minutes on Self-Assessment. In that Self-Assessment stage, roughly half the time is devoted to "assets," and then the candidate has the opportunity to turn "developmental needs" to their advantage by showing that they are capable of a realistic self-appraisal instead of just taking a virtue and calling it a flaw.

You want to hear the candidates' perspective on themselves not necessarily because you're going to buy it—they may be completely mistaken about their own assets and developmental needs. You're going to make you own judgments about them based on the data you've collected throughout the interview; as a matter of fact, one of the things you'd like to know is whether they have a realistic understanding of themselves. Suppose Richard is really quite talented but there's an area in which he needs to develop further, such as presentation skills—say he hasn't had experience in doing formal presentations with slides and charts. Perhaps you would like to provide him with an opportunity for development, and it so happens that your company has a program specifically designed for that. Now your turn to the Self-Assessment section: Not only does Richard think he needs no improvement in that area, he thinks he's good at it. How likely is it then that he is going to be willing to change?

On the other hand, if Richard already knows he needs to develop in that area then he might be quite receptive to it, especially if he expresses interest in improving. In that case, his remarks might provide an opportunity to influence him a little later in the information-giving phase, at which point you could say: "Richard, earlier on in our interview you indicated that you wanted to develop yourself in this particular way. Not only do we feel strongly about it, we actually have a training program designed for that very purpose, because often people come in without this kind of experience. If you come on board with us, within six months you'll have acquired that skill."

With some people, that Self-Assessment category may reveal little new or vital. With others, you'll get at some really interesting material, or add a valuable dimension to the things you already know. In any event, it only takes a few minutes and it's worth doing.

By the way, if you skip it, when you turn to asking people, "Is there anything else about your background you want to cover?", candidates with any savvy at all will take the opportunity to summarize! They'll say, "Well, I guess one thing I'd like to do is pull it all together. . . . " and they'll summarize because that's what they've been trained to do. It's much better to give them the opportunity to summarize under your direction, in the context you've chosen for that purpose—one that encourages them to give you a more balanced picture, and gives you the opportunity to ask a lot of detailed questions.

≡≡≡11≡≡THE ART OF ASKING GOOD QUESTIONS

Once you have introduced a topic such as Work Experience or Education, how do you probe to get details and subtleties from candidates and how can you be sure they'll be the details you need?

In the last few chapters I've laid out an overall structure or plan and a strategy for the effective interview—but so far that structure has no depth. It introduces a subject but gives no clues as to how to get substance and detail. Strategy is useless without tactics. Those are the areas I'm going to address in the next few chapters: the fine points, the tactics of getting detailed, relevant information.

THE FUNCTION OF QUESTIONS IN THE INTERVIEW

Testing Assumptions

In general, we make too many assumptions. For one thing, we assume that someone who's been doing something for five years is better at it than someone who's only done it for two years. Yet, while that may be the case, things don't always work out that way. No doubt you know someone who has had the same job for five years who is no better at it than someone on the job for two years.

Another common assumption is that someone who has done something is better at it than someone who hasn't done it. If two students, for example, have the same grades and same general background but one has actually performed some of the tasks involved in the particular job for which you are interviewing, it is tempting to decide that the one who has the relevant experience would be a better choice than the one who has no relevant experience. Of course, that might be the correct choice, or it might not: What about performance? Did the candidate demonstrate the qualities we know are related to success on our job—or did the candidate demonstrate the opposite behaviors? We don't know until we test the assumption. If there was nothing else to go on, certainly I would go with the person who had the relevant experience. But I want you to get past that.

The only way you can find out whether your assumptions really are correct is to test and validate them. For that you need to have a pool of effective, well-researched questions to choose from. Equipped with these, you can unpack, delve into, and probe each experience in the candidate's background until you have answers you can rely on.

Getting Beyond What They Did to How they Did It

Remember, people do not bring to you their accomplishments from their previous job or educational background. They leave their accomplishments behind. What they bring with them is how they achieved their accomplishments.

They bring their initiative, analytical thinking, motivation, stick-to-itiveness, their capacity to work under deadline pressure, and other qualities that made them successful. One of the functions of the interview is to move us past the knowledge of what they did to how they did it. That's what we "buy" when we hire someone.

Why Do We Need These "Ready-made" Questions?

You may think you already know how to ask questions, and maybe you're right. But you might not be when it comes to the special context of the interview. Like so many other things regarding the interview, the effective questions and the probing techniques are derived from solid research into areas that are usually taken for granted. The questions I'm going to provide for you are not magic questions, or questions you or the candidate have never heard of—there are no such questions. But they have been determined to meet all five of the following criteria:

1. They're easy for the interviewer to ask.

2. They're easy for the candidate to answer.

3. They're seemingly casual questions.

4. They don't telegraph what qualities you're looking for.

5. They're easy to follow up and probe for more detail.

But before I show them to you I'm going to review questions that don't meet these criteria, yet are frequently used by interviewers.

INEFFECTIVE QUESTIONS

Predictable Questions

Most interviewers automatically ask the same two or three questions about every job with every candidate. The questions usually are: "What were your duties and responsibilities on that job?" "How long were you there?" "What did you like best about it?" "Why did you leave?" "All right, what was your next job?" The order might change, but those are the basic questions. Some of them have probably been answered on the candidate's application or résumé. If you are seeing several candidates in a row, as happens in campus interviews, you are at the very least, too predictable. By the afternoon the word has spread, and the last few students seem very articulate—partly because they know your questions in advance.

Now if you've been using them yourself don't be offended. Most interviewers ask them. They're not illogical or silly, but they're not very productive. The trouble with these questions is that they don't differentiate between candidates effectively. Eight out of ten candidates will respond to these questions with virtually the same answers. Also, an alert (or coached) candidate will use them as a pretext for delivering a canned presentation.

Ridiculous Questions

Many well-intentioned interviewers, out of utter frustration and in an effort to help differentiate between candidates, have been known to ask, "What's your favorite color?" or they might suddenly fire the question, "If you could be an animal, what animal would you choose to be?" In fact, there are many interviewers who swear by such questions. Here's a list of questions culled from applicant debriefings:

- ☐ Quick: how much change is in your pocket?
- ☐ You're walking down a path and come to a fork in the road. In one direction is a lake. In the other, a forest. Which would you choose—and why?
- ☐ Describe the silliest thing you've ever done.
- ☐ What mistake might we make in hiring you?
- ☐ Do something that will infuriate me! (a favorite of the lovable Admiral Rickover).

☐   Give me one reason I should hire you rather than one of the many other talented candidates I've seen!

☐   Quick, sell me this (pen, ashtray, etc.)!

Would you like to be asked these questions? Your answer should be an emphatic yes! . . . if you're prepared for them you can really impress the interviewer—obviously that doesn't add much to the real usefulness of these questions. It is true they are often unpredictable and candidates do answer very differently, but the answers are usually both uninterpretable and, at the same time, overinterpreted by interviewers. Also, talented candidates with choices tell us they go elsewhere when they encounter interviewers asking these questions.

Whether you are asking this sort of question or whether you've been the puzzled recipient of such questions, I hope you can appreciate my point—this business of questions is trickier than it looks at first blush. There are pitfalls. It is not something that you can necessarily do right automatically, without thought.

WHAT KINDS OF QUESTIONS ARE EFFECTIVE IN THE INTERVIEW—AND HOW THEY WORK

The questions I'm going to introduce in the following chapters fall into two groups. The questions in the first group—the key, well-researched questions referred to above—comprise a menu of basic questions that I call one-step probes. These appear on the Interview Guide (see Chapter 9, Fig. 6) under each topic. Chances are you won't ask all of these questions; you'll choose the ones you need to probe a particular job, educational experience, or any other area of the candidate's background you want to explore.

The questions in the second group—the deeper follow-up questions or two-step, three-step, and four-step (and so on) probes—are the questions you'd ask whenever a line of inquiry opened up by one of the questions in the first group looks like it might be promising.

Is it clear yet? Maybe not—but let's get on to the actual questions you should be asking in an inteview. Then we can refine the probing techniques I've sketched out so far. When I show you how these questions operate during the interview, you'll see it isn't very complicated—just very powerful.

While I warned against relying on "social conversational skills" for the interview, I do not mean to say that the interview doesn't use verbal skills. It is a purposeful conversation. It follows branching pathways. Decisions are being made all the time by you and the person you're talking to about whether to go on discussing a particular topic or to change the subject; the difference is that the interview is a guided conversation, and what guides it are the structures we're talking about now.

Tools to Help You Probe for Details

Here's another way of thinking about it. Imagine a tract of land, 10 thousand acres owned by an oil company. You have stock in that oil company. You wouldn't be too thrilled to hear that the head geologist was bringing in the drilling crew and saying things like, "All right, tell you what, let's drill over here today." When nothing is found, he says: "All right, too bad. Okay, today's a new day, let's try over there. Okay, how about over here?" In other words, all the geologist is doing is drilling at random on this tract of land. What a nightmare that would be, not what you would expect. You would assume that the geologist would be doing what he's been trained to do . . . grid out this landmass, number every element of the grid, take soil samples from each one and study them, take infrared photography from above, study rock formations . . . and do whatever geologists do to make judgments from surface indicators as to where it would be reasonable to drill, where you've got a chance of getting oil or gas, and where it would be irrational to drill.

You're going to do the same kind of thing that a conscientious geologist would do. Instead of a tract of land, you have a particular job or educational experience or outside activity in front of you. You're going to use the one-step probes (the Follow-up Questions from the Interview Guide) the way a geologist would use soil samples to touch the surface of an event—in this case, a single job. You're going to ask the one-step probes. Like a geologist, you'll study the results of your soil sample. Except you're looking for job-relevant information. In the back of your mind are the Can Do, Will Do, and Fit factors—the Knowledge, Skills and Abilities, Behaviors, and Environmental Issues—that you've researched beforehand. So you say, "What were some of the difficult problems you faced?" Now, it might happen that you find the candidate's answer fascinating, and personally you'd love to hear more about it, but it has no relevance to any of the job criteria for which you are searching. If this were a social conversation you might go down that path another 10 minutes. There's no time for that in a business interview. So you'll say, "That's really fascinating, I'd love to talk to you more about it if we had time, but, what were some of the things you liked best about that job?" and shift the candidate to another question, touching the surface of another aspect of that job. If this doesn't turn up anything of a job-related nature, you go on to the next one-step probe, "What were some of the things you learned from that experience?" or, "What opportunities were there for advancement or promotion?" If any of these answers trigger off the hint of a Can Do, Will Do, or Fit factor, then you will pursue it, through the two-, three-, four-, or five-step probes.

You will only pursue an area of inquiry when you have some job-relevant reason for doing so—and you will do it systematically; the process will be tight and efficient. Apply this simple principle of asking the basic questions about an event such as a single job and probing further only when you've got something that is job-related, and the efficiency of the interview will be sharpened dramatically. There will be none of the drifting and wandering that happens when interviewers haven't any idea what they're looking for or any plan for pursuing it once they're on the trail.

≡≡≡12≡WHAT QUESTIONS SHOULD YOU ASK: ONE-STEP PROBES

I am about to introduce the set of recommended, well-researched, basic questions you should start with when probing a job, an educational experience, or any other facet of a candidate's background. Since some of you are skipping around in this book—or may have even jumped to this chapter for the questions to ask in your next interview 30 minutes from now—I'm going to review the source of these basic questions here. Then in subsequent chapters I'll deal with testing the answers they elicit.

You may recall my saying earlier that these questions have been selected out of a large universe of questions because they meet the following five criteria:

1. They're easy for the interviewer to ask.
2. They're easy for the candidate to answer.
3. They're seemingly casual questions.
4. They don't telegraph what qualities you're looking for.
5. They're easy to follow and probe for more detail.

Questions that meet these criteria are wonderfully helpful to you in the interview. Why shouldn't they be available to you? When you look at these questions you'll see that there's nothing astonishing or unreasonable about them. These are not magic questions: there are no such questions. Nor are there likely to be any questions you haven't heard of before. Remember they are in part selected because they're seemingly casual and therefore disarming. Your aim is not to be unique or startling, your aim is to get detailed answers from each candidate so you can differentiate one candidate from another. When the same questions elicit different responses in each interview, you know the differences derive from the candidates, not from your approach. By the way, we won't accept the answers at face value—the ways to probe past the initial answer, to test it for accuracy and to get even more detail are covered in later chapters.

There are no questions here like, "Tell me about yourself," or, "Why should we hire you?" because those questions don't meet the criteria referred to above. They just don't help you differentiate one candidate from another very well.

Notice that on the Interview Guide (see Chapter 9, Fig. 6) there is a separate set of one-step probes for the categories of Work Experience, Education, Activities and Interests, and Self-Assessment. Take a look at the Work Experience section. Most of the one-step probes provided could be asked about any single job—the only exceptions are the last two—"What kind of environment would you prefer to work in?" and, "What are you looking for in a job or a career?" You would ask those questions only once, at the end of your review of a candidate's entire Work Experience. All the other questions—what they liked about a particular job, what they didn't like, what they learned, what they accomplished, their relationships with the people they report to, the frustrations they experienced—could be asked about any job.

TOO MANY QUESTIONS? NO, A "MENU" OF QUESTIONS

In one sense, this list contains too many questions, and in another sense, too few. There are too many because you couldn't possibly ask every question in the Work Experience category about every job the candidate ever had from day one and expect to be out of that room before the end of the week. Obviously, you would not ask them all. When you start with the earliest job, ask one or two questions. For the next job, a couple more, on to the next, a few more, until you get to the most recent full-time, professionally, or technically relevant jobs, at which point you might ask all these questions and more perhaps. You should regard this as a menu of questions from which to pick and choose at will— and at random. They're all statistically equivalent; none of them is predictably better than any of the others. They all have equal potential to open up a job-relevant facet of the candidate's background.

In situations like campus interviewing, where you see many candidates in a row, one advantage of having a reasonably large pool of questions to choose from is that candidates will not be able to predict exactly what you're going to ask. To avoid being second-guessed you don't have to ask random, inappropriate questions, nor do you need to have an infinite universe of questions from which to choose. Equipped with a pool of questions in each area of the candidate's background, you'll be asking some questions about one job, some about another, some of one student, some of another. When the students get back to the dorm, they'll be telling one another, "You can't predict what this interviewer is likely to ask," because you were apparently (they think) making up questions on the spot. With even a limited universe of questions you will have more than enough flexibility.

TOO FEW QUESTIONS? ADD YOUR OWN JOB-RELEVANT QUESTIONS

However, there are also, in a different sense, too few questions from which to choose. You have to decide, among other things, if the candidate is technically competent, "Can Do" the job. It would be up to you to develop some targeted questions in this area. The Can Do's include other qualities besides technical competence, but there are usually, among the Can-Do's, certain hard-and-fast requirements that are very specific to the particular job. Whether you're hiring an engineer, a programmer, a secretary, an auditor, a marketing person, or a sales person, there are certainly things you need to know to determine a candidate's knowledge base of technical expertise. Can they operate a Wang? Do they have experience with cost accounting procedures? Do they know COBOL? Whatever the particular Can Do requirements of the job, add the necessary questions to the list for that interview. If you are the "technical interviewer," you would have to add a great number of them in order to accurately judge the candidate's technical competence.

However, for the Will Do and Fit factors, knowledge of the job requirements would probably influence your choice of questions and how you ask them, but would not make it necessary for you to create many new ones. Remember, it isn't particularly effective to ask the candidate, "Do you like to work under strict and close supervision?" It's really better, even though it seems less direct, to ask, "What did you like best about the kind of supervision and direction you received on that job?" and then ask, "And what were some of the things you liked somewhat less about it?" Ask this type of quesion for many of their jobs, and equivalent questions for your review of the candidate's educational background and outside activities. From these questions, you should get the data you need to make a judgment regarding the candidate's ability to handle the type of direction and authority likely to be experienced on your job. The answers to these more general questions will be more reliable. Of course, we'll also be probing more deeply into the answers, as you'll see. Also, note that while the questions are seemingly general or even vague, they meet all five of the criteria for a good question mentioned earlier. And, they apply to everybody. Remember, one of our goals was to set the candidate to do 80–90 percent of the talking. These questions alone go a long way toward making that happen (they're easy to answer!).

HOW DO YOU KNOW WHAT QUESTIONS TO FOLLOW UP?

As I'm sure you have noticed, one-step probes are easy to follow up (criteria number 5 of a good question). While for the most part this can work to your advantage, there's also a trap involved: For those one-step probes you do choose to ask, you simply will not be able to get through that interview in any reasonable period if you follow up on every answer the candidate gives you. That's a process more appropriate to social conversation.

Why Social Conservational Skills Are Inadequate for the Task

In a casual social conversation you might actually ask a question of someone because you want a factual answer. You might actually want to know, "What was it like going on a cruise for a vacation?" because you yourself have a vacation coming up. You might be asking, "What was this particular movie like?" because you are considering seeing it. On the other hand, often when you ask a question in casual social conversation, you either already know the answer or you're not that interested in the answer. You ask questions in order to facilitate the conversation. Say you're at a cocktail party and you find yourself face-to-face with a person you don't know, and perhaps even don't want to know. But you're a reasonably polite person, so you ask a question: "Where are you from?" or, "How do you know Bob?" or, "What do you do?" and he answers that question and then he asks you, "What do you do?" Questions help move the conversation along. That's just right for a cocktail party.

Let's suppose I met Phil at the Waldorf Astoria cocktail lounge last night and we both realize we're attending the same seminar the next day, and we start to talk. The next day you're sitting next to me at a seminar and I tell you that Phil and I talked for two hours the night before. "Really? Your backgrounds are so different, what did you talk about?" And I could say, "Oh, I don't remember the details but he's a bright person, I really enjoyed talking with him, it was great." That's fine for those circumstances.

Ah, but suppose I told you I interviewed Phil for a job and you said to me, "Well, what did you learn?" and I answered, "Well, I don't really remember the details, but he's really a bright person, I really enjoyed talking with him, it was great."

You recognize the problem. In the social situation my intention was only to facilitate the interaction. The content of any communication that went on between us was irrelevant; only the flow mattered. If Phil said something that lent itself to another question, I would ask it, because that would be the easiest way to keep things rolling.

That's what usually passes for interviewing. Of course, words are exchanged in both contexts, but in the interview your goal is considerably different. Your goal is to answer three questions: Can he do this job? Will he do it? Will he fit into my environment? I'm not going to answer those questions by chitchatting with him. First, I need some kind of organized plan. That was the Interview Guide (see Chapter 9, Fig. 6), which ensured a valid and complete sampling of the candidate's background.

The next step is to choose from a pool of effective, well-researched questions, and to probe below the surface whenever there is a job-related reason for doing so.

When you ask Phil, "On that job, in what ways were you most effective with people?" who knows what he will say. He might talk about the relationships he had with his co-workers, or about customers, or about phone contacts, or about the degree to which he had to interact with people in other departments. You have no way of predicting his response. Phil might answer: "Well, actually, I was pretty much working by myself. I sat at my terminal and of course I had a department manager to report to once a week, but outside of that I was pretty much on my own, there wasn't much interaction with people there."

Depending on the job criteria, you can now choose to pursue one of many paths, or move on to another general question, such as: "What were some of the things you liked about that? What were some of the things you didn't care for so much? ..." Maybe there you would hit pay dirt.

On the other hand, you might ask that first question of another candidate (or of the same candidate, but in connection with a different job) and get the answer: "Well, I think I was particularly effective in dealing with complaints. We had a lot of complaints in those departments about reports being late." This particular answer could have any number of meanings for you in connection with the job you have in mind. Perhaps this kind of behavior would bode well for the candidate, perhaps not. In any event, at this point a door has opened that you'll probably want to explore with some of the "deeper probes" I'll introduce in a later chapter.

≡≡13≡HOW MUCH TIME SHOULD YOU SPEND IN THE INTERVIEW?

Now, perhaps, is the time in your review of this book to say something like this: "I'm supposed to cover the candidate's Work Experience, Education, Activities and Interests, and Self-Assessment and ask all those one-step probes. Then there's the in-depth probing I'll have to do to test their answers—this is going to take at least two hours!" Fortunately, that's not true in practice. You're going to be pleasantly surprised and pleased with the efficiency of our approach once you try it out. But the question raises another important issue: Should it take two hours? Probably you don't have that much time but suppose, with a little stretching, you could manage to give two hours to every candidate. Would it be worth it?

When asked about the relationship between the time they

invest in the interview and the accuracy of the judgments they arrive at, most interviewers would say that as time increases, accuracy goes up. In other words, they'd say that on a graph the relationship between these two factors could be represented by a straight line. The more time put in, the more accurate the judgment. Perhaps they would acknowledge some point of diminishing returns, because obviously you can't go on forever; nevertheless, they'd probably maintain that until several hours or even days have gone by the straight line relationship would remain true. An incremental increase in time would result in an equivalent incremental increase in accuracy of judgment. That's not an unreasonable notion, but neither is it correct.

Figure 7 represents the true relationship between the investment of time and accuracy of judgments in the interview. Time intervals of 10, 20, 30, 40, 50, 60 minutes, and up are represented along the horizontal axis, and percentages of accuracy of judgment are represented on the vertical axis. You might notice that while the vertical axis represents "Accuracy of prediction," the graph doesn't say what it is specifically we're trying to predict. That is because this demonstration graph is based on the results of scores of studies done over the years in which everything you could possibly want to predict in an interview was assessed against the factor of time. Different studies focused on accuracy as a function of time in predicting turnover rates, technical competence, sales success, success at the end of training, the dropout rate from training programs—virtually any issue you could think of. There were even studies comparing performance reviews of people who were hired after interviews of varying duration. In these studies everything except time investment was kept constant. We're assuming we're using the same structure, the same logic, the same plan, the same probing techniques; we're assuming that we understand the job requirements and that everything else is constant. The only variable here is time. The question then becomes: Whatever we're trying to predict, how does time affect the accuracy of our judgment?

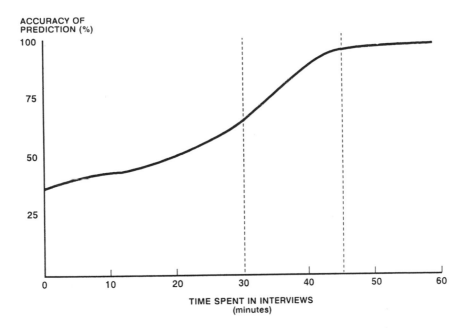

Fig. 7. Interview accuracy as a function of time.

REASONABLE TIME FRAME FOR THE DECISION-MAKING INTERVIEW

While screening interviews and campus interviews can be briefer, let's examine the research results on the time spent in the decision-making interview. You can see from Fig. 7 that for the first several minutes of the interview, accuracy of judgment is below the chance level (50 percent being chance). The reason for this is that in the first several minutes of the interview, you don't have sufficient data to make accurate judgments. During that initial period of time the interviewer's judgment is overinfluenced by factors such as the quality of the candidate's handshake, the degree of eye contact, and whether the candidate seems comfortable or nervous or inadequate in some way. The interviewer may, also, be unduly influenced by the candidate's appearance or by the fact that he or she reminds the interviewer of someone who was very successful or who caused some problems. These issues are not very powerful predictors in any event, and when that's all the interviewer is responding to, it reduces the accuracy of prediction to less than the 50 percent level. Considering this, one could argue that if you only have five minutes in which to interview somebody it would be better to guess, or to decide on the flip of a coin. As an aside, this is why interviewers, on meeting a candidate at the elevator and chatting for a few minutes, come up with an opinion about them that is often unshakable, but to which there is often little validity. There's no substitute for spending a reasonable amount of time in the interview.

Now let's talk about the issue of minimum times in the interview, and the points at which the interview diminishes in efficiency. While, as you can see from Fig. 7, it is true that as time increases, accuracy goes up, it doesn't go up in a straight line. As time increases we reach, at the 30-minute mark, a level of accuracy that is significantly enough above chance to make the interview minimally worthwhile. In 30 minutes you capture enough data at least to make minimally rational judgments about how the person will behave in the future on the job. Thirty or thirty-five minutes might be sufficient for interviewing for a secretarial or entry level position, where the job is not that complex and/or the candidate's background is not that complex. However, as the job becomes more complex and/or the candidate's background becomes more complex and involved, then you need to spend more time, and as you can see, going from 30 to 45 minutes results in a rapid increase in the overall accuracy of our decisions. Forty-five minutes is not the upper limit, but rather it represents the point past which efficiency diminishes rapidly. Thirty to forty-five minutes is referred to in the literature as the "window of efficiency" for the interview. If, however, you have a special reason to go beyond 45 minutes, you should do it. If the candidate has three advanced degrees and has had 19 full-time jobs, obviously it will take more time to interview that person, because there is more ground to cover. Senior positions or very technical jobs might require an hour or more. We ought to recognize, however, that if 40 minutes is good, 80 minutes is not twice as good, and that routinely going beyond 45 minutes to an hour is not justified. Remember that in most instances other interviewers are also going to see the candidate. Interviewing every candidate for an hour or an hour and a half is usually not an efficient use of time. If you employ the Interview Guide and Follow-up Questions (see Fig. 6, Chapter 9), probing techniques, and listening skills, you can collect a tremendous amount of information in a 30–45 minute time frame. Try it. It proves itself.

Of course, one could look at the graph and say, "Well then, barring cases where the candidate has an especially complex background, every interview ought to be 45 minutes because that maximizes your effectiveness." That would be a correct interpretation of the graph. However, you don't always have 45 minutes. So the question is, how far below 45 minutes can we go before the interview becomes nonproductive? The answer to that is: 30 minutes. Any interview less than 30 minutes is dramatically less effective. Thirty minutes is the minimum of time to invest—and again, with candidates with less background, 30–35 minutes might be the optimum, as well as the minimum time.

I should also point out that once you get past the 45-minute mark, the curve on the graph should, as any math major knows, "asymptote out," that is, get closer and closer to the top but never reach it—we never reach perfection. Accuracy continues to increase after 45 minutes, but it increases at a much slower rate.

If you follow the procedures and the structure and the probing techniques we presented earlier in our program, then, in fact, in 30–45 minutes you'll get all the information you need in most instances to make very accurate judgments.

≡14≡HOW TO MAKE THE INTERVIEW SEEM CONVERSATIONAL— AND STILL MAINTAIN CONTROL

The interview, as I have presented it so far, looks something like this: An interviewer sits down with a candidate, asks a question and gets a response. And asks another question, and gets another response. And asks another question and gets another response. And so on. What is wrong with this picture?

Q. ――――――→ R.

Q. ――――――→ R.

Q. ――――――→ R.

Q. ――――――→ R.

Q. ――――――→ R.

This is not the diagram of a conversation or a conversational interview. This is a diagram of an interrogation. If you were to actually follow this rigid a format—ask a question and get an answer and ask a question and get an answer—you might find the candidate doing 90 percent of the talking at the beginning, but by the time you got to the fifth question you'd probably be getting articulate answers like: "Yeah, that's true," or "Uh huh." This kind of approach is bound to tighten anyone up. It's just too constricted to work to your advantage. How to avoid constricting the candidate like this, how to guide the flow of information effectively, but subtly, is the subject of this chapter.

LISTENING SKILLS

In everyday life, when people talk about listening skills, you hear things like, "Be a good listener" or, "Don't talk too much" or, "Be quiet, just let the other person talk." And in my opinion, that's not being a good listener—that's being a good tape recorder! Even in the context of everyday life, that passive approach to "being a good listener" isn't very effective. Being a good listener might require you to be quite active, verbally and nonverbally—and you're a good listener, then, not because you're passive or quiet, but because you're helping the other person, in our case the candidate, to open up. At the same time, you're reaping the benefits by guiding the interview process.

First, I'd like to show you that there are a number of serious and important advantages that accrue to you in the interview if you have command of genuine listening skills. Then I'll discuss how to use them to your advantage. There are two different types of listening skills, verbal and nonverbal; in practice, all the verbal skills are various types of comments. Any verbal behavior on your part, other than a question, which you use to influence the interview process is a type of comment. There are six clear advantages to using comments in the interview.

THE ADVANTAGES OF USING COMMENTS IN AN INTERVIEW

Creating a Smooth Conversational Flow

You ask Larry, "What were some of your accomplishments?" and he answers. Instead of continuing to fire questions at him, suppose you comment on it. You might say: "Well, it sounds like you did a lot in a relatively brief period of time, and you made a pretty good dent in that problem— and that's to your credit. I'm glad you mentioned it. But tell me, what have you learned from that job in the two years you were there?"

Here are two specific questions being asked about the same job (what was accomplished and what was learned), but after Larry answered the first question, and before you went to the next, you commented. Perhaps you've already asked three or four questions in a row. Had you not commented, casually, before you went on to the next one, the effect would have seemed aggressive or high-pressured. In a social situation, most people would find it objectionable; in an interview, they might be more willing to accept it but will still find the process far from pleasant.

So the first advantage to commenting is that it creates a smooth conversational flow. Pretty obvious, right? Yet most interviewers ask 6–10 questions in a row, not realizing its effect on the flow of data from the candidate. These interviewers are so focused on "collecting data" that they lose something that they do automatically and naturally in social conversation.

Eliciting Spontaneous Information

But that's the least of it. Let's go on to other advantages of using comments in the interview. Let's go back to the same comment you made before: "Well, it sounds like you did a lot in a relatively brief period of time, and you made a pretty good dent in that problem—and that's to your credit. I'm glad you mentioned it." But this time, instead of going on to another question, you briefly but deliberately pause. Sometimes at this point the candidate may actually volunteer some additional information. The second advantage, then, of commenting is that it creates an opportunity for eliciting spontaneous information. In fact, it's almost the only way to get information spontaneously. Questions yield logical, rational, and perhaps prepared answers. When you comment and pause, occasionally candidates will give you details, often as an "aside," which are quite revealing. You want these data!

The pattern of question–answer–question–answer–question–answer prohibits spontaneity; candidates get the sense that they are fielding the questions. Once they've caught one of them—by coming up with an answer—they'd better get ready for the next one.

But if you comment and pause, candidates will be encouraged to add more. Comments signal that their answers are not disappearing into a vacuum; the pause (in place of another question) gives them permission to dwell a little longer on the subject—you don't seem to be in such a hurry, so there's no reason for them to be either. Since the comment was positive or neutral in tone, the pause isn't threatening. It does, however, take advantage of that natural human tendency to fill a brief silence in a conversation with an elaboration or explanation. While you may not always get that extra sentence or two, pausing encourages the candidate to come forth with more. Notice I'm not recommending a long, tense silence to force the candidate to speak, but just that you occasionally pause briefly to give them the opportunity to add more. If the candidate doesn't, move on with another question.

Giving You Time to Think

You have asked several questions in a row and Larry has answered. The last time he answered relatively briefly, and you're not quite sure what you're going to ask next. By commenting and kind of dragging it out as if you were thinking about what he just said (don't overdo this, obviously), you can give yourself time to think of a more sophisticated, better targeted question. While you are quietly commenting and summarizing, the candidate can't jump on to another subject. You're holding their attention.

Without this advantage of commenting, you might be forced to just pull a question out of the air. But look at what you can do: If you're not sure where to go next, instead of pausing after the comment (a technique that is designed, remember, to encourage the candidate to elaborate), try dragging it out, "That's very . . . interesing, Larry . . . ah . . . I didn't realize there was that much to it . . . it seems like it was a pretty complex job with a lot of responsibilities . . ." (and now you've finally come up with a question!) ". . . but tell me, how did you manage to do that while you were committed full-time to this other project?" While you're commenting he can't speak because you're speaking. You're holding his attention momentarily . . . and then you ask the follow-up question. This question might not have been in your mind a moment ago, but you gave yourself the microsecond you needed to think of it. As you know, you can think three or four times faster than you can speak.

Forcing Yourself to Listen

Although most of the time there is a lot of excitement connected with the art and science of the interview, you attention won't be riveted by every candidate. Yet you owe it to all of them not to let your mind wander while they are in good faith answering the questions you've asked them. In this connection it may help to note that you cannot summarize back to the candidates what they said to you unless you are paying attention. If you train yourself to comment on what people say, it forces you to listen. This is more important as a discipline for you than for its effect on the candidate, but its effect can be very positive.

Giving Candidates Feedback

By commenting you are also giving the candidate feedback. If you replay what someone said back to them, they get the message that you're listening, you're paying attention, and you're really interested. Candidates realize that what they are saying is being understood and processed.

Controlling the Direction of the Interview

The ability to move the candidate onto another subject (or pull them back to the one they've strayed away from) when necessary is an essential skill for the interviewer to master and one that can be greatly facilitated by commenting. As we have already established, by commenting and pausing you can encourage candidates to come forth with spontaneous information. But there are some candidates for whom the last thing you would ever want to do would be to encourage spontaneity. In cases such as these, instead of commenting and pausing, comment to interrupt them and gently move them on to another subject.

This may seem a little mechanical at first, but it works very smoothly in practice. If Ben is going on and on and on and on, you could of course wait for a period at the end of a sentence and then change the subject. But it might be a long wait. Maybe Ben has a habit of not stopping at the end of his sentences; it is not only getting more and more difficult to be patient, it clearly isn't going to work. You don't want to be rude, but you have to interrupt. How can you do this pleasantly, without damaging rapport?

It's very simple. It involves using a combination of the verbal and nonverbal. You start talking (commenting, summarizing) while he's speaking. Do it quietly and look away momentarily as you speak. He realizes then that he no longer has your full attention. He sees you're caught up processing what he just said. He hesitates for a moment for you to catch up, and in that moment's hesitation you change the subject. Here's an example. While he is still talking you say (quietly to yourself), "That's real interesting, Chris, I didn't realize it was that complex, there certainly were a lot of things going on at one time," (and now he pauses for an instant), "but we have a lot of ground to cover in such a limited time, why don't we move on, and if we have time perhaps we can come back to this. What was your next job?"

What have you just done? You started to talk while he was speaking; he paused, and you came back in and changed the subject. Notice that in this case, structure was used as your rationale for doing this—a valuable face-saving excuse; the implication is that while you personally are fascinated, and would give any amount of your own time to get to the exciting conclusion of Chris' record-breaking declarative sentence . . . sadly enough, the necessity of getting a full picture of his background requires that you and he go on to the next job.

On the other hand, if you have to interrupt Chris every three minutes, you needn't refer to structure every time. Just do it. When Chris goes on and on again, start talking quietly as he's talking, "Well, Chris, I didn't realize how much responsibility came with that assignment, I can see how you learned a lot from that project . . ." (and he finally stops) and you say, "But let me put it in context. Where'd you go to from there? What was your next job?"

The Candidate Wants Direction from You

An interruption of this sort makes perfect sense in a conversation even though it might look disruptive in print. The interview is a directed, purposeful conversation. In a conversation, how many times have you been telling a story to somebody who interrupts you and says. "Oh, that reminds me—"and then introduces a totally different subject—now the conversation goes down that path. That's the way conversations go.

Remember, also, the candidate is hungry for direction from you. So if you pause momentarily, get Chris' attention and come in and change the subject, or if you're in the middle of the interview and notice that he's drifting and you need to regain control, you're going to easily be able to move on to a new subject or pull back to an existing one by saying: "Well, Chris, that's really an interesting aspect of that job, but before you go any further, let's just back up a second; you mentioned on your previous job what your team did—but it wasn't exactly clear to me what you did. What was your role exactly under those circumstances? How long was that project? When did you first get involved?" He was drifting on to the next job, but you pull him back, because you're not leaving this one until you're finished with it. But it's all done very pleasantly.

These are all reasons why commenting can serve as both an effective listening skill and an effective means of controlling the interview.

TYPES OF COMMENTS

While there are other verbal interventions that can be used, the types of comments I'm going to review now relate to the substance of the candidate's message. The casual comments like "I see," "Great," "That's interersting," or grunts and exclamations like "Oh" and "Uh huh" have limited utility. They don't give you all the advantages I've mentioned above.

Now I'm going to discuss, and try to give a practical demonstration of the four types of comments that are most useful in the interview:

- ☐ Restatement
- ☐ Pat on the Back
- ☐ Downplay Negative
- ☐ Reflect Feeling

Restatement

Restatement is the type of comment I've used most often in the illustrations above. If you just think of it as summarizing back to the candidate the essence of what they said, it is not difficult to use. The problem is that if you want to get the advantages we reviewed, it has to be done just right. You should make sure not to add anything, not to subtract anything, and not to reveal your opinion of what the candidate said. Make sure to give a neutral, accurate summarization. Why? Suppose you're interviewing Stephen. He answers one of your questions and you summarize his answer back to him, but you leave out some critical piece. Instead of getting spontaneity, getting more and new data out of him, you get the same information over again, because he has to correct you; he thinks you have missed something. He says, "Well, I guess I did say that, but I also meant to suggest that ..." and he brings back the part he thinks you didn't hear. On the other hand, if you seem to be evaluating, if you seem to be judging him: "Well, Stephen, it seems as if you're the kind of person who ...," he might say (or think), "Now, wait a minute, I didn't mean that I was that kind of person; I just did it that way. I thought it was practical. But I'm usually very flexible in other instances." He might get defensive. None of this is productive. So if you want to reap the advantages described above, it is critical that your summarizations be neutral and accurate.

Pat on the Back

I would like you to think of the pat on the back as a replacement for compliments. Don't try to give candidates compliments. You're a total stranger. Compliments will bounce off them. While compliments won't necessarily damage the process, they don't add much to it either. Of course, it's still worse to suggest that they're just what you're looking for. That sets them up for expectations that may not be met—even if you really think a given candidate is right for the job, you may think the next one is better; in any case you shouldn't be making that decision yet and it would be deceptive to suggest you are.

You can achieve the same advantages without compliments or deception, a pat on the back. The candidate has told you about some everyday accomplishment. It isn't deserving of a medal of honor, but it did require going a bit beyond the minimum. Make it known that you recognize this.

You might say, "Well, Kathy, you just mentioned it in passing, but I have to say that a lot of people wouldn't have bothered to do it that way. You did it conscientiously and went out of your way to make sure others were not inconvenienced; I think that's a nice touch and I'm glad to know it about you."

The recognition of little things in passing and in context gives the candidates the sense that you're truly processing what they're saying, and you understand where they're coming from. Little things, not big things.

Downplay Negative

This would be an important point for maintaining rapport, of course. There's nothing to be gained by saying to a candidate, "Well, Karen, if I understand what you're saying it sounds as if you were rather ineffectual in that role." That may, in fact, have been a perfectly accurate restatement of what she said. But the restatement of negative information comes across as negative. Therefore, it's better to downplay it. Tell her: "Well, Karen, I appreciate you mentioning that to me. It must have been difficult for you at the time. Of course, we all have little awkwardnesses in our first job which we look back on with some degree of concern, but you were obviously a lot more successful in your next job, why don't we focus on that one?" I'm downplaying the negative issue and moving on. A few seconds later I could write in my notes, "Spilled coffee in main computer; cost company $50,000." One way or another, I will make a note of it; it's not as if it wasn't important; there just isn't any need to beat the candidate over the head about it, so I postpone making the note for a few moments. If instead of moving on you wanted to explore that sensitive topic, you could adjust your comment by saying: "But you were there and know better than anyone else what happened. I'd like to hear your view."

Reflect Feeling

If you are going to get the candidate to be open with you, you should acknowledge their reaction when you notice them reacting strongly to something.

We are not talking about deep psychological techniques here. In the context of the interview reflecting feeling would be something like this: "Well, Kate, it seems to me that you put a lot of your own personal time and energy into this project and that's one of the reasons you were so successful. But I guess it must have been a little disappointing when it came time for your performance review that it wasn't even mentioned; you had to bring it up yourself." You want Kate to know that you understand the position she was put in by that incident, and how she felt about it.

≡≡≡15≡HOW TO PHRASE YOUR QUESTIONS: AVOIDING CLOSED-ENDED QUESTIONS

————————————————————————

Any question you ask—any question you ever ask, in life as well as in the interview—necessarily falls into one of two categories: closed-ended or open-ended. The use of open-ended questions as probing tools is discussed in the next chapter. For now the seemingly simple issue of closed-ended questions needs review. While it's not a complex issue, it is a bit more subtle than most treatments of the topic would suggest.

We'll start with some definitions. A closed-ended question is one that can be answered with the single word "yes" or "no." An open-ended question, on the other hand, is one that will encourage the respondent to come fourth with an answer of greater complexity and length; at least they cannot answer merely "yes" or "no."

WHY YOU SHOULD AVOID CLOSED-ENDED QUESTIONS IN THE INTERVIEW

There is nothing inherently wrong with closed-ended questions. They are quite appropriate in any number of other situations. In the performance appraisal, for example, or a sales situation, everday business or personal life, they are pragmatic and work very well. However, they can be deadly in the interview.

Closed-ended questions usually start with one on the following words:

☐ Is   ☐ Are
☐ Can   ☐ Should
☐ Will   ☐ Did
☐ Could

For example:

"Is the meeting still scheduled?"

"Are there any alternatives to that approach?"

"Could you give me a second option to consider?"

"Are there any alternative ways of doing that?"

"Did the TV service technician come today?"

"Have the contractors called with the estimate?"

"Are my shirts back from the cleaners?"

"If we could resolve that, would you be able to sign the contract?"

"Did you meet the objectives we set last year on this issue?"

In the interview it is more effective to ask open-ended questions, that is, questions that cannot be answered by a simple "yes" or "no": "What were some of your accomplishments?" "How did you go about solving that problem?" "Why did you do it that particular way?" "Tell me about some of the alternatives you considered." "Describe to me the step-by-step process you took." "Explain to me your rationale for that approach." "Give me an example of how you went about doing that."

None of those questions can be answered by the single word "yes" or "no." If I asked, "Carol, How did you solve that problem?" Carol wouldn't be very likely to say, "Yes"— not if we were speaking the same language, she wouldn't.

Some Candidates Will Answer Literally "Yes" or "No"

Candidates who are nervous or shy, or beginning their careers or who have a limited education . . . or even a very advanced candidate with a narrowly focused technical orientation . . . might actually answer your questions with the single word "yes" or "no." If you've ever been through an interview like that you know how painful it is. The candidate says in answer to all your questions: "Yes. Uh . . . yes. Mmmm . . . yes. Ah . . . sort of, sometimes. Yes."

Responses such as these are excruciating for you, and they are no fun for the candidates either. After the interview Dan walks out of your office and goes to the nearest phone booth to tell the news to a friend: "Oh, it was a terrible experience. I was terrible, I didn't say anything. The interviewer must have thought I had nothing to say. I'm certainly never going to get that job."

Although you had done everything you could to make Dan comfortable, he was too nervous to do anything to break the pattern you set with your questions—he's just not the sort of person to take the initiative. So the outcome was that he didn't get much information out; you didn't learn much about him. The whole experience was like pulling teeth and you had nothing to show for it.

True, you are not responsible for the candidate's personality. But suppose you've gone to the trouble of building and

maintaining positive rapport, and Melissa, a new candidate,
is also a bit constricted in her presentation. She occasionally answers literally "yes" or "no" to questions that can,
but do not have to be, answered in that way. Her personality
may be a factor in her behavior, and you are not responsible
for that. But after she answers one question with a "yes" or
"no," further answers of the same type are your responsibility. She could only answer in this way if you are asking
closed-ended questions. When the candidate says to you
"yes" or "no" you might say to yourself, "Well, I wish this
person wouldn't answer so briefly." But you should also say,
". . . I guess I'll stop asking closed-ended questions because I
don't want any more of those brief responses." From then
on, you should avoid closed-ended questions entirely.

Closed-Ended Questions Elicit Brief Responses

But that's the least of it. Let's go further. The use of
closed-ended questions also has the potential to constrict
the range of response, even of articulate candidates. Closed-
ended questions inadvertently instruct the candidate to
answer briefly; the effect of asking a series of such questions
is like saying: "Stick to the point. I don't want to hear a lot
of extraneous information, just give me the facts." Did
you . . . ? Are you . . . ? Is there . . . ? Can there . . . ? Should
there . . . ? Could there . . . ? Were there . . . ? You risk giving
the candidate the impression that you are in a hurry, that
you want to get out of there, so their answers had better be
crisp and brief.

Using Closed-Ended Questions Endangers Your Control
of the Interview

Another hidden pitfall of using closed-ended questions is
that they can cause you to lose control of the interview.
This particular pitfall is especially dangerous if you are
dealing with college students who have had a two-week
course in interviewing, or an executive who has been

through outplacement counseling, or anybody who has been to a How-To-Get-A-Job seminar or read a book on the subject. Individuals with strong verbal skills (salespersons, attorneys, or anyone used to doing business presentations) are especially skilled at wresting control of an interview from you. Whether they are specially trained or they intuitively know what to do, when these candidates are asked a closed-ended question, chances are they'll answer "yes" or "no," and immediately change the subject, introducing a prepared statement or topic they would prefer to focus on.

Watch *Issues and Answers* or *Meet the Press* next Sunday morning and you'll see this happen. The Senator is not there increasing his or her vulnerability to the press for nothing. The Senator has a particular agenda to put forward. The reporter asks, "Senator, do you feel that economic aid to El Salvador is in our long-range foreign policy interests?" A closed-ended question. The Senator says: "Yes, I do. And only last week I was speaking to my constituents about the energy crisis. And I feel that the deregulation of gas is one of the most fundamental problems facing our society. Only yesterday I read a staff report that clearly indicates . . . ."

Responses like these could go on for several minutes—as long as the candidates can talk without taking a breath, getting out their point. If you ask closed-ended questions of people who know how to redirect the interview, they'll answer "yes" or "no" and throw your structure out the window. The topic they introduce might be one you want to hear about, but you want to guide the interview so that it comes up in context. You, not the candidate, should determine what is discussed, at what point, and at what depth.

HOW TO STOP USING CLOSED-ENDED QUESTIONS

This is not an intellectually challenging issue, and I'm sure that by now you understand my point and may be willing to reduce the use of closed-ended questions you use in the interview. The trouble is that asking closed-ended questions is so automatic you may not even know you're doing it. You've never had to be conscious of them before. It made no difference in everyday life (although, incidentally, parents and teachers should be aware that children usually answer closed-ended questions with a literal "yes" or "no"). But in the interview it's important to have control over this question form. Learning not to ask closed-ended questions really just amounts to learning to break a habit. Catching yourself in the middle of a closed-ended question and rephrasing it might seem a little awkward at first, but it helps break the habit. If you start a question with, "Susan, did you . . . ?" catch yourself and say, "Let me rephrase that: tell me what you liked about that job."

Finally, lest you think I'm overstating this point, let me make my intention clear. I want you to have conscious control over this question form so you can handle any situation that comes up in the interview. If you purposely and consciously ask, "Did you take a course in accounting?" I don't object. Just be aware that achieving that kind of conscious control over the use of closed-ended questions usually takes effort. I promise that there is no danger of you asking too few of them.

≡≡16≡HOW TO PROBE FOR DETAILS AND TEST FOR TRUTHFULNESS

- ☐ What
- ☐ Tell me
- ☐ Review   One-Step Probes
- ☐ Explain
- ☐ Describe

- ☐ How
- ☐ Why
- ☐ Who
- ☐ When   Two-Step Probes
- ☐ Where
- ☐ Which
- ☐ Give me an example

The words in the first list appear at the beginning of open-ended questions. These typically begin what we called the one-step probes, the basic questions on the Interview Guide and Follow-up Questions form (see Chapter 9, Fig. 6). The words in the second group are the basic building blocks of the two-step, three-step, four-step, and five-step probes.

ONE-STEP PROBES

A one-step probe is a question that begins the exploration of the surface of an event.

What is an event? Well, one single job in a candidate's background is an individual event. An individual educational experience is an event. A particular outside interest or a community involvement you want to discuss is an event.

We explore a candidate's background by taking each event, such as a single job, and asking detailed questions about it, in order to unpack it, to probe it in depth. But we do it in stages. The first tools we apply to the event are the key questions or one-step probes—those are the "soil samples" we take to determine if an area will reward further "drilling" or exploration. If the one-step probe unearths something of a job-related nature, we probe into it in more detail.

TWO-STEP PROBES

You should ask the next level of question—the two-step probe—if you decide to explore the answer in more detail. It is not necessarily a more sophisticated question; it's just a question that leads you deeper into that subject. It does not introduce a new subject itself but drills below the surface of the topic unearthed by a one-step probe.

"How," "why," "who," "when," and "which" are examples of words that introduce two-step probes. Rarely can you begin an inquiry with, "Why did you do it that way?" or, "How did you resolve that problem?" or, "When did you first get involved in that project?" All those questions assume that some issue is already under discussion. They probe deeper into answers received from one-step probes such as: "What alternatives did you consider?" "What problems did you face on that job?" "What were some of your accomplishments on that job?" But remember our strategy—we're not going to ask a two-step probe just because an opportunity to do so presents itself. Even if you asked a one-step probe and were fascinated by the answer and presumably wanted to know more, you still wouldn't continue with that line of questioning unless there was a job-related reason for doing so. Throughout the interview you will be making decisions about whether to penetrate deeper or to move on to another surface question . . . that is, go on to another one-step probe.

Here's an example. "What were some of your accomplishments?" you ask. You are aware that just knowing what somebody accomplished isn't enough—candidates leave their accomplishments behind, and what they bring with them to you is how they did it. So now you ask the two-step probe: "How did you do it?" "Why did you do it that way?" "Who else was involved?"

These techniques allow you to get to more details. Let's take a look at another one-step probe. You ask Karen, "What were some of the difficult problems you faced on that job?" and she describes a very difficult problem. You find that her answer by itself is interesting, and the problem she described a complex one. We could assume many things about Karen from her answer . . . but only after you know how she dealt with the problem, or why she dealt with it that way, or who made the final decision . . . only then will you have the data necessary to interpret the significance of the information and its relevance for your job criteria.

Using Two-Step Probes to Test for Truthfulness

The obvious value of two-step probing is that it gets more detailed and specific information from the candidate. But another striking value of this seemingly simple process is that it helps you determine whether somebody is misrepresenting the facts. It helps you test the validity and accuracy of what people tell you, as well as enabling you to get more details.

Naturally, it is of great interest to interviewers to be able to determine whether the information the candidate is supplying is correct. Now, I must say that if candidates were willing and able to bold-facedly lie throughout the entire interview there would be nothing you could do about it, and there would be nothing I could help you with.

Fortunately, applicants are neither able nor willing to absolutely and bold-facedly lie in the interview, at least not at the level of depth you're going to go. For three reasons: (1) They don't know how much you can check. When you ask specific detailed questions, you require them to reveal confirmable information. (2) If you do probe in depth, in the context of the comprehensive structure, they have to remember what they told you earlier in order to avoid contradicting themselves. (3) In an in-depth interview, I assert that they cannot possibly be prepared, no matter how many questions they've rehearsed answers to. I'd like to explain what is behind each of these points.

Candidates Don't Know How Much You Can Check. When you ask a question at the surface level, candidates could characterize their answers in such a way as to put themselves in the best light, and probably they will. Chances are they won't blurt out details if such details might have negative connotations. What they do is omit critical facts, allow you to believe, they suggest, imply and otherwise twist and turn the facts to create a positive impression. But when you start asking specific questions that ultimately get to such a level of detail that can be easily checked, candidates have little choice but to give accurate information. There's always the chance that, by calling a reference or by some other route you'll find out that the candidates misrepresented themselves. That would not only rule them out for this job, it might follow them the rest of their career, for all they know.

They Have to Remember What They Told You Earlier. Another reason candidates are reluctant to lie when you probe in depth is that by doing so they build a house of cards that could come tumbling down on them during the interview. You're not going to begin an interview with: "Tell you what, Warren, let's conduct this interview in a very creative way: Why don't you just give me the four or five points you memorized last night in front of the mirror, and that'll be our interview."

Of course, that would make it easy for the candidates to misrepresent themselves. But you're not doing that. You'll be going through their background in a very systematic and comprehensive way: earlier jobs up to the present, earlier education up to the present, and their outside interests. Each individual event is going to be touched on with many different surface probes; many issues will be probed with even more detail. This puts enormous pressure on their concentration, their mental agility, and their short-term memory. If they're making up things to impress you as they go along, they're going to have to remember, 20 minutes into the interview, what they said 20 minutes before. That's one of the reasons Work Experience and Education are covered separately, even though there were some instances in which the candidate worked and simultaneously was in school. It helped "triangulate" on the candidate's past behaviors. Under these circumstances, rather than risk being caught in a contradiction, even candidates who might be tempted to misrepresent themselves tend to give accurate information.

Candidates Cannot Prepare in Advance for In-depth Questions. Candidates cannot avoid revealing accurate information by exhaustive preparation in advance: That's the third reason they don't absolutely lie. They cannot possibly be prepared at the level of depth you're going to go even when you only drop beneath the surface a couple of steps. As much as candidates might prepare answers to questions in advance, they can't be prepared for all the possible tributaries you can take with two-step probes. Theirs is the problem faced by a literal-minded chess player who tries to envision every possible response of her opponent to every move she might make, and then her every possible next move to each of those hypothetical moves of her opponent—the complexity increases exponentially with each move, and with each conceivable probing question: it is an impossible task. Candidates are only prepared at the surface level, and if they are probed below the surface they start giving accurate information.

Suppose you are going to be interviewing me. I've prepared for the interview by buying a book that gives me the 50 questions most often asked in the interview. I've made the effort to memorize answers to 30 or 40 of them. It is already a monumental task to memorize detailed and specific information in answer to that many questions. But maybe I could do it. Among the questions that I've prepared for are some of the one-step probes you've prepared to ask. That is certainly possible. The one-step probes are not magic questions that no one has ever heard. They are good, solid, fundamentally effective questions that unearth information, but they are not unpredictable. So it is theoretically possible that, in addition to my preparing for the ridiculous questions and ineffectual questions and questions of very little value, I could also prepare answers for some of your one-step probes. In that case, when you ask, "Well, tell me, what were some of your accomplishments on that job?" I could give you a well-rehearsed, detailed, and very impressive answer. But now that you know about the two-step, and, by extension of the same principles, about the three-step, four-step, five-step probing process, you can go beyond my initial answer. After any one-step probe question, you can probe in many unpredictable directions. You can probe for initiative, you can probe for motivation, for technical skills, for teamwork—you can pursue so many different directions below the surface that I can't possibly be prepared. I can barely be prepared for the 40 or 50 questions on the surface. I can't be prepared for the 10 tributaries you might go into on each one. It's not humanly possible.

In that case, how do candidates ever get away with being deceptive? They get away with it because interviewers say, "Tell me about yourself," and ask only surface questions.

Perhaps now you're saying to yourself, "Okay, I got it. Ask the candidate: 'What did you accomplish?' and follow up by asking, 'How did you accomplish it?' Then ask, 'What problems did you face?' and follow that up by asking, 'How did you handle those problems?' Then ask them to review a difficult problem they faced and follow that up by asking, 'Why did you approach it that way?' " "Well," you might be thinking, "it doesn't seem all that sophisticated or monumental." It's not brain surgery. But on the other hand, even though it is not very complex, interviewers who have been interviewing for 20 years don't seem to arrive at this process by trial and error. They ask mainly one-step probes, and accept at face value what people say. The typical job interview goes like this:

Interviewer: "Well, tell me, Jeanne, what were some of the things you feel you accomplished on that job?" And after she answers, the interview continues: "Sounds like you accomplished a lot. And what were some of the things that you liked best about that job? . . . Well, you liked many things, you accomplished a lot, that's great. But no job is perfect, what about some of the things you had difficulty with or problems you had to face . . . Well, that's a thorny collection of issues to deal with, but obviously despite that, I can tell from your résumé that you were there a reasonable period of time and you accomplished a lot while you were there and you enjoyed the challenges you faced, that's good. Now let's go on to your next job."

The interviewer may actually think they're accomplishing something, but there is no detailed substance to this line of inquiry. While the interviewer asked questions, they were all surface questions—all one-step probes. Without the two-step probe I'm really just poking around, and the inevitable result would be that I get a lot of information from the candidate but the significance of that information in terms of my job criteria would be left unclear. If, however, I had dropped just one level below the surface I'd have gotten dramatically more accurate information.

Perhaps a demonstration will help show how comprehensive probing cuts through a haze of assumptions. Recently, an engineer was being considered for a project manager position for a major defense contractor. I will call the interviewer Cynthia and the candidate Mike. Cynthia was a trained interviewer and she used a structure essentially the same as the one outlined in this book. About five minutes into the review of Mike's work experiences she said, "Tell me, Mike, what were some of your accomplishments on that job?"

"Well," said Mike, "I haven't thought about it all that much, but when I was there I created, established, and brought into being three different projects which I think might be specifically related to the kinds of things you might be looking for." And Mike continued with his well-oiled, well-rehearsed, very sophisticated and very impressive accomplishment. Cynthia was impressed. "That's great! We could use someone who has had all that experience and exposure," she thought. "I wish I had 10 people like that. I wish I had one person like that." Those were her unedited thoughts. But she also knew about two-step probes, so instead of just admiring Mike's accomplishments, she asked him a fundamentally simple question (leading into it with a brief comment to maintain a smooth, conversational flow): "Well that's great, Mike, that's quite an accomplishment. By the way how long was that project and when did you first have the opportunity to get involved in it?" Although it was not a sophisticated question and there was nothing particularly combative or intimidating about it, it worked very well at piercing Mike's less than completely candid account of events. For all the reasons I mentioned earlier as to why candidates give more accurate information when you probe below the surface answers, Mike was not going to lie at the next level down. But he did try to cover himself. "Well the project was a year long and I was there for the last," Mike mumbled something that was not quite audible, ". . . weeks."

"I'm sorry—how long was that?"

"Um, oh. Three weeks," and he quickly added. "But I was there for the implementation phase, which I feel was very important . . . ," and Mike began to try to run past the issue. Because Cynthia is human, and was a little annoyed at this point, what she wanted to say was: "Now, wait a minute. You were there for the last three weeks for this year-long project. I guess that means that you weren't there for the analysis of the problem stage that you talked about in such detail! And you couldn't have been around for the development of the alternate scenario solutions, because that was six months ago. And obviously you weren't around for the field test in that one department, and you obviously weren't around when the cost analysis was done. Basically, what you're telling me is you were there when they plugged the equipment into the wall. Is that right?" She did not say that, of course, because saying it would have served no purpose. But she would have liked to. She was really annoyed.

Suppose Cynthia took it even further and said: "Well, Mike, I'm just shocked, I'm really shocked that you would have lied to me. As a matter of fact, I don't know if I want to continue this interview." Mike, who was without shame, could have said: "Well, you'd certainly have a right to be shocked if you thought I lied to you, but I'm sure I never claimed that I was involved in the project from the beginning. I talked about the project, and the team, and what we did, and where it was going and where it was coming from so that you could have some background to ultimately understand my contribution. I thought you understood that I was there at the implementation phase. I'm sorry if I didn't make it clear. But, uh . . . ."

IMPORTANT NOTE: Of course, Cynthia shouldn't and didn't say, " . . . what you're telling me is you were there when they plugged the equipment into the wall . . . " and certainly not, " . . . I'm shocked . . . ," nor should you. What she did do at that point was say to herself: "Boy, was I sharp. I had made some assumptions about the candidate but I've been able to adjust them. Now I know precisely where Mike's contribution lay—it was in the implementation phase of the project. I can now proceed to probe into the implementation phase and the possibly subtle part he played there (maybe he did in fact do more than push the button and flip on the terminal screen)."

Candidates might claim to have a great deal of experience with something, but when you get right down to it they were in the room when it happened—they themselves never did it. It's a thin line that many candidates are willing to walk, especially since most interviewers do not probe and test for accuracy. Fortunately, it does not take much to ask that two-step probe, or by analogy, the three-step or four-step probe that will quickly bring the discussion to that level of depth where everything but the truth will buckle under the pressure.

When an Articulate Answer Fizzles Out.   Sometimes when you compare the answer to a one-step probe with the answer to a two-step probe, you notice a dramatic difference in the quality of the candidate's delivery. When this happens, it should alert you to the fact that the first answer was probably rehearsed. Now the real candidate is starting to emerge. An ability to spot this distinction is important not merely as a way of penetrating misrepresentation. Even if the rehearsed answer were true, you should try to get to the unrehearsed one. The ability to be articulate and to think analytically and logically on demand may be an important job requirement. Pay close attention to candidates' performance when you've gotten beyond the one-step probe responses where candidates might have had a chance to think through or rehearse their answers.

By the way, the fact that there is a discrepancy between the one-step probe and the two-step probe does not mean that you are dealing with a dishonest candidate—it simply means that you now have the accurate information where before you did not. It might turn out that a viable candidate lurks behind the veil you've insisted on lifting.

Remember, there are many pressures on candidates to perform as well as they can in the interview; they will put themselves in the best possible light because they know other candidates are doing the same, and also, because like anybody, they want to be accepted—who wants to be rejected? Even if they don't want the job, they'd rather be in a position to reject you when the time comes. Finally, it should be borne in mind that job seekers are often confronted with interviewers who have no idea what they're doing; in view of this, they feel justified in coming to the interview with some kind of prepared review of their background. Otherwise, for all they know, their genuine merits might not get any consideration at all. Chances are that if you were going on an interview, you would want to be prepared for it.

When candidates come across as very glossy, a little too airbrushed to be believed, probe below the surface to see whether they're telling you the truth. When the opposite happens, and they come across right from the start as a bit awkward in their presentation, you should also probe and test below the surface.

Neither a good theatrical presentation nor a less than 100 percent effective presentation is decisive evidence. You need facts to relate back to your job criteria. That's the difference. That gives everyone a fair shake.

How to Prevent a Series of Probes from Becoming an Interrogation

The entire design of this book rests on the premise that the interview is the smooth integrated use of a number of individual skills. Here is where probing and commenting work in combination.

Suppose you asked a basic one-step probe, followed immediately by your deeper probes: "What were some of your accomplishments? How did you go about doing that? Why did you do it in that particular way? How long was that project? When did you first get involved?" If you fired all those questions just as they're written here, with no comments, the effect would be pushy and confrontational—in fact, it would be analogous to interviewing in a bare room with a harsh light shining in the candidate's eyes. You are unlikely to elicit an open, spontaneous dialogue. To get subtlety and details you need to comment in between some of your one- and two-step probes; do it skillfully enough and it can seem as if you're asking merely out of curiosity and interest.

You might ask, "Mike, what were some of your accomplishments on that job?" And he answers. Before you ask another question you're going to comment: "Well, it sounds like you did a lot in that relatively short period of time and that's really to your credit, and I'm glad to know that. But I am kind of curious—how long was that project and when did you have the first opportunity to get involved?"

Now he tells you he was there for the last three weeks, the implementation phase.

.But wait . . . that was a year long project. . . .

There's no point in antagonizing him or making him feel awkward. You're not going to challenge him—that really wouldn't be productive. You're going to use the "downplay the negative" comment, while making a note of the reality of the situation. "Well at least you were there for the implementation phase, Mike. But since you had to use information from people who proceeded you, before you were involved with the project, how did you go about organizing that information? . . . I see. Well, it sounds like you did it quickly and rather efficiently. By the way, who made the final decision on how to proceed?"

You just made a one-step probe, a comment, a two-step probe, a comment, a three-step probe, a comment, and a four-step probe. Then you might do two or three questions and another comment at the end of them—obviously you shouldn't make your comments mechanically in a conspicuous rhythm, but you ought to pepper your conversation with them. This lends a more natural and conversational quality to the deeper probing, just as comments earlier were shown to make the one-step probing process more conversational.

≡≡≡17≡PRESENTING INFORMATION PERSUASIVELY AND CLOSING THE INTERVIEW PROPERLY

The time comes during every job interview when it is the candidate's turn to find out something about your organization. Most interviewers recognize this as an opportunity to influence candidates' decisions, and this is absolutely correct: After all, the most effective interview techniques in the world aren't much use if talented candidates can't be persuaded to say yes when you make them an offer.

In this chapter I'm going to show you how to adapt your presentation and closing to your level of interest in the candidate—specifically, to three different levels of interest: talented candidates you've decided to pursue; inappropriate candidates you'd like to let down easy; and star performers for whom you'll want to make a special effort. Since the

approaches you take for these different groups have a certain amount in common with one another, I'll model it for
you with one group first, and then show you how that model
varies for the other groups.

You may recall, from Chapter 2, "Common Errors Made
by Interviewers," that I advised you to postpone giving
details about the job until after you reviewed the candidate's background. I said it was because we wanted to avoid
contaminating the interview. There's no point in telling the
candidate the "correct" answers to your questions before
you've asked them.

Another reason that giving the details of the job up front
as a matter of routine would be unwise is that it's just not
efficient. In many cases once you review the candidate's
background you may realize that you're not interested in
that particular person, and you'll wish you hadn't bothered
giving so much data up front. It would have been more
efficient to do it more briefly at the end.

Finally, and most important for our current discussion,
you should hold off giving details until the end because it is
measurably more persuasive to do so.

If you tell the candidate about the job at the beginning,
you're forced to give an encyclopedic presentation, essentially consisting of a bunch of facts. Out of the universe of
things you could talk about, you select whatever you think
is the most important and present it without reference to
the candidate as an individual. You make the same speech
for every candidate. Under those circumstances, that's the
best you can do.

Ah, but suppose you knew something about the candidate
first. Suppose that while reviewing Susan's background you
listened not only for information with which to evaluate
her, but also for what she'd like to get from a job, what she
hopes to get, what she needs to get, what turns her on, what
frustrates her . . . ? Then when you turn to giving her data,
out of the many things that there are to talk about you
could pull out the ones that are most important to her.

While I don't mean to limit you to five minutes, I can

assure you that as little as five minutes of information tailored and adapted and modified to a candidate's particular interests is by far more persuasive than 25 minutes of mere facts.

MAKING THE TRANSITION FROM COLLECTING TO GIVING INFORMATION

First, though, you have to make a clean break with the information-collecting phase before moving on to your presentation. This can be easily accomplished with the transitional question (shown in Chapter 9, Fig. 6): "All right, we've covered a lot of ground, Bruce. I appreciate your sharing the information with me and I've enjoyed talking with you. Before we turn, however, to my review of us as a company and the job, is there anything else about your background that you'd like to cover?" It's purposely a closed-ended question because you want to encourage the candidate to say "No." You want them to know that they don't have to tell you any more, but just in case they want to, you're giving them the chance.

The next step is to say, "All right. Do you have any specific questions and concerns?" Another closed-ended question. You ask it just to make sure there isn't something that might affect what comes next. Most of the time when you ask that question the candidate will breeze right through it, saying, "Well, really, I have nothing specific at this stage, I'm sure I'll have questions later," and allows you to give your presentation. But every once in a while somebody asks about something that affects what you cover or do next in your presentation.

Be Complete

One other general word of advice before we proceed to consider how we will vary our presentation by level of interest: Even if you are sure that in your circumstances most people will accept an offer, or for some other reason do not feel it is necessary to invest much effort into influencing candidates' decisions, it is nevertheless always a good idea to be complete when you give information. That is, at the very least, you should make sure that no one ever comes on board and says, "You never told me that—I don't want to do that, and I don't think I'll be able to." By being complete you are able to ensure that there will be no misunderstandings later.

DIVIDE CANDIDATES INTO CATEGORIES, ACCORDING TO YOUR INTEREST IN THEM

In Fig. 8 there are three general categories. Each represents a different possible level of interest in a candidate. Say you've finished collecting information. You're about to shift to presenting data. At that point you need to make a general assessment: Which of these three categories does the candidate fall?

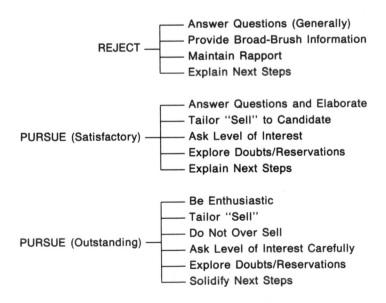

REJECT
— Answer Questions (Generally)
— Provide Broad-Brush Information
— Maintain Rapport
— Explain Next Steps

PURSUE (Satisfactory)
— Answer Questions and Elaborate
— Tailor "Sell" to Candidate
— Ask Level of Interest
— Explore Doubts/Reservations
— Explain Next Steps

PURSUE (Outstanding)
— Be Enthusiastic
— Tailor "Sell"
— Do Not Over Sell
— Ask Level of Interest Carefully
— Explore Doubts/Reservations
— Solidify Next Steps

Fig. 8. Pursue (satisfactory), Reject, and Pursue (outstanding).

Group One: Pursue—Talented Performers

Most candidates fall into this group—worthy of serious consideration. They're talented performers, and you want to retain their interest, though you will also want to compare them with other people you've interviewed before you make a final judgment.

Group Two: Reject

Totally inappropriate. There should be relatively few of those if your screening procedures are good, but it could happen.

Group Three: Pursue—Star Performers

This group consists of the star performers, candidates you consider to be outstanding and whom you want to pursue vigorously.

There is at least one possible objection you might have to this procedure: At this stage of the interview you have not yet completed your evaluation of the candidate; you've collected a lot of information relating to his or her background, but the systematic processing of these data into a selection decision still lies before you. It is a process that will not begin in earnest until after the candidate has walked out the door. Nevertheless, your best—perhaps your only—chance to influence this person's decision is now, while he or she sits in front of you. How do you resolve this paradox?

Fortunately, this is one problem that looks much knottier in theory than it is in practice. To adapt your presentation to the individual candidate, you don't need to make final, fine-tuned selection decisions. All you need to do is decide into which broad category the candidate fits: Do they seem to be a good, viable contender, a star performer, or are they totally out of the running? Your remarks will, of course, be contingent on your level of interest in the candidate, and you will tailor what you say to that level of interest.

As you can see from the outline in Fig. 8, the procedures for each of these groups overlap. There are some procedures that can be applied to all of them, and some procedures that would be applicable for one and not the other two. To present them to you I'm going to describe, first, the approach I recommend for the middle group—Pursue (Satisfactory). Then, using the approach to the middle group as the basic model, I'll show you how to modify the basic strategy for the top group—Reject—and the bottom group—Pursue (Outstanding).

Group One: Getting Talented Candidates to Say Yes

As I've said, a persuasive, as opposed to merely informative, presentation is one that takes into account what you've learned about the candidate during the interview. Fine. How do you do that?

There are four principles involved:

Principle Number 1: Connect Your Job with the Specifics the Candidate Wants. During the course of the interview Barbara has identified certain things that she wants or needs to get out of a job. If she hasn't volunteered any information regarding this you have inquired about it by asking questions like: "Tell me, Barbara. What are you looking for in your next job?" "What type of environment is important to you?" "What are you looking for in the long run?" You've been trying to get a sense of what's important to her.

Now when you make your presentation about the job you can say: "Barbara, you indicated to me earlier that in your very next job it was important to you to have the opportunity to manage or supervise people. You also said you wanted to have the opportunity to work on more complex projects. I'd like to point out to you that this job will have these challenges." And then you go on to explain specifically just what you mean by that. You make sure that she doesn't leave that room without knowing that this job offers her what she wants.

The principle at work here is not difficult to understand. Few people dispute its usefulness for influencing candidates, but some are reluctant to put it into practice because they feel it's too obvious. Won't Barbara know you're trying to influence her? Well . . . yes, she might. She's intelligent, that's one of the reasons you're interested. So it may well be that if you do give information that overtly connects what she's looking for with what you have, she'll assume that you're interested in her. But what's wrong with that? It's the truth. It doesn't mean she's got the job, it means she's in the running. You are interested; most candidates will feel good about that.

However, some interviewers feel awkward even hinting to candidates how interested they are in them. Instead of isolating and highlighting those features of the job that they know the candidate will find desirable, they choose to embed them in their presentation. They think it's more subtle that way. The trouble is, it's too subtle.

As you go on with your presentation you casually and surreptitiously insert the things that you think are important to Barbara, relying on her to pick up on what you're saying. If the two of you were sitting at home or chatting over lunch, she might be able to process the data as you intend her to. In the formal setting of an interview, however, she is not likely to be so receptive. Even if you've succeeded in building a relaxed atmosphere, the situation, by its very nature, still has some tension built into it, and she is therefore unable to perceive the subtleties that you wish to convey. Her attention for the last 30–40 minutes has been focused on making the best impression that she can make on you—it's not easy for her all of a sudden to stop thinking about her presentation and give full attention to what you have to say, much as it might be to her advantage.

It's like the difference between sitting at home watching a game show on television and actually being on the game show. In your own chair, in your own living room, you may get all the answers right (and pile up thousands of dream dollars)—but in the studio with the lights and the action and the camera you might find it more difficult.

Your responsibility is to make sure Barbara doesn't leave the room without knowing that the specific things she's looking for in a job are available in your job.

Now I'm not suggesting that for the sake of making a favorable impression you invent advantages that the job or the organization doesn't have to offer. If they don't exist you can't invent them; but the extent to which there are aspects of the job that reflect the candidate's concerns and desires, you should make them known, clearly and forcefully.

Principle Number 2: Sell Benefits, Not Features. Yet there is room for subtlety. If you have any sales experience, you know the importance of the distinction between "Features" and "Benefits." I'll show you how this concept applies to the interview.

A feature of a job is a mere fact about that job. Simply reading the job description would be the worst type of encyclopedic presentation: bald facts. Take some of those features and rather than just recite them mechanically, show how they are of benefit to the individual—now we're being persuasive.

During the course of your review of Phil's background you've collected data about his talents and abilities. You know about some of his hopes with respect to future jobs, because, at you request, he's stated them directly! That's one of the questions on the Interview Guide (Chapter 9, Fig. 6).

But that's not your only source of information. As you walked through his background, you've also noticed patterns. There are patterns that concern things he liked, didn't like, paths not taken, things that frustrated him, things that excited him . . . themes running through his career. You've learned things about his preferences and style. You've learned what motivates him and what discourages him, even though he may not have stated it directly. You've been systematically examining his background, and you'll probably have picked some of these things up—it's almost impossible not to pick up some pattern. Now you should be able to take at least a couple of the facts or features about the job, and select, out of the universe of things you could talk about, those with a special meaning for Phil.

Notice the distinction between these two kinds of information about the candidate's wants and needs. In the first instance the candidate said, "I want x," and you responded by saying, "You said you wanted x, we've got it." In the second instance he hasn't said it directly but you've inferred it from your review of his background. You've connected what he's hoping to get out of a job, or needs to get out of it or would appreciate getting out of it, with what you can offer.

Again, I don't find many interviewers objecting to that process in theory. I don't hear anybody saying, "Oh, that won't influence candidates." I do, however, hear interviewers say: "Isn't it hard to do? I'm not a psychologist after all." Well, you don't need to be a psychologist to do this. You just need to be awake during the interview!

You're already doing it in your personal life. Ask yourself if the following scenario sounds familiar. You're talking to an old friend over dinner and he is lamenting his love life and you're feeling in a frank and forthright mood and maybe a little irritated with him because you've heard this story so many times before, and so you say: "Look, you know how many times you told me that story? It's driving me crazy. Sure the names change, but you have the same arguments about the same issues at the same point in the relationship and you break up for the same reason—don't you see the pattern?"

Seeing the Patterns.   It's pretty easy, even in a complex life issue, for you to see the patterns emerge. In the interview it's actually even easier, because that's what the interview is designed for. You walk through Phil's background systematically, chronologically, forward in time, through various jobs, various educational experiences, asking what he liked and didn't like, what he learned, and so on. Soon it's pretty obvious that every chance Phil gets to do six things at once, he takes it. If he has six things to do he's happy as a lark. If he has three things to do he looks for more to do; if he gets it he's happy, if he doesn't he's not. If he has six things to do and finishes three, he doesn't wait to finish the remaining three, he grabs more. He does it in his earlier jobs, later jobs, in school, outside interests—everywhere he goes, that's the way he is.

So then, Phil needs to be kept pretty busy and that's one thing that makes him happy. If you're able to fulfill that need, you should emphasize it. Tell him how your company rewards and encourages people who take on more and do more. Tell Phil that if he wants to operate that way that's a real plus for him, because there are plenty of things to keep him busy. If Phil really is the sort of person you have every reason to believe he is, then pointing this out will make the job more attractive to him.

In addition, you might have noticed that every chance he gets he likes to work on special projects by himself, independent projects without a lot of people looking over his shoulder, without sharing it with anybody else. He doesn't mind working with others on teams as a part of his regular routine, but he likes to have some special project of his own as well. He did extra book reports in high school. He took on extra tasks on various jobs he's had. In his various community involvements he serves on committees. He declines repeatedly chairperson roles, but volunteers to work independently on a particular issue: "Oh, I'll study that," he says. "I'll research it and report back to the committee." This is also quite different from working on a joint project with others. Well, if this pattern is obvious to you, pick up that theme. Every chance you get you should let him know that he will have the opportunity to work on his own in your setting (if this is true), and you should explain to him just what you mean by that.

So, based on your information from two sources during the interview—the candidate's responses to direct questions, and your inferences based on the patterns you've been able to detect—you're going to show how a feature of the job is a benefit to the candidate. Let me give you a less effective, then a more effective version of this.

Less effective. "Well, Carol, you've given me a lot of information about yourself; now let me give you some information about us. We all work on a small project team basis here. We have a strong training program and I also think you might want to know something about the kind of career opportunities that exist here, so let me kind of chat about those a little bit. Beyond that, you might also be interested in this, this, this, and this." And you give her lots of information about those three topics. And she's bobbing her head and she's asking questions and taking notes, it's going fine.

Compare that presentation with this one.

More effective. "Well, Carol, you've given me a lot of information about yourself; now let me turn to giving you some information about us as an organization and the job in some detail. And let me start with an issue that I think will be of particular importance to you. If we were to make you an offer and you were to come on board, you would immediately be assigned to a small project team. And every member of the project team is involved in every aspect of the process, from the analysis and the problem stage to the development of the alternate scenario solutions, right down to implementation, and they may even carry it through implementation in some cases. Now the reason I am emphasizing this facet of the job first, Carol, is that I got the impression that in some of your previous jobs you felt like a small cog in a big wheel, and how what you did fit into the bigger picture wasn't all that clear to you. As I recall, you said that in one job you felt like an automaton. You were basically just doing you're little job and people would take what you did and apply it somewhere, but it wasn't very satisfying—you even left one job early because of that. Well, around here we work on a small project team basis. The way we operate you'd be able to see the immediate results of your efforts, and you'd be able to see how what you did fit into the bigger picture, and I believe that would be ultimately more satisfying for you."

In the first example I mentioned working on a small project team basis at the start, but only in passing. This time I said: "You see this facet of the job? This has meaning for you. Let me explain for you how it has meaning."

Principle Number 3: Create a Picture in the Candidate's Mind. Last but not least, you're inevitably going to have additional features about the job to share with the candidate, but no other way of connecting them back with benefits, so you can apply this third principle: Create a picture in their mind of them doing the job or task. When you have more information to share, and no other way of connecting it back with benefits statements, you can still do a better job than just firing a bunch of data at the candidate. You might say: "Well, Phil, if we were to make you an offer and you were to come on board, let me describe to you the training you would receive. As a matter of fact, here's a copy of the curriculum. Let me review it with you. Let me give you some detailed information about how this operates. Let me walk you through a typical day, let me describe to you the numbers of people, let me talk about the kind of equipment you'll be using; you go into the field for a month and then you have another week of training."

At the very least you can make it clear. You can help Phil picture what the job will be like in his mind so that he can see that it's believable, that it can work, and that he can picture himself doing it.

Principle Number 4: Maintain Positive Rapport. If all other things are equal, where would you rather work— where the interviewers were cold, mechanical, distant, and played games with your head, or where they seemed sincerely interested in you as a person? An influence factor that can make as big a difference as any other is positive rapport—but of course that isn't something you start doing now. You've been doing it all along. It's the kind of tone you used for relaxing the candidate. The same tone that's best for getting spontaneous responses from candidates is best for persuading them that this might be a nice place to work.

All right. Having dealt with presenting the information on the assumption that we're interested in the candidate, we need to shift now to how you close up the interview, still working on the assumption you're interested. Then I'll address the question of how to modify the basic strategy for presenting information and closing the interview if you're not interested in that person . . . or if you're very interested.

Closing the Interview

Answer Questions. If Phil has any additional questions, any loose ends that he wants to see tied up, you should make sure he has the chance to let you know about it. Simply ask, "Do you have any other questions, about us, the job, or anything else?" You're wrapping things up. You've given him the chance to ask questions before this point, but now you're just checking to see if there are any loose ends. If there are you deal with them, if not you move on.

Ask for Level of Interest. Then you ask a question that goes something like this:

"Well, Phil, we've covered a lot of ground up to this point. You've given me information, I've given you information, and while neither one of us is in a position to make a decision at this moment, I am curious, what's your level of interest?"

"Degree" or "level"—phrase the question in one of those two ways. Not, "Are you interested?" Not, "What about the job interests you?" Those are okay questions to ask earlier on, but now that you're at the close you're asking this question for a very specific reason. Your intention in asking people their level of interest is to try to encourage them to express any doubts, reservations, concerns, or conditions they might have so you can deal with them.

There may be a realistic concern that somehow hasn't come up prior to this point. And, while some candidates will pump the interviewer for answers and raise all sorts of personal concerns or issues, others haven't found the opening to do so. This is the candidates' last chance to ask about some concern that's in the back of their minds. A question about their level of interest can sometimes prompt them to express that concern. It only takes seconds, usually you breeze through it, but you never know when it's going to be useful.

Explore Doubts or Reservations. Now, how often will something of that sort come up? Maybe one or two times out of ten. Most of the time when you ask candidates their level of interest, they'll say, "Well, I'm really interested, it sounds like a wonderful opportunity," and you move right on. But every once in a while, and you never know when it's going to happen, some specific obstacle will be mentioned. A candidate might say: "Well, I am very interested in the opportunity, but I heard there's so much weekend work and overtime I might not be able to take advantage of your tuition reimbursement plan. Is that really true?" Or, "I understand that if I want to be able to afford housing I may have to live 90 miles away. Is that really true?" In certain areas this might very well be true.

Explain Next Steps. Having explored the candidates' doubts or reservations, if there were any, you tell them what's going to happen next. How complicated that might be will vary with the circumstances. It might be just a matter of explaining who the candidate is going to see next in the sequence. You might simply say, "Well the next step is for you to meet with Jeff, let me give him a call, make sure he knows we're coming." Or the next step may be when they hear the results of the interview process, if you're responsible for that. It's best to be as conclusive as possible. That is, while you may not be able to let Barbara know exactly when she is going to learn the results of the interview, you can at least explain the process. If you're evaluating lots of other people between now and the time she's going to hear—or if at the end of that cycle, due to some bureaucratic delay, it's going to take an extended period of time . . . you can tell her about it to prepare her, explain why there's a delay, and maybe tell her who she should contact in the meantime if she hasn't heard anything and has questions. Be as clear as you can be regarding what will happen next. The acceptance rate of talented people drops off rapidly after the interview if all they've heard is vagueness at the end. "Well, Barbara, we really enjoyed having the opportunity to talk with you, thank you for coming in. We'll be in touch." But if at the end you can at least give some clarity regarding what the process is all about, why there might be a delay, who should be contacted, you can hold on to people's interest longer.

End the Interview. And finally, last but not least, you want to get the candidate out of there. It might seem like a simple step, but many people linger at this point and say, "Um, all right, we have a couple of extra minutes, Don, what other questions do you have?" Don doesn't have any extra questions at this stage, because, assuming you've gone through all these other steps, he's already had the chance to ask them. If you ask him for more questions now, he might feel that you're expecting a question and that he'd better come up with one. In cases like this, candidates report afterward: "I did okay in the interview up until the end, and then I really messed it up. There was something the interviewer wanted me to ask about and I couldn't figure out what it was."

Even if Don is not going to leave the building because he's scheduled for another interview after yours, you should at least let the candidate know plainly that the interview has ended. Suppose you call Jeff, the next interviewer in sequence, and he says, "I'm a little late, bring the candidate up in five minutes." "Okay, no problem," you could say to Jeff, hang up the phone, then tell the candidate: "Well, Don, Jeff will be available in five minutes, he's a little bit late. We'll sit here and chat for a few minutes, but I want you to know that our interview is formally over."

No matter how sophisticated they are, many candidates at whatever level, visibly and physically relax. Because it's over.

That's the basic pattern for presenting information persuasively, that's what you do for the majority of candidates who fall into the Pursue (Satisfactory) category. What about the others—the person in whom you are not particularly interested, and the star performer for whom you want to make an especially vigorous effort?

Group Two: Reject

If George is, in your view, totally inappropriate for the job, then there's nothing to be gained from encouraging him to leave the interview feeling that this is the job that's right for him, that really suits his personal needs and interests— after all, he's going to get a letter in three days that says, "Thanks, but no thanks." So with the people in his group, you're still going to maintain rapport, you're still going to provide information, but you're not going to get that specific, you're going to do it in a kind of broadbrush way. You'll answer his questions, but in more general terms. What you won't do, as you can see from Fig. 8, is tailor and adapt your presentation to his particular needs and interests, as you would if you were interested. You won't show how features are benefits. You will simply give the information. In other words, you will go back to the ency-clopedic presentation, but still maintain rapport and show enough interest in him as a person so that he won't leave feeling you've counted him out. He should leave thinking: "This is a fine organization; the interview is very profes-sional, the interviewer took time to explain things to me and gave me time to explain myself. It was a fair interview, the company sounds like a nice place, the job sounds inter-esting—even though of course it's a job I could do in lots of other places."

You want George to leave feeling good about you, about the process, and the company . . . but you don't want him to be all that excited about the job. There's nothing to be gained from that. Notice, however, that you do nothing to discourage him. You don't say anything to make him feel that this is not the place for him, you don't say anything to turn him off. You simple make sure not to add fuel to the fire. You can't stop people from wanting or needing the job, but you can avoid adding that extra measure in.

Group Three: Star Performer

Let's suppose you are faced with someone who falls into the third category: a star performer. The basic strategies for presenting information and closing up the interview that you would use for the Pursue (satisfactory) group apply here, but now you need to add some extras.

Note the first item under Pursue (outstanding) in Fig. 8, "Be Enthusiastic." This piece of advice takes into account an observation about the nature of star performers, which is that they know who they are, they know they have choices, and they don't want to settle for just a job. They want something special. They want to feel excited and enthusias-tic about what they do. The problem is there's no way in the world they can know in advance whether a particular job will make them feel that way. They have to guess at it, and it turns out that one of the things they base their guess on is you! And if you seem enthusiastic about what you're doing, they say, "Oh, maybe there's something here for me." Therefore, it's your job to express some enthusiasm, toward the end of the interview.

This is not something that you express in an effusive manner. Instead, make some kind of statement such as, "Well, Judith, I just want to let you know that I made the decision five years ago to come on board here, and I'm excited about what I do and I really think this has been a wonderful experience for me, I've grown a lot and I'm pleased I made the decision." And then move right on. No response needed from the candidate. But lest you think it is meaningless, or that nobody's going to be influenced by that or even remember it, you should know that this is one of the issues star performers talk about. "You know the people at that place really seem excited about what they do. That helped me make my decision." It's a small thing, but when you're trying to ensure that a talented person with choices will accept your offer, every little thing you can do counts.

In addition, all the items that apply to the presentation you give to people in the Pursue (satisfactory) category in Fig. 8 apply to the presentation you give to star performers, so you tailor your presentation to their needs and interests as you would with the middle group.

Note, however, that there's a danger of downplaying negative information and overselling to star performers. You don't want to discourage these people, so you may have a tendency to hint at things that may not be true, or say: "Well, I don't know if we should discuss it at this point. I mean, we might be able to work that out, but that's for later on . . ." and sweep things under the rug. And later on, when you can't deliver, they feel something has been removed from the table.

They might end up not accepting the offer if they feel something you hinted at has been removed from the table; or, more likely, they'll use your mistake as a bludgeon with which to hit you over the head. They say: "Well, in the interview the interviewer said that it would be possible, and I really feel now this is quite different. If you can't do that you'll have to give me an extra week's vacation."

You can avoid being put in that position. If there's something they ask for that you can't deliver and you know about it, then you say: "Judith, I understand why you'd want that. But let me say that there's no precedent for it. The likelihood of that happening here is quite low. But I'd be happy to look into it just in case I'm missing something, but I can't promise it to you at this stage. So far as I know it can't be done."

Star performers are trained to ask for the moon. They don't expect to get the moon, they expect to get half of it. So don't feel bad about not giving in to every little thing they want. They're not going to run out the door because of that.

Explore Level of Interest. You ask candidates in the Pursue (satisfactory) category their level of interest in order to trigger off some doubts and reservations, so you can deal with them if they exist. With the Reject group, however, since you're not concerned about resolving their doubts and reservations, there's no point in dredging them up. But with the star performers, not only do you ask them their level of interest, but if they don't express a doubt or reservation you should say: "Well, Judith, I appreciate the fact that you're interested in us, but let me just take it one step further. If we were in fact to make you an offer, is there anything at all that would cause you to lean away from accepting it, anything at all?"

With a star performer you might want to push that a little bit, because you might learn some valuable data that would help you.

Explore Doubts and Reservations and Explain Next Steps. Of course, you should explore doubts and reservations if they come up. Once that has been taken care of you should go on to tell the candidate what's going to happen next, and perhaps even make an appointment to get back to them with more data. With the star performers you should always make sure to solidify what the next steps will be so that you will have some reason to keep in touch with them.

Close the Interview.   Finally, the last step as with every candidate is to get them out of there, end the interview in a reasonably crisp manner, just as you began it.

IV ═══ MAKING
DECISIONS

This section of the book is brief compared to what's preceded it, but it would be hard to overestimate its importance. Here's where you learn how to use the rich information you collected in the interview to arrive at an accurate good selection decision.

In Chapter 18, "How to Take Notes During the Interview— Have an Accurate Record and Avoid Distraction," you'll learn how you can take accurate, complete notes unobtrusively so that you'll have a good clear basis for your judgment.

In Chapter 19, "Organizing and Interpreting the Information Collected," I'll show you a way to organize the raw data in your notes. Then I'll introduce you to the Interview Analysis Worksheet (Fig. 10), a training tool and ready reference that can do for the decision-making process what the Interview Guide (Chapter 9, Fig. 6) does for the interview. I'll show you how that piece of paper can help you refine everything that has gone before into a decision that's fair, that's rational, that can be justified and explained to others in your organization . . . and that can be expressed briefly but clearly.

≡≡≡18≡HOW TO TAKE NOTES DURING THE INTERVIEW—HAVE AN ACCURATE RECORD AND AVOID DISTRACTION

Y ou may recall the following fact about human memory from your introductory psychology course: We remember best those things that occurred at the beginning and end of any sequence of information; and we remember a lot less clearly whatever occurred in the middle. (Does the name "Ebinghaus" trigger any memory traces?) In the classic studies done by him and others on the subject of memory and retention, subjects were read a list of information and then were asked to write down whatever they remembered. The results were consistent. Individuals remembered more and more accurately what they heard at the beginning and end of the sequence of data. Information in the middle was either lost or distorted. Of course, the interview is also a sequence of information.

"PRIMACY AND RECENCY"

The principle derived from these studies is called "primacy and recency." After any sequence of data, we remember most clearly what was said at the beginning—or the "prime" things—and those that occurred most recently. Human memory works that way despite a person's willpower, intelligence, or ability to concentrate. We have no control over it, just as we have no control over the physiological fact that as volume decreases human hearing loses the high notes and low notes first, and then, as volume decreases further, we lose the ability to perceive the middle notes. That's why audiophiles (or teenagers) like to play music loud. The fact that you're a bright person doesn't mean that you can hold on to the high and low notes longer. By that same logic, you have no control over the psychophysiological facts of human memory.

WHY NOTE-TAKING IN THE INTERVIEW IS SO CRITICAL

Studies done on the selection interview have given many interviewers the opportunity to contrast what they remembered immediately after the interview with the actual transcript of the interview. Of course, the transcript is more complete and more detailed—it's word for word and it comes as no surprise that the quantity is different. But the quality is dramatically different too, and that is often a shocker. When they listen to the interview again, on tape, or read a transcript, interviewers say: "Oh my, I forgot about that. I didn't realize that. If I'd seen this in connection with that I'd have realized . . . ."

The interview is a sequence of the information. If at the end of the interview you do not have the advantages of some memory jogger to help you recall what occurred, you will remember best and be influenced most by the things that occurred at the beginning (including your initial impression), and by the things that happened toward the end. What will be lost will be a lot of the subtle, detailed information that occurred in the middle of the interview, when the complex, in-depth, two-step probing was going on. The solution is to take notes during the interview. Taking notes will mute this primacy–recency effect—the notes will act as memory joggers, and you will not be left at the mercy of your "memory."

COMMON NOTE-TAKING ERRORS

As important as it is, most interviewers don't take notes during the interview. Either they've tried it and found that note-taking interfered with the process, or they anticipate that it will. Their feeling is that in the feverish effort to get everything down on paper they will miss more information than they preserve, and they are concerned about the effect on candidates who might be put off by the sight of an interviewer with his or her nose buried in notes.

These are real problems. Arguably it would be better not to take notes at all than to take them so ineffectually. Let me highlight for you what some of those common errors are, and then talk about some solutions.

Stopping in the Middle

One of the observations made by candidates about note-taking is that the interviewer seemed to abandon the note-taking process. After taking notes consistently or periodically for several minutes, the interviewer has finally gotten to the good stuff. They've turned to those subjects that get rich, detailed information—most likely the most recent work experiences or education. A tremendous amount of information is coming out. It's flowing freely. Two-step probes are eliciting valuable information. Comments are encouraging spontaneity—and the interviewer gets so caught up in the content and the verbal interaction that they forget about taking notes.

Of course, the moment this happens the candidate, who has been watching closely, notices and wonders why. What does it mean? "The interviewer stopped taking notes," they tell us. "Does this mean that what I was saying was no longer of value? Maybe they were at some stage of the interview where they're just chatting with me, like at the beginning? Maybe they were just being polite and they'd already ruled me out. Or maybe it's something good. Maybe it means I got the job and they didn't need to write anything down because they were already sure they were going to make me an offer!"

Or if none of those things occurred to them, they just say to themselves during the interview, with some justification, "Just when it got really complex they stopped taking notes: I wonder if they're going to remember any of this."

In addition to being self-defeating (you stop taking notes at the very point of the interview that covers the most complex information), this kind of behavior is highly distracting to the candidate.

Obvious Highlighting

Some interviewers highlight certain items. Periodically, when the candidate mentions something of critical importance (usually a negative issue) they might even say, "Oh— excuse me one second," and they write down on their pad the issue that was just discussed. More commonly they underline items, circle items, inset asterisks, draw arrows, write in big letters, print . . . they do all sorts of things that make it very difficult for the candidate to concentrate. Even if this obvious highlighting doesn't immediately follow the disclosure of negative information, it's bound to stifle spontaneity because the candidate wonders—Was it something good I said? Was it something bad? Is it something I should worry about? Should I clarify?

Allowing the Candidate to Watch You Taking Notes

Finally, another common error interviewers make in note-taking is to put their notepad right on the table or desk in front of them or next to them. The applicant can actually read the notes, or at least can watch them being taken. Most candidates find their gaze being drawn to those notes like a magnet—if they're not looking at them, their neck muscles are going to ache later from the strain of fighting the urge to look. They can't help being curious what you're saying about them.

While sitting in on interviewers, I've actually seen candidates resort to numbering items out loud as they give their answers and wait for the interviewer to jot down Point 2 before moving on to Point 3. I've seen candidates notice what the interviewer wrote and then try to refute it.

Fortunately, all these mistakes can be avoided rather easily so that you have an accurate record of what the candidate said without it being a burden for you or a distraction for the candidate. All you have to do is follow the five principles of effective note-taking that I have listed below.

HOW TO TAKE NOTES EFFECTIVELY AND UNOBTRUSIVELY

Use a Clipboard, Not a Plain Pad of Paper

A valuable procedure is to remove the surface plane of your notes from their "visual field"—a fancy way of saying, tilt your notes up so that the candidate can't actually follow along as you write. This reduces the "distraction factor" considerably. Notice that you're not hiding or disguising the fact that you're taking notes. You're simply making it impossible for anyone to actually follow along. To accomplish this, you need to use something that will keep you from putting your notes on the surface of your desk.

While a steno pad would serve your purpose, I've given up suggesting that since interviewers are reluctant to use it; nevertheless it's quite well-suited to our purpose. A plain pad of paper with cardboard backing will not work well because it's too flexible. So use some kind of clipboard—a plain old medical clipboard with a clip on the top, or a leather one that folds. Would you rather use a designer clipboard, translucent, with your name in gold? Feel free to do so. As long as you can put it in your lap so candidates can't follow along with you while you're taking notes.

This one technique, simple and mechanical as it might seem, lowers the distraction factor by a considerable margin—and that's the important issue. It's a small thing, but it works well.

Do Not Record Information That Is Otherwise Available

Why take down in your notes any information that is already available someplace else? Why make a painstaking record of where the candidates went to school, what they majored in, where they worked, their duties and responsibilities, their title—if that information is available on their application or résumé or some other document in your possession?

It may seem like an obvious point, but the fact is that when interview notes have been analyzed, fully 80 percent, four-fifths of what interviewers write down in their notes turns out to be information already available someplace else. By not recording the information you'll reduce the burden of taking notes considerably. You'll spend much less time writing and that much more time paying attention, without losing any information. Of course, this also reduces the risk of distracting the candidate since you are writing much less.

Avoid Taking Verbatim Notes

There is no need to write down quotes of what the candidates say. Get the essence of what they say that's job-related. You're not writing a transcript of the interview.

Record Results of Two-Step Probes

If you're not going to write down information already available someplace else, and you're not going to write down everything the candidate says, what are you going to write down? The answer is: You are going to write down the results of the two-step probing process.

It may help to explain what I mean by this in a little more detail. You'll recall that on the Interview Guide (Chapter 9, Fig. 6) there were one-step probes that were intended to touch the surface of any individual job or educational experience or outside interest. Those one-step probes are like soil samples, each touching the surface of an event. If through using a one-step probe you learn something of a job-related nature, you drilled into that subject for more detail. It logically follows that if you ask a one-step probe about a particular job or educational experience and do not learn anything that's job-related, you do no further probing in that area. You save your in-depth probing for those surface inquiries or one-step probes that reveal job-related information.

Well, having reminded you of that, consider this sequence. You ask a one-step probe about a particular experience, do not learn anything that's job-related, and therefore do not probe into it in any more detail. Do you need to make a note of this exchange? I don't think so. For the most part, you needn't take any notes concerning one-step probes, which are exploratory questions—unless you hit pay dirt. If you ask a one-step probe and follow up with two-step, three-step, four-step, and five-step probes, then that's information you will want to remember.

Take "Telegraphic" or "Key Word" Notes

But even in those instances you're not going to write down everything the candidate says. After the inquiry is over, all you need to write down are a couple of key words, a symbol, a little telegraphic summary, some little, quickly written message that will remind you of what the candidate said that you thought was important.

Notice I didn't say write down your conclusions. Your notes should not consist of words like "Initiative— Initiative—Motivated—High Energy . . . Initiative . . . ." Instead, mark down some cryptic reminder that later on will help you recall an entire complex incident. Let the incident itself tell you something about initiative, analytical ability, logic, common sense, teamwork ability, or whatever else is implied by the candidate's response. Based on that concrete information you can look for patterns; not only will you be able to make decisions for yourself, you'll be able to justify your conclusions to others.

The same "memory jogger" principle that governs note-taking governs multiple choice tests. In multiple choice tests, rather than drawing on recall memory, we draw on recognition memory—we look up and down a list of choices and, if we've done our homework, the right answer jumps off the page at us. That's much easier than simply being given the question and having to recall the answer.

Memory joggers work the same way. At the end of the interview, each one of your notes—your memory joggers—will trigger off a memory trace—and through this process you will be able to remember a very complex incident much more accurately than if you had tried to summarize without the aid of notes. I recommend note-taking very highly to you as a tool for remembering accurately the rich information you collect. If in the course of half an hour or 45 minutes you ask 40, 50, 60, or 70 questions, then you'd better be taking notes if you want to remember the essence of what the responses were.

If you have had any exposure to memory training, you may recall the basic principles of good memory joggers. Write down something that exaggerates the issue at hand, some little symbol or a few words that remind you of an exaggeration of the issue, and you'll remember it better. Do this, and at the end of the interview you'll have 5, 10, 15 of these little memory joggers. Not many; but each one will contain job-related information not available any place else.

No one who's only seen the paperwork on this candidate will know what you know from your notes—it's new information—because you didn't write down any information that was already available on paper. It's not just new inform-ation, it will all be job-related information, because you wouldn't have probed below the surface with a two-step probe unless you had a job-related reason for doing so. Your notes, remember, are only records of your two-and-more-step probes.

Finally, every one of those little memory joggers that represents new and job-relevant information will in fact do just that—jog your memory and remind you of what was said in detail. Even though your note consists of no more than a couple of words and perhaps a symbol, you will remember what was said accurately and you will be able to share it with others. You'll be able to use it to explain your point of view, or to make decisions or compare it with other things that the candidate said in order to come up with judgments that are accurate.

One of the chief advantages of this method of taking notes is that it is incomparably less time-consuming than ordinary methods, so much so that it answers the chief objections to note-taking: distraction and time.

Suppose you have just completed a 40-minute interview, and after the candidate leaves you have 10 of these little telegraphic or cryptic notes to yourself. How long might it take to write a single one of these little notes?

Say, at the outside, your hobby is calligraphy, 10 seconds. Ten times ten is 100 seconds, a little more than a minute and a half—let's wildly exaggerate and almost double it and call it three minutes. Out of the 40-minute interview, maybe 10 minutes was spent presenting your own information. That leaves 30 minutes of data collection. Ten percent of that 30 minutes was spent actually writing and the 10 percent (or 3 minutes) was spread out over the entire 30 minutes. Hardly a distraction; most of the time you're relating to the candi-date, maintaining good eye contact. And you can even be writing, sometimes, while you're talking, which reduces the distraction. You say: "Well, Ken, I didn't realize it was that complex, and there were that many aspects to it, I'm glad you mentioned that. What was your next job?" and while you're commenting you've made your note.

PRACTICE TAKING NOTES IN OTHER CIRCUMSTANCES

By the way, you don't have to wait for the interview to practice anything I've said here. Next time you're in a meeting with one person or twenty people, every once in a while write down some little key word or memory jogger relating to the subject being discussed. At the end of the meeting you'll be able to reproduce an accurate record of the meeting, no matter how complex it was. You'll certainly be able to do that much more accurately than someone else next to you who paid very careful attention, but is relying on unaided memory.

≡≡≡19≡ORGANIZING AND INTERPRETING THE INFORMATION COLLECTED

The interview is over, the candidate has walked out the door and you are sitting at your desk: What do you do now?

At this point, in what often passes for decision making, interviewers look over the random information in their notes and say: "Well, let's see what I have here...highly relevant work experience, that's good, and thinks analytically and logically, good, familiar with our hardware and software, that's good, shows initiative only when they're interested in something, that's a potential problem. And, ah, let's see, works well on a small project team, good, but doesn't work so well as an individual contributor, a potential problem. I don't know—There's evidence for yes, evidence for no...."

. . . and they weigh and balance the conflicting evidence in their mind and say, "Okay, let's make this a hire!"

. . . or they say, "Na, I don't really think so!"

Most interviewers make an educated guess at the end of the interview, based on an accumulation of impressions. This "global impression" is not irrational, especially if the interview was conducted using the principles of structure and in-depth probing presented in Part III of this book. But even after a good interview, an "eyeballing the data" approach is far from the best way to make use of the in-depth information you've gathered. That's why I want to take you one step further and show you how to organize and interpret your information before making a decision. The tools I'm about to show you will sharpen the accuracy of your decisions considerably and even enable you to make fine-tuned comparisons of different candidates.

HOW ORGANIZING THE INFORMATION INCREASES ACCURACY OF JUDGMENT

All the research on the decision making after an interview tells us that organizing our information before arriving at a decision results in a much more accurate judgment. But what does that mean?

Remember the fundamental task of the interview is to answer three questions. Can the candidate Do the job? Will they Behave in the ways needed?, and Will they Fit into your unique set of environmental circumstances?

Prior to the interview you therefore started out making sure what the true job requirements were. During the course of the interview you then reached for evidence related to these criteria. Now you have to match up what you learned in the interview against the job requirements.

Figure 9 is a visual representation of the process of organizing and synthesizing all the information available to you at this point. Along the top are the three questions you are expected to answer after an interview: Can the candi-

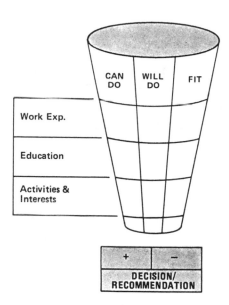

Fig. 9. The "hopper": Organizing and interpreting the information.

date Do the job? Will they Behave in the way that we need?, and Will they Fit into the particular environment?

During the interview you couldn't directly ask about the many factors represented by each of these questions, so you needed a plan to help you capture relevant information indirectly. You therefore covered the candidate's Work Experience, Education, Outside Interests and Activities, and then their own Self-Assessment. This framework was very helpful in collecting information. But now that the interview is over, that structure is in your way. From a decision-making standpoint, the information you collected is in almost random order—chronological by category. To put it another way: The rows in Fig. 9 were very helpful in collecting information, but the questions represented by the columns are now the important issue. After, all once the interview is over no one is going to ask you: "Where in your structure did you learn that the candidate was analytical and logical in their decision making? Where in the interview structure did you learn that the candidate can work on a small project team?" No one cares about that. They just want to know if the person is right for the job, and why. They want to know if there is sufficient evidence to justify the conclusion that the candidate Can Do the job, Will Behave in the necessary ways, and Will Fit into their environment.

In effect, I'm going to recommend that you take the information gathered during your interview (shown on the left side of Fig. 9—Work Experience, Education, and Activities and Interests), and shove it into the hopper-shaped structure beside it. Organize the information against the columns of criteria, and then extract out a judgment about the candidate's appropriateness for the job. You will reach a much more accurate decision through this process than by making a global judgment by "scanning" the data.

A TOOL FOR ORGANIZING AND INTERPRETING INTERVIEW DATA: THE INTERVIEW ANALYSIS WORKSHEET

The Interview Analysis Worksheet (Fig. 10) is the practical tool you can use for organizing and synthesizing the raw information from your interview; and in fact, if you compare it with Fig. 9, you can see that, in a way, they are essentially the same: The hopper is a graphic depiction of the logic built into the Interview Analysis Worksheet.

Of course, the Interview Analysis Worksheet, in turn, is just a guide to acquaint you with the process and lead you through it a few times. Once you understand the process, you will probably find that you can dispense with the Interview Analysis Worksheet; by then a piece of blank paper will work just as well.

Takes Only Five to Ten Minutes

I'm about to launch into a detailed explanation of the worksheet and how you use it, but first I would like to make the following point: I'm well aware that if I give you a way to organize and interpret information that took 20 minutes to do, no one would use it! I could argue with you—hey,

INTERVIEW ANALYSIS WORKSHEET

Applicant _____   Position _____

Date _____   Interviewer _____

POSITION CRITERIA	SUMMARY OF JOB RELEVANT INFORMATION (from notes)		
Can Do Factors (Skills and Abilities)	**OVERALL IMPRESSION**		
_____			
_____			
_____			
_____	**WORK EXPERIENCE**		
_____	CAN DO (BOTH + AND −)	WILL DO (BOTH + AND −)	FIT (BOTH + AND −)
_____			
Will Do Factors (Behaviors)			
_____			
_____			
_____			
_____			
_____			
_____			
Fit Factors			
• Environmental Circumstances			
_____	**EDUCATION**		
_____			
_____			
_____			
_____			
• Knockout Items			
_____			
_____			
_____			
_____			
_____			
_____			

Fig. 10. Interview Analysis Worksheet.

Consider Can Do, Will Do and Fit Factors from reverse side.	ACTIVITIES, INTERESTS AND SITUATIONAL CONSIDERATIONS		
Also consider: • Travel Restrictions • Relocation Obstacles • Overtime Requirements • Evening or Weekend Schedules • Physical Requirements			

SYNTHESIS OF ALL AVAILABLE JOB RELEVANT INFORMATION

A. SUMMARY OF ASSETS (+)	B. SUMMARY OF DEVELOPMENTAL NEEDS RESTRICTIONS OR LIMITATIONS (–)

OVERALL SUMMARY AND RECOMMENDATIONS (Incorporate Into Your Organization's Report Form)

1. Summarize from A above the candidate's strengths and assets in a sentence or two.

2. Summarize from B above the candidate's developmental needs, restrictions and/or limitations for this position in a sentence or two.

3. Weigh and balance strengths and developmental needs, highlighting the most important factors. Then make a final recommendation, considering this candidate's match for this position, including placement options, training, supervis and future potential.

Fig. 10. Back.

you're making a $20,000 or a $40,000 decision, don't you think it's worth 20 minutes? But as a practical reality very few interviewers would do it. A process that would take 20 minutes would be worthless to most interviewers. But you will use it if it takes five to ten minutes, and once you're familiar with it that's how long it will take.

What the Interview Analysis Worksheet Is For—And NOT For

Notice the form does not say, "Report form (fill me out, type me up, take an hour to do it, and be ready to be criticized for everything you write, especially in court)." No one is going to see this except you. It is just a worksheet to help you organize the evidence.

It does not say on this form, "Please take notes on me," because it's not for that, either. It is designed to help you organize information after the interview is over, after your notes are taken. From it you will extract your report, decision, or recommendation.

TOUR OF THE INTERVIEW ANALYSIS WORKSHEET

Now I'm going to take you through the Interview Analysis Worksheet (Fig. 10) step-by-step, explaining the function of each box, in the order in which you'd use each box. When necessary, I will give examples to help clear up ambiguities. When I'm finished, you should have a pretty good grasp of how you can use this form—or the logic behind the form—to arrive at accurate, justifiable decisions. Remember, it's essentially the same as the logic I reviewed in explaining Fig. 9.

Position Criteria

The column that says "Position Criteria" (see Fig. 10) on the left side of the front of the form is used to record the Can Do,

Will Do, and Fit factors you analyzed in advance. Filling this section out on the form may not be necessary. If you've filled out the Job Analysis Worksheet (see Chapter 3, Fig. 1), you have already recorded the job criteria there and you may not need to write them down again. This section is on the form for intellectual completeness (and remember, once you are familiar with this process you can dispense with the form entirely). If, on the other hand, putting the information in these boxes will help you to keep the job criteria in mind, feel free to do so. The important thing is for you to have the job criteria clear in your mind and available to you as you organize information from the interview.

While it is important to have the job criteria available to you in some place or other, the heart of the Interview Analysis Worksheet (Fig. 11), the place where you do your organizing and analyzing, is the part I'm going to review now.

Overview of the Core of the Inverview Analysis Worksheet

The form contains sections for summarizing the evidence you collected from your "Overall Impression" and your review of their "Work Experiences," their "Educational Background," and their "Activities and Interests." Into each of these sections on the form you will enter the evidence you've acquired during the interview, placing it into the appropriate column, and indicating its positive or negative value.

The two boxes on the back of the form, labelled "Summary of Assets" and "Summary of Developmental Needs," refer to your extraction of all the evidence summarized previously on the form. These two sections are the same as those two lists referred to at the bottom of Fig. 9.

In the last section, "Overall Summary and Recommendations," we turn the two lists into the three statements that are the end product of our efforts.

That's the overview. Now I'll go over each section individually.

INTERVIEW ANALYSIS WORKSHEET

Position _____

Interviewer _____

SUMMARY OF JOB RELEVANT INFORMATION (from notes)

OVERALL IMPRESSION

WORK EXPERIENCE

CAN DO (BOTH + AND −)	WILL DO (BOTH + AND −)	FIT (BOTH + AND −)

EDUCATION

Fig. 11. Core of the Interview Analysis Worksheet.

Overall Impression. As I've emphasized throughout this book, final judgments based primarily on the candidate's momentary behavior during the interview are notoriously inaccurate: This is not to say, however, that such behavior is irrelevant. Notice, however, that we are not focusing on only "initial impression" or "gut reaction." Instead, ask yourself what did you learn through direct observation during the interview (as opposed to the things you were able to deduce from the answers to your questions) that relate to job criteria? Was the candidate articulate and logical? Were the candidate's answers thoughtful?—These are possible Can Do factors. This is the place to summarize each observations.

Work Experience. Look at the next section, Work Experience, and the corresponding columns, Can Do, Will Do, and Fit. During your review of the candidate's entire work experiences you collected lots of data. Now the interview is over. You look over your notes, you look over all the available paperwork relating to the candidate, all the forms, performance reviews in the case of an internal candidate, whatever other documentation you have, which now of course includes your notes. What did you learn from this documentation and from that 15–20 minute segment of your interview about any of the Can Do, Will Do, and Fit factors?

You might have learned that Bill has a highly logical and rational approach to problem solving, some highly relevant experience; you record these in the Can Do column and put "pluses" next to them. He might have demonstrated that he has behaved in the way we defined as "high energy"; note this in the Will Do column with a plus. He doesn't work well as an individual contributor; that's a small minus under the Fit column. He does work well on a small project team; that's a plus under the Fit column. He seems to have displayed the kind of behavior we mean by "motivation," that's a plus under the Will Do column. But on the other hand, he only shows initiative when he's really interested in the project at hand; that's a minus under the Will Do column. And his experience was with a previous generation of the software you use; that's a minus under the Can Do column.

You take whatever you learned during that part of your interview during which you covered the candidate's work experiences and just place it in the appropriate box under the Can Do, Will Do, or Fit headings and give it a charge— positive or negative.

Education. You do the same thing for Education. Bill's taken some highly specialized courses, or has a gap in his technical background or training, demonstrated teamwork ability or leadership skills or a disinterest in attending to details, or displayed some other positive or negative qualities relevant to the Can Do, Will Do, or Fit factors. You plug these observations in as pluses and minuses in the Education section of the form.

Activities and Interests and Situational Considerations

You look over your notes on Activities and Interests and you do the same thing; you enter what you learn that's job-relevant, giving each a charge, positive or negative, as appropriate. Include in this section any special circumstances or restrictions you learned in the interview that might interfere with the candidate's ability to meet the job requirements.

Why Is There No Box For "Self-Assessment"?

There is no box for "Self-Assessment" because that category of the interview was the candidate's summary of his or her assets and developmental needs—as such it served either to reinforce or attenuate what we learned and should be reflected in information recorded in the boxes for Overall Impression, Work Experience, Education, and Activities and Interests.

The process so far should take a maximum of five to eight minutes: Just organize your evidence by category into columns.

Anything in your notes that is not relevant to the job requirements gets ignored and eventually thrown out.

Next, in the "Summary of Assets" section, create a list of all the most important positives, and in the "Summary of Developmental Needs," a separate list of all the most important negatives. To create these lists all you have to do is extract and summarize all the positives and negatives recorded in earlier sections of the form.

Overall Summary and Recommendations (Fig. 12)

Once you've done that you are two-thirds of the way toward writing what I would call your "Evaluation Report." The bottom third of the back of the Interview Analysis Worksheet (Fig. 12) represents the guts of your report. The first sentence is simply a summary of the candidate's assets; the second sentence is a summary of his or her limitations or developmental needs; and your third sentence includes your

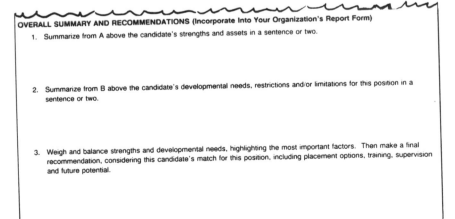

OVERALL SUMMARY AND RECOMMENDATIONS (Incorporate Into Your Organization's Report Form)

1. Summarize from A above the candidate's strengths and assets in a sentence or two.

2. Summarize from B above the candidate's developmental needs, restrictions and/or limitations for this position in a sentence or two.

3. Weigh and balance strengths and developmental needs, highlighting the most important factors. Then make a final recommendation, considering this candidate's match for this position, including placement options, training, supervision and future potential.

Fig. 12. Overall Summary and Recommendations.

weighing and balancing of those issues and, finally, your recommendation.

Notice the recommendation should be more than just "hire" or "don't hire." Compare the candidate's assets and limitations to explain your reasoning. Additionally, you may want to make specific recommendations, or a recommendation for supervision or training, or you might want to recommend the candidate for another more suitable role in your organization.

Here's an example: Marcia has a candidate named Ed who needs to be interviewed on a day when she's going to be out of town, and so she asks you to conduct the interview for her. You're trained to interview so she is confident you can do a good job. She has given you the specific Can Do, Will Do, and Fit factors required by this job, so it's clear what you're looking for, and you know how to take notes and organize information afterward. You conduct the interview. After Ed leaves, you organize your information in the way I've outlined so far, and extract out your two lists of the candidate's job-relevant assets and limitations. You finally write three sentences. The next day Marcia comes in and asks you, "Well what did you think of the candidate?"

In response to her question you make three statements:

1. A statement about the candidate's job-relevant assets

2. A statement about the candidate's limitations and restrictions with respect to the job

3. A recommendation, with your reasons

In this scenario you're presenting your views orally, face-to-face, but it could just as well be done over the phone, in a memo, or at the bottom of your organizations' evaluation form. If your organization has such a form, the place for these three statements might be anywhere on it where it says, "Other Comments or Summary."

Here is what you might have said:

Statement 1

"Well Marcia, for this particular position, Ed had a number of strong assets. For example, he had very relevant prior work experiences and he worked effectively on projects at least as complex as the ones we have. He has an analytical and logical approach to problem solving. He's demonstrated that he has the behaviors we labeled as initiative and high energy. There is an indication that he works well on a small project team, and he seems to have the kinds of interests that would enable us to keep him sustained and focused here. Ed also seems to have a solid familiarity with the hardware that we're using, and it seems as if nothing would prevent him form working on an occasional weekend if he gets a little advance notice, and he's willing to do it: He sees that as part of the job."

You might notice that those are all positives, and they include some of the Can Do, Will Do, and Fit factors since they have been extracted from the three columns or organized evidence in our chart.

Statement 2

"On the other hand, Marcia, no one is perfect, and I have to say that for this particular position Ed presents us with some concerns. For example, he has worked with previous generations of the software we're using, and while that gives him some familiarity with it, the software has changed dramatically and it will take a good period of time and some work on our part to get him up to speed. We have to take that into account. For another thing, he always seems to show the greatest initiative when he's really interested in something, and as you know, some of what we do here is pretty mudane, but it has to be done right and with some degree of creativity. On top of that there is a problem with his availability the fourth weekend of every month because of a personal commitment. We'll have to see if we can reschedule weekend assignments around that. While he works well on a small project team, as an individual contributor on special projects he is not at his best, and to the extent that this job would include occasional independent projects that's a potential concern."

On my list of concerns, limitations, or reservations I have some Can Do, Will Do, and Fit factors, again because this list was extracted from the three columns of organized evidence in our chart.

Now for your last statement. I'll give you three different versions of it.

Statement 3

Version One

"Even taking these factors into consideration, Marcia, I can recommend Ed unequivocally for this job. His strengths far outweigh his limitations and there's nothing about the limitations that would prevent him from being fully functional on day one. And once he comes up to speed in some of these areas that need to be developed he'll really be great."

Version Two

Or you can say: *"I can recommend Ed for this position, but only conditionally. That condition being that we can quickly, within the first 30 or 60 days, bring him up speed on that software. I know he can learn and is willing to learn, so the question is, Do we have the resources to do that quickly? If we do, then I would recommend hiring him. But if we can't do it quickly, then he's going to be twiddling his thumbs for months around here; he's going to discourage and demotivate other people, and he himself may even leave after a while. Make an offer to Ed only if we can get him up to speed on the software within the first month."*

Version Three

Or, in your third statement you might say: *"I cannot recommend this candidate at all. It's true we started out with 10 candidates and we narrowed it down to 3, and Ed is one of them. In terms of assets he's far superior to any of the people we eliminated. He's really strong in many ways. My obstacle, though, is that without immediate command of the current generation of our software, he won't be able to be fully functional on day one, and that's a serious problem given the backlog of work. He hasn't got the skill now, and we have to have it on day one. So no matter how strong he is and how much he impressed me and everyone else in the interview, in my opinion that eliminates him."*

One of those three would be the last statement.

Why a Summary Is Better Than Just "Hire" or "Don't Hire"

Compare those three statements—a summary of the candidate's strengths, a summary of his or her limitations, and your weighed and balanced recommendations—to what I've seen on many a report form. All the following are real statements I've seen over the years: "Great Candidate" written diagonally across the evaluation form. "NG." A drawing of a thumb, pointing down, done in pen and ink across the form. (How seriously was this interviewer taking the interview process?) Then there was, "Good technical skills"—compared to what? In any event it does not provide us with much insight into the basis of the decision.

The muddy thinking that these types of summation suggests is bad enough if the interviewer is the decision maker. But there are additional problems when an interviewer passes on "gut feeling" to others to help them make a decision.

Suppose when Marcia came back and asked you what you thought of Ed and you said: "He's great! I really like him. One of the 10 best I've seen all year?" Marcia couldn't make a decision based on what you said. She may say: "Okay, I guess Ed's not totally inappropriate then. But I can't make my judgment purely on one interviewer's say-so. I guess I'll have to interview him, too." For her to exercise any judgment of her own she would then have to see the candidate. But if you summarized Ed's strengths, summarized his limitations, and gave Marcia your recommendations, she might be able to make a decision for herself; even if she disagreed with your conclusions, she would find enough information in your earlier statements to think her way to a different conclusion. She might say, "Well, I can see his point, but, based on what he's told me, if I were to change this aspect of the job, have Ed supervised here, or just remove that little bit of responsibility, or remove independent projects from the tasks assigned to Ed, the most substantial negative would then be eliminated, and we'd be left with all the assets."

By making some adjustments Marcia can now come to a decision different from yours because you were able to show her the evidence and the reasoning that led to your conclusion. In this way she can participate in the process without actually having to interview the candidate. Or if she wants to, she can build on your interview to go even further with her own interview.

Coordinating Decisions Made by More Than One Interviewer

Of course, that's still assuming one person is doing everything immediately connected with the interview: organizing information afterward, reading your lists, and making the selection decision. In reality, there are usually others involved. An additional advantage of using this approach to articulate your decision is that it can help coordinate a decision made by more than one interviewer after multiple interviews. In a case like that I recommend that each interviewer takes the process to the point of creating individual lists of assets and limitations, but not go any further. Suppose there are two of you involved. Produce your individual lists. Get together and each of you present your findings. Compare notes and refine it until you come up with one list you can both agree on. Give your reasons back and forth for your opinions, compare notes, and you will make a better decision based on two interviewers seeing the same candidate. That's better than having you come into the room thinking, "This person is going to work in this department and that's it, I want him," while I come in thinking, "This person is never going to work for us," and deciding the outcome with a battle. Instead, we both pool our data and arrive at a much more accurate judgment.

To sum up, your "report" consists of three sentences: a summary of the candidate's job-relevant strengths, a summary of their limitations, and your decision or recommendation. The bottom third of the back of the form (Fig. 12) is the substance of any report, memo, or summary you must prepare as a result of the interview. This represents all anyone sees and hears about the process. The rest was just a way to get you there.

After you've done this three or four times you won't even need this piece of paper anymore. You can take a plain piece of paper, create three columns representing the Can Do, Will Do, and Fit factors. Then create horizontal sections to separate the categories of Work Experience, Education and Activities and Interests. Fill in the boxes with the appropriate information from your notes.

Overall Impression	Demonstrated natural, relaxed manner throughout Interview Presented info logically	Followed direction and guidance of interviewer yet willing to make suggestions	Able to relate to a new person easily
Work Experience	Directly relevant work experience Has organized tasks on complex projects Lacks experience with latest version of our software (-)	Initiative - starts new tasks w/o waiting for instruction Shifts to new situations smoothly High energy - can juggle several tasks	Works well on small project team Not available to travel extensively (-)

	CAN DO	WILL DO	FIT
EDUCATION	Analytical/logical approach to problem solving	High energy	Not strong as individual contributor (-)
	Lacks clarity and brevity w/ writing tasks (-)	Shows initiative only when work is interesting (-)	Makes choices indicating interest in our type of work
	Few business courses (-)		

	CAN DO	WILL DO	FIT
ACTIVITIES AND INTERESTS	Oral skills - formal presentations to community groups	High energy - copes easily with several conflicting demands on time	Avail. to work weekends with little notice
	Depth of experience with budget process on local water board	Makes serious commitment to long term projects	Not available 4th weekend of every month (-)

Make two lists . . .

ASSETS	DEVELOPMENTAL NEEDS
• relevant work experience	• no experience with our latest version of software
• has organized tasks on long, complex projects	• no evidence of strong writing skills
• high energy	• few business courses
• good oral presentation skills	• initiative only when interested
• works well on small project team	• not strong as individual contributor
• avail. to work weekends w/ little advance notice	• not avail. to travel
• analytical approach to problem solving	• not avail. 4th weekend of month
	• doesn't adapt easily to new situations

Write sentence one, write sentence two, think about it for a minute, and write sentence three.

1. Ed's verbal skills and relaxed natural presence make an excellent first impression. He's got solid, relevant work experience, an analytical approach to problem solving, and shows ability to handle serious commitments to complex, long projects. He's got the kind of energy we need here, works well on a small project team, and he's available to work weekends even with little advance notice. Especially helpful for this job are his strong oral presentation skills.

2. Ed lacks experience with the latest version of our software. He lacked interest in business courses in school, and seems to show initiative only on projects that are intrinsically interesting. His strength is not as an individual contributor, and he's not available to travel extensively, nor is he available the 4th weekend of the month.

3. Given Ed's strong work experience, high energy, and oral presentation skills, Ed should be a finalist for the position. The lack of current software experience is critical for this position, but we could assign him to Dave Johnson's department since Dave has the time and staff to help get him up to speed in that area. His strengths for this position outweigh concerns or limitations, so I conditionally recommend him, pending comparisons with other finalists and a review for placement in DJ's department.

This whole process takes under 10 minutes. It's no more time-consuming than what you do now. But when those 10 minutes are over, you'll have three crisp sentences that summarize the degree to which the candidate meets the job criteria. You are not doing an English composition on each candidate. You are matching what you learned about the candidate against the job. Once you've tried it a few times, you will find that this is easier than the usual agonizing and time-consuming process, and a more accurate and powerful decision-making tool.

Should You Give Topics Different Weights?

The question that often arises when I explain this process in my seminar is a very natural one—not all the factors we're going to mark with a plus or a minus are equally important. How can you make the process reflect this fact? Well certainly in preparing for the interview, during the job-analysis process, you should start to prioritize your job requirements and indicate minimum criteria in each column.

In fact, a variety of systems has been developed that purports to allow you to assign a numerical value to each of the Can Do, Will Do, and Fit factors. Then you can rate candidates from one to ten (or whatever) on each of the abilities, traits, and behaviors from the evidence in the interview. I urge you, however, not to go into that kind of detail. At every stage of the process there is too much room for inaccuracies and too high a margin of error. These errors compound one another. Finally, you will find yourself comparing Candidate A, who has 157 points, against Candidate B, who has 194 points. You might be tempted to take the one with the higher points when in fact the difference is irrelevant. I've shown you how to make sure that your thinking is rational and objective in the sense that it will have a sound basis in fact, and you will be able to justify your decision and discuss it with other people—but it can not and should not be completely formal and automatic.

What has been proven to be effective and practical is to organize the evidence from the interview by category of job criteria, and to extract out the key positives and negatives. At that point you can apply your judgment. You have two sets of relevant information. Individual items within each set can be weighted approximately, and the candidate with the best blend of pluses and minuses will stand out. If, however, you're considering a single candidate against the job, gauge the degree to which that candidate meets the minimum criteria. This will be equally apparent. By weighing and balancing the two lists one against the other, you can make quite subtle comparative judgments about candidates.

V ═══ FITTING THE INTERVIEW INTO YOUR SELECTION SYSTEM

The face-to-face interview doesn't occur in a vacuum. We've already addressed the importance of preparation (which precedes the interview) and decision making (which follows the interview).

In this last part of the book I'm going to take up some issues that relate the interview to your organization's selection procedures and system.

For example, except for screening interviews and campus interviews, there are almost always other people besides yourself who interview the candidate and participate in the decision. In Chapter 20, "Sequential Interviewing—When the Candidate Will See Several Interviewer in Succession," the major variations and models that can be used when the candidate will see more than one interviewer in sequence are presented; you can then determine which is best for your particular situation. If you occasionally use the panel interview, where several interviewers interview a candidate at the same time, you can find out in this same chapter how to make this approach as accurate and effective as it can be.

Finally, I'll try to shed some light on an important topic that causes many interviewers a great deal of unnecessary worry. In Chapter 21, "How to Conduct Fair and Legal Interviews," I'll show you how what looks like a maze of arbitrary rules and regulations can be understood as the application of a few simple concepts. I'll also show you how you can get all the job-relevant information you need without ever asking an insensitive, personal, or illegal question.

≡≡≡20≡SEQUENTIAL INTERVIEWING—WHEN THE CANDIDATE WILL SEE SEVERAL INTERVIEWERS IN SUCCESSION

Up until now I have been talking as though one interviewer were doing everything. That is, as if you and you alone would analyze the job criteria, conduct the interview, take notes, review the notes, organize the information collected, and make a judgment. In reality, with the exception of campus interviews or screening interviews, there are usually several interviewers involved. In this chapter I'm going to present alternative models to cope with the logistics of several interviewers seeing the same candidate. The special case of several interviewers participating in the interview at the same time (the panel interview) is discussed later in this chapter.

HOW MANY INTERVIEWS ARE NECESSARY?

How many interviews should there be? There is clear evidence on this. Assuming that the same criteria and a similar or comparably organized approach are employed, then two interviews are dramatically better than one. It is much better for two interviewers to see the candidate for 45 minutes or so than for one interviewer to spend 90 minutes with the candidate.

For that matter, three interviews are better than two. The increase in accuracy of judgment is not as great as in going from one to two, but it is better by a significant margin. Four adds a small gain in accuracy.

The most common model is this: The first interviewer is a professional in the Employment, Personnel, or Human Resources department. He or she may set the schedule for the day and/or be the last interviewer to see the candidate. Issues such as relocation and benefits may be covered by this interviewer. In instances where this interviewer starts off the day with the initial screening interview, a decision might be made at this point for the candidate not to go on to others. Of course, if there's a chance of that happening it would be better not to lead the candidate to expect four interviews, but, rather, to tell him or her that other interviews may take place if the manager or supervisor is "available."

In most cases, any more than four interviews will not increase the accuracy of the judgment, nor (with a few exceptions I will describe a little later) will it add much to your ability to influence a candidate. I don't mean to imply, however, that it is inappropriate to conduct more than four interviews, or that there would never be any justification for doing so. There may be political reasons why six or seven people have to see the candidate. It may be that two people in each of three departments have to "sign off" on the candidate—that's six right there. I only want to point out that from the standpoint of accurate decision making and the ability to influence the candidate, it is ordinarily inefficient to go beyond four.

Even when many people see a candidate, a formal interview might not always be necessary. A few years ago I conducted an interview training program for a prestigious firm based in Washington. This organization regularly brings in potential employees from overseas. The candidates travel in from Jakarta, cross the international dateline, and arrive on a Sunday night, still suffering from jet lag. Starting the following morning and going through Tuesday afternoon they have no fewer than 22 and as many as 28 interviews. When I asked what possible justification there could be for such a marathon, the firm's chief of recruitment told me: "Well, a lot of people have to meet the candidate. These candidates go back to Jakarta and for the next five years communicate with many people here only by telex. They won't even speak with them by telephone. So while they're here it's important they meet them all."

I said to him, "Hey, give them a cocktail party!" You don't have to have that many interviews to accomplish such a goal.

MODEL I

In Fig. 13 I've assumed that there were four interviews, two in the morning and two in the afternoon with lunch in between. This is an arbitrary suggestion for visual purposes—I had to indicate some plan. If you have four interviews scheduled, the interviews needn't take place all

Fig. 13. Four interviews.

in the same day. You could just as well conduct three interviews in the morning and the remaining interview on another day.

Won't it Seem Mechanistic to the Candidate if Several Interviewers in a Row Use the Method Presented in This Book?

This is a question that may occur to you at this point: If everyone who interviews the candidate in a single day does it the same way (Greeting, Small Talk, Transition Question, Work Experience, Education, Activities and Interests, and Self-Assessment), aren't they going to come across like a bunch of automatons? Wouldn't it be a good idea to have some variety? Of course it would. But you must also have validity. All too often, organizations in an effort to provide "variety" wind up doing four chaotic and ineffectual interviews. Not a particularly effective solution, in my opinion.

I'll describe in a moment ways of adding variety to the sequential interview process. However, first let me argue for a pure version where each interviewer does exactly what this book has advised. By exactly, I don't mean reading the Interview Guide (Chapter 9, Fig. 6) to the candidate. As I've said before, the idea is for the interviewer to put the Interview Guide in his or her own words and just retain the logic. Still, all interviewers will follow the same logic or structure.

Is that repetitive? When Interviewer A sits down with Ronnie, the candidate, he tells her what he is going to do, and then he does it: He covers her work experience, her educational background, gives her a chance to talk about her outside interests and activities, gives her a chance to summarize at the end, and gives her some information. Then Ronnie goes on to Interviewer B, who also tells Ronnie what she's going to do, and then she does it. She covers the candidate's work experiences and her education, gives her the opportunity to talk about her outside interests and activities, gives her a chance to summarize, and finally gives her some information. Interviewers C and D follow exactly the same procedures.

Is it a surprise to Ronnie that these four topics in her background are covered? On the contrary, if Interviewer B doesn't give her a chance to summarize, she might choose to do it herself. If Interviewer D doesn't ask about her education or give her a chance to talk about some outside interest she's proud of, the candidate might regret that she didn't have the opportunity to give a full picture of herself. The fact that those topics are covered is no surprise to any candidate. They are not repetitious in themselves. They are necessary components of a complete picture of the candidate.

Furthermore, keep in mind that Interviewer A introduces the topic of work experience, what one-step probes he chooses, what two-step probes he asks, what comments he makes, what specifics he focuses on, will be different from those of other interviewers.

While structurally all the interviews should be the same, they're not going to be lock-step, mirror images of one another. This is not like taking a survey, with all the same questions asked in the same order, mechanically.

That's the basic version, the simplest way to do sequential interviews. It does not require a lot of coordination between interviewers. It does assume they know how to conduct an effective interview and are all using the same criteria. Afterward they can pool their information, using the approach I suggested earlier when talking about team decision making in Chapter 19.

The Problems of Haphazardly Attempted "Variety"

If dividing tasks between interviewers is important to you there are other routes you can take. Some interviewers respond to the techniques I've shown in this book by saying: "Well, this guy Swan has a good thing here, I like this structure but I'll tell you what, let's add some variety; let's mix it up. Anne-Marie, you cover the candidate's work experience, and David, you cover the candidate's educational background, and Josh, you cover the candidate's activities and interests, and Helene, you cover the candidate's self-assessment. Then we'll pool our information. We'll cover the whole structure and we'll add variety because there will be no repetition."

While this approach might add a lot of variety, there is a notoriously low rate of accuracy for interviews done in that fashion. The difficulties intrinsic in this approach are similar to the problems that come with concentrating on too narrow a band of a person's background—only the most recent work experience, only the most recent education, and getting an invalid sample of the candidate's background. Also, an interviewer covering just one part of the candidate's background may not see the significance of a single incident. It wouldn't stand out enough to seem important. But if it came up over and over and over again (in Work Experience, Education, and Activities and Interests), the significance of it would be more readily apparent.

How to Divide up Tasks Between Interviewers

You can divide up the interview so that each interviewer has a different focus. The question is how to do it. Instead of violating the structure by dividing the interview up "horizontally," by subject or area of the candidate's background, I recommend dividing the interview up "vertically"—by having interviewers focus on different job criteria areas, according to the ultimate questions the interview is meant to answer—the Can Do, Will Do, and Fit factors.

That is: Anne-Marie conducts a complete and thorough interview, covering all the basic categories of structure. But since she knows the most about the technical side of the job, she is assigned the task of concentrating on the Can Do factors. She concentrates her two-step probes on the Can Do factors. For those of you familiar with the so-called "technical interview," this is similar, but more expansive. In addition to the strictly technical components of the Job Requirements, she also looks for other qualities that fall under the heading of Can Do factors—analytical ability, intelligence, writing skills, listening skills, ability to learn, leadership, etc. With that concentration on Can Do factors she proceeds through the complete interview structure: Work Experience, Education, Interests and Activities, and Self-Assessment. Other interviewers take responsibility for evaluating some or all of the Will Do and Fit factors. Again, they would cover the complete interview structure.

This model is simply a formalization of common practice. The interviewer who knows the most about the technical aspects of the job is often expected to focus attention on these issues anyway. Interviewers at the senior level are usually concerned about the Will Do and Fit factors—Is this candidate going to have personality conflicts with other employees? Is the candidate promotable? Can the candidate do other tasks? Will the candidate do his or her share of the work on weekends if we get an overload? Is the candidate reliable and dependable?

This practice is so widespread, in fact, that the most senior members of the evaluation team often assume the candidate has been assessed on the technical issues. This procedure makes sure that it really does happen by specifically assigning the responsibility.

MODEL II (Fig. 14)

Model II is designed to overcome a problem that commonly arises in the information-giving phase of the interview. It is

Fig. 14. Dividing up the information-giving phase.

not uncommon for a candidate to go through four interviews and hear the same relentless, repetitive story about the history and mission of the organization four times. By the time Michael gets to Nick he can still manage to keep a bright look on his face and say, "Really?" By the time he gets to Marlene he can't even say that much anymore; he's too bored. Or, he hears during the course of the day two different versions of the company's mission and its future or what a particular department does or what its intention is; he'll hear two different stories about the possible relocation to Delaware or other things that are going on behind the scenes. Or, the candidate will go through four interviews and never get an answer to a very critical question that is very important in his decision making. He'll ask it of Chuck who says, "I'm out of date, check with Patricia." He checks with Patricia and she says, "Well frankly, Mark has the details on that." Mark says, "No, I think you ought to check with Nick," and Nick says, "Oh, you didn't ask Chuck?" And now Michael is on the plane flying home and he hasn't been given an answer by anybody.

Or the company has been in the news the night before—right there in section D of the *New York Times* the headline reports a takeover rumor, or the sale of a subsidiary, or a product recall, or a possible change of corporate headquarters: Is it true? What does it mean? The candidate wants to know and everybody stumbles and fumbles because nobody knows the policy answer.

This problem can be easily resolved by using the second model. Each interviewer conducts an effective and thorough interview using the techniques and structure explained in this book, but when it comes to giving information each covers a different "subject." The first interviewer may discuss the organization's history, where it's going, its mission. The second interviewer may talk specifically about the division or department. The third interviewer may talk about the actual job in technical detail. The fourth interviewer may talk about relocation policy, benefits, or some other subject.

This approach avoids repetition, and it makes sure a lot of

information gets out. All questions are answered, all interviewers know who is covering what so they can trade off. If the person scheduled to conduct the second interview is out sick that day then somebody else, armed with a list of things to cover, can fill in. We make sure we cover everything and not only is it complete and professional, but as a byproduct it adds variety to the process without having to vary the information-collecting phase at all.

Of course, you can take that second model and combine it with the first to get a hybrid; you divide up the information-collecting phase in terms of criteria, and in addition you divide up the information-giving phase. Obviously, though, it would make sense for the interviewer who searches for technical detail to be the interviewer to talk about the job in technical detail.

MODEL III: FOLLOW-UP INTERVIEW BASED ON CONSULTATION

What should we do if, after narrowing the field down to one or a few candidates, one or more interviewers decide to bring the candidate back? Figure 15 illustrates a possible plan for this circumstance.

The first two interviewers have interviewed the candidate and then discussed the candidate together. The questions they are trying answer for themselves are: "What do we know and what don't we know and why don't we know it? What should we do differently in the next interview? Are there some things we don't have information on—are there certain things we have hesitations or concerns about?"

Fig. 15. Follow-up interview.

Armed with the results of this consultation, either one of these individuals (or, more likely, a third interviewer) conducts one or more follow-up interviews that build on the results of the first interview.

Alternatively, if we already know we want to make an offer to the candidate, the follow-up interview can really be a focused attempt to sell the candidate. The result of the consultation between the interviewers in that case would have been a decision to make an offer to the candidate, and a strategy for persuasion.

If one or more interviewers are going to discuss the candidate with the next interviewer, it's important that these first interviewers do not contaminate the third interviewer by sharing their conclusions, such as saying, "I don't think the candidate is an analytical thinker." What they should say is something like this: "We don't have any information on that individual's ability to work on a team; somehow we didn't get any data on that, so be sure you check into it. We thought we covered their work experience thoroughly, but we didn't get much detail on the job just before their current one. Please look into it." Give suggestions for a follow-up interview that builds on the first two interviews.

MODEL IV: THE PANEL INTERVIEW

The panel interview, in which candidates see two or more interviewers at the same time, is notoriously ineffectual. Notice I didn't say inherently ineffectual. But as is usually practiced, it starts off with all the problems of the regular interview—no structure, no planning, no two-step probing, no building of rapport—and added to all that are the potential tension between interviewers, a lack of coordination, increased formality, and heightened tension and constriction of the candidate.

Municipalities, government agencies, and school systems tend to use the panel interview because they claim it is a fairer process. It does have the appearance of fairness; all interviewers have seen the exact same data base. You could argue this point with me only if you could demonstrate that it was a valid data base. Seven people watching an invalid interview doesn't sound fair or effective to me. However, assuming that you have practical reasons for conducting a panel interview, you can make it as effective as possible— not that I'm recommending it as an alternative to the one-to-one interview. It is never as effective as that approach. Yet, by drawing on the procedures and techniques that make a one-to-one interview valid, we can make the panel interview meaningful. Keep in mind that doing a panel interview doesn't save us time. It is still two or more person-hours for us. It does, however, save the candidate time, or it reduces the total number of interviews experienced. If the candidate's time is limited, if they can only be interviewed in a narrow window of time, the panel interview may be a reasonable alternative.

There are two basic versions of the panel interview. In the first version, only two interviewers are present; in the second version, there are three or more interviewers in the room.

Panel Interview Case 1: Two Interviewers Present (Fig. 16)

Let me start by taking the case of two interviewers in the room at the same time. In addition to the reasons already given for the panel interview, you might employ the two-interviewer model when someone from another department wants to see the candidate, but is unable to personally interview him or her (or you don't wish to alert the canddate to the possible alternate placements you are

Fig. 16. Two interviewers present.

considering). In addition, you can use the two-interview model to train a new interviewer, who can sit in and observe the complete interview.

Here are two interviewers, but there's some difference between them. The solid figure is Susan, she's the principal interviewer. She goes to meet the candidate, calls him by name (his name, for purposes of this explanation, will be Mark), introduces herself, thanks him for coming, and tells him that her colleague, Bill, will be meeting them in her office. When she brings Mark in she introduces him to Bill and explains the secondary interviewer's role: "... and Bill will have some information for you about the specific job and opportunities here, and he may have some questions for you at the very end. But I'll be conducting the basic interview. In fact, let me give you an overview of how I'm going to proceed...." And she introduces the structure contained in this book. Bill does not speak during the information collecting phase, nor does he fidget... at least in the ideal version of this model.

In this way we can approximate the basic one-to-one interview with, in effect, an observer. It's not perfect; it will be slightly distracting for the candidate; but if Bill has been introduced, and his role explained; if he's where the candidate can see him (not at the other end of the room staring off in the distance, or breathing down the candidate's neck); if he's not fidgeting too much and he occasionally responds with a smile, if (to sum up) the candidate is not pressured to relate to two people simultaneously, this method can be made to work.

Allowing the Other Interviewer to Participate

What if you want to divide the labor up more equitably between the two interviewers? In that case, break the interview down according to topic. Susan begins the interview as described above and covers the structure through Work Experience, and then she says: "Well, we've covered your work experience pretty thoroughly. Now let's shift to your educational background, and for this portion of the interview let me turn it over to Bill." Bill handles the next unit or more, while Susan keeps quiet. This "horizontal" division of interview chores is not open to the objection I raised against such a division earlier, because in this case both interviewers are present throughout the interview, and able to note and compare patterns of behavior in different areas. Again, it's not perfect. But if there's going to be more than one interviewer in the room at the same time, the least you can do is see to it that the candidate does not have to concentrate on more than one person at a time.

I should remind you that I wouldn't use this routinely. It may save the candidate time, but it does not save you time since it still takes two person-hours to get the job done, without the added effectiveness you might have got from two consecutive interviews. I would only do it if I had some special reason; if, for example, the candidate has limited time, or some person from another department wanted to check the candidate out without personally conducting a separate interview.

Panel Interview Case II: Three or More Interviewers Present

This is the full dress panel interview, beloved of the civil service and the military as well as some corporations. If there are several interviewers involved, the best results will be achieved by letting one interviewer be the moderator. For purposes of illustration, you are the moderator, and once again you're interviewing Mark. You go out and get the candidate, call him by name, introduce yourself, thank him for coming, bring him to the conference room, sit him down, and explain the process. Then you go out and get the panel. You bring them in all at once so they don't come in dribs and drabs and the candidate isn't subjected to 10 minutes of repetitive chitchat and introductions. They come in, they sit down, and you say: "Mark has been nice enough to come in and talk to us. Before we go into his background, though, let us introduce ourselves and let him know who he's talking to." One by one the panel members briefly introduce themselves. Then, in your role as the moderator, you start the interview by saying, "Well now, Mark, why don't we begin with your very first full-time job," and you ask a specific question. He answers that and when he's done you turn to the panel ask them, "Would anyone like to ask Bill any questions about this job?" And if they don't two-step probe the answers to their own questions, you do it. If they're getting interrogational, you add some comments. If they're dwelling on one area too long, you say to the panel: "Well I'm sure you have more questions for Bill about this particular job, but perhaps we can come back to that later if we have time. Let's move on to your next job, Bill." You move the candidate through the structure, step-by-step. It's the application of the basic model you learned in this book—even though there are several interviewers involved.

MODEL V: THE CONFERENCE TABLE MEETING (Fig. 17)

This may look like a panel interview, but it's not. During two, three, four, or more interviews over the course of a week or weeks, we decide we want to hire Susan and now we bring her in to meet with a number of key people. This model is used for hiring attorneys at the partner level in law firms and hiring top scientists at think tanks. We bring the candidate to meet the many senior staff around a comfortable conference table, with danish and coffee, perhaps. Each person introduces himself or herself casually, and talks a little bit about what they do. Susan shares a little about herself, and the whole group, guided by a moderator,

   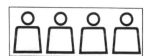

Fig. 17. Conference table meeting.

discusses professional issues or just talks casually for a while. Susan leaves feeling she's part of the team. Everyone gets a chance to observe one another and a professional, comradely discussion ensues with a certain amount of structure as each person is introduced and the candidate gets to say a few words. This is a very good technique for drawing candidates closer to accepting an offer and for putting the candidate into contact with people at a very senior level.

These five models do not represent everything that can happen when more than one interviewer is involved in the process, but they certainly cover a lot of ground and they will give you some tools to work with when it comes to moderating and modulating your own organization's interview process.

≡≡21≡HOW TO CONDUCT FAIR AND LEGAL INTERVIEWS

It is not the intention of the law to require you to hire candidates who are not capable of performing the job. The intention of the law is to fulfill the all-American spirit of fair play. Anyone with the capacity to perform a job should have a shot at it—and aspects of that candidate's background that are not relevant to the job should not be reviewed or discussed, to insure that information is not available to be used—or misused—after the interview.

Who could argue with that? It makes perfect sense. But because of the fact that people don't like being told what to do, and because of the bureaucratic structure from which rules and regulations spring, many interviewers react to this issue more strongly than they need to.

It is true that the Equal Employment Opportunity (EEO) rules and regulations require us to be more alert to certain aspects of the interview process than we were, 20 years ago; but just about every aspect of our business and personal lives has become more complex over the past 20 years. Why should the interview be an exception? Whatever your feeling on the subject, EEO considerations are just another business reality, which require a businesslike approach.

Many interviewers think of EEO as a mine field of risk in which one little navigational error will lead to disaster. Fortunately, that's not the case, so long as you have a basic understanding of the rules and regulations, are reasonably sensitive, and know how to phrase your questions.

THE INTERVIEW IS MORE VALID BECAUSE OF EEO

Participants in my interviewing seminars tell me that some of their fellow interviewers mutter to themselves when they are told about the restrictions and limitations imposed on them. "Oh, all these complexities and details I have to worry about—and all for *them*," say the mutterers, who, for some reason, always point to the upper right when referring to *them*. Although these individuals are not aware of it, the "them" they are referring to happens to include every one of us. Every interviewer, everybody reading this book either is in or will be in one or more "protective groups" at some point in their lives. This includes all women, all men and women older than 40 years of age, veterans of Vietnam, people with certain health problems or handicaps (or those who will develop them in the future and thus join that protected group)... as well as other categories you are more familar with, such as racial background, country of origin and religion.

A protected group is a category of individuals in our society with something in common, who are protected as a group by law against unfair treatment in employment or housing or other areas. To take the most inclusive category, if you aren't over 40 already, you will be some day, and if at that time you are denied ready access to a job or promotion because of someone's arbitrary notion about the capacities of a person your age, you're going to resent it. You're going to wish you had some recourse, and fortunately for you, you would have recourse—because you'd be in a protected group. The rules and regulations are designed to make the interview process fair and equitable for everyone.

While the goal is fairness, as a byproduct EEO rules and regulations have made the interview more valid. There was a time when an interviewer could deny someone a job based on irrational and irrelevant criteria. We know how unfair that is. But then the interviewer is also hiring people based on the mirror image of the same irrational criteria. It isn't smart from a business standpoint to deny ourselves the services of talented individuals or to bring people on board on the basis of less than relevant criteria.

IF YOU'RE KNOWLEDGEABLE YOU NEEDN'T BE OVERCAUTIOUS

On the one hand, it is possible that during the interview you may inadvertently make an error that could precipitate a lawsuit. On the other hand, however, it is also conceivable that you will be so wary of making some unconscious error that you'll be overly careful; you might even hire people you think are marginal because you don't want to take any risks. That really isn't necessary. The intention of the law is to be fair to you, the employer, to make sure you get talented people, and simultaneously to be fair to the candidates, to ensure that they are not eliminated for irrational, non-job-related reasons.

Below are a series of subjects that should either be eliminated from the interview as an area of inquiry, or asked about in a job-related way. Among them are the specific subjects that repeatedly come up as areas of uncertainty or confusion in my seminars. I'll cover them in greater detail.

GENDER, MARITAL STATUS, FAMILY STATUS

This happens to be the single largest area of complaints nowadays. Asking candidates questions about their personal background and life circumstances is inappropriate for both men and women of any age, under any circumstances. Have I lost you already? What about the fact that the job may require last-minute overtime? Or weekend work? Or extensive travel? Of course, you need to make judgments about the candidate's ability to meet these requirements. I can show you a legal and effective way to do it. First though, I need to review some problems.

There are three problems with a personal line of inquiry.

That Line of Inquiry Is Insensitive

The interviewer's heart may be pure. He or she may be asking those questions out of mere friendly curiosity—"I have three kids. How many do you have?" In the belief that when personal issues come up in small talk, or while chatting in front of the elevator, or over lunch, it's okay to ask more about them. But any conversation you have with a candidate prior to making an offer is a part of the selection process, and therefore those questions are inappropriate in any of those arenas even if they are not asked as part of the formal, sit-down review of the candidate's background.

Interviewers' hearts may also be pure because their intentions, they think, are appropriate. They're simply trying to determine if there is anything that will prevent the candidate from meeting a specific job requirement like last-minute overtime or weekend work. They feel that personal questions are okay, given the business intent. However, even if the intention is pure and job-related, the question is still insensitive. Look at the position it puts the candidate in. Perhaps knowing very well that you are not supposed to ask that question, the candidate must either answer it or actively refuse to answer it. While more and more candidates are willing to refuse to answer, that doesn't mean anyone likes being put in the position of having to say, "I'm sorry, but you have no right to ask me that question and I prefer not to answer it." If you're concerned about the acceptance rate of talented people who have choices, you should consider this, and you should also consider your organization's reputation in the business, professional, and local community.

It Doesn't Work

The second problem with asking people questions about their personal backgrounds is that it doesn't even work. Suppose Linda sits in front of me and I am very impressed with her. She has the skills and abilities, the initiative and motivation and energy I need, and she fits the job in every other way. But I have a couple of other concerns about the job availability in the back of my mind. Either I don't know about the EEO rules and regulations, or I don't care. I ask every conceivable question of a personal nature that I can think of, and Linda answers them all—and she answers them honestly and completely. I now breathe a sigh of relief, certain that there is no obstacle in her background that would prevent her from meeting my very specific job requirements. I make Linda an offer and she accepts.

Six weeks after she's on board I need her to handle a weekend assignment. She nervously refuses, saying: "Well, I'm sorry, I'd like to, but I have an irrevocable family commitment. I'm not available this weekend."

When she explains why she is not available this weekend, I suddenly realize that I made a mistake during my original interview—I don't know how I could have overlooked this but somehow during my original interview I forget to ask the following question: "Excuse me, in addition to everything else I've asked you, do you happen to have a second cousin with Down's syndrome that you're responsible for every third weekend of the month and therefore are unavailable for assignments those weekends?" Of course, you probably wouldn't have thought to ask such a specific question.

But think of all the complexities in your personal life, in your own family, in your extended family, in the families of your neighbors: children with developmental disabilities, in-laws or relatives with Alzheimer's disease, or a cousin with cerebral palsy. A great number of people are separated or divorced with children who spend one week with one parent and the next week with the other. There are so many complexities in people's lives nowadays that you couldn't begin to think of all the questions you would need to ask to cover all the bases. And when you ask in an insensitive way, people may reluctantly answer your question, but nobody volunteers anything. As a result, you might miss some critical obstacles because you couldn't possibly have thought to ask them.

Furthermore, even if you get the candidates to talk about their personal backgrounds by asking these specific and insensitive questions, you might very well be drawing the wrong conclusions. Furthermore, does the fact that someone is married with 2 children and a dog guarantee that he or she is more stable than a single person? On the other hand, you may suppose that a single person would be more willing or available to travel, but single people also have personal lives that may attach them to a particular place.

It's Illegal

Finally, just in case you may not be aware, inquiring into a candidate's personal background is not just a little grey area you should avoid if you can, or ask about, if possible, in a whisper. It is just plain illegal, and has been since 1971, to ask candidates about their personal lives, personal circumstances, husbands and wives, family backgrounds, number of children, and all those sorts of questions in an interview.

Here's the paradox—it's illegal, insensitive, it doesn't even work—yet it's the single largest area of EEO complaints nowadays. Men and women are both formally complaining in large numbers about being asked personal questions. Young people just coming into the work force are particularly sensitive and aware of the inappropriateness of questions of a personal nature.

The Right Way to Find Out About a Candidate's Availability

The paradox exists, I believe, because interviewers simply are trying to do their job. They know of no other way of finding out about the candidate's availability to meet special job requirements like last-minute overtime and weekend work. Luckily, there is another way, a solution that's legal, fair, more sensitive—and it's the only way that has at least the potential for working. The formula is simple. State the job requirement as clearly as you can and then ask a closed-ended question. Here's an example. Say to all candidates (tall, short, young, old, male, female):

> *"This job will absolutely require you to be available for work on Saturdays. . . ."*

(or "every Saturday" or "every other Saturday" or "You'll need to keep a suitcase in your office and when there's a problem in the field you're going to have to run to the airport and catch a plane; you'll have time for one phone call.")

> *"If you are unable to meet this requirement you would be unable to function in this job. Therefore, let me ask you—"*

You've stated the job requirement as clearly as you could; now comes the closed-ended question:

> *"Is there anything you're aware of, anything at all, that would prevent you from meeting this absolute requirement?"*

That's the formula. Say: "This job will require X. Is there anything that will prevent you from meeting that requirement?" And they answer. That's what you really need to find out. You're not after gossip. The nature of the obstacle is not the question; the question is do they have an obstacle? And aside from the legal or fairness issue, remember to ask this of every candidate, not just those you think might have a problem with availability (women, for example)—because anyone can have some obstacle to meeting your requirements. You want to be sure every candidate is asked about their availability to meet your specific requirements.

You ask them. If their answer is, "No, there is no problem; I understand what will be expected of me; I can do it," then there's no need for you to go any further. Document their answer and go through the rest of your interview. It helps to make the consequences of failure to meet the requirement crystal clear.

If they say: "Yes, well, I do have some commitments. How far in advance before a weekend would I know?" that is a reasonable question on their part. At that point you could go down one of two paths. The wrong path is to say: "Oh, personal commitments? Do you mean children? How many do you have? How sick have they been in the past year?" The appropriate path is to modify the formula you've already used. State the requirement more precisely, and ask if it can be met. Say: "Usually you'll know by Wednesday or Thursday at the latest. If you were to know by Thursday, would that be sufficient time for you to be able to make the commitment to be here on the weekend?"

You could push it further if you wanted to. Still talking about the job and not the candidate's personal background, you could say: "And since failure to meet this requirement would be so disruptive, I am required to document your answer now so we can reflect back on what you said during the interview." You want to go to the extreme? If it's true you could say, "Failure to meet these requirements would be grounds for disciplinary action or dismissal," or, as I've heard some of my clients say, "It will severely affect your promotability and your performance reviews."

Obviously, you want to avoid saying something like that in a way that would make the room seem warmer and the candidate's collar seem tighter. You might or might not say it at all depending on whether you felt it was necessary, whether the consequences of the requirement not being met were so significant, or whether you've had a history of problems in the past.

In any case, that's the formula. State the job requirements, and ask the closed-ended question. It's the legal way, the more sensitive way, and the only way that has a chance of working.

What if the Candidate Volunteers Personal Information?

You are responsible for all the information you collect, whether you asked for it or the candidate volunteered it. Therefore, when candidates volunteer information about their personal backgrounds, you have an obligation not to do the following three things:

Do not ask anymore about it. You can say, "Well, I appreciate you mentioning that, but what have you learned from that experience that might be relevant to the job?" or change the subject completely. But do not simply allow them to run on about it, and don't ask any more questions about it. The fact that they raised the issue doesn't turn it into a legitimate subject of inquiry.

Do not write it down. It should not be in your documentation.

Finally, you do not pass it on to anyone else orally. If you interview Ralph and he happens to mention in passing that he's married and has three children and the next interviewer says to you: "Oh, by the way, is he married? Does he have children?", your answer should be, "I don't know," even though you do know, because your responsibility is not to pass on such information.

If you and other interviewers in your organization do not routinely pass on inappropriate information and there is an EEO complaint, the investigation will make it quite clear that you, as an organization, are meeting both the letter and the spirit of the law, even if in a particular instance there may have been a technical error. But if interviewers are willy-nilly passing on inappropriate information, writing it down, allowing candidates to divulge it at length, or talking to other people about the candidates' personal lives, that fact will become apparent to investigators. The original complaint will now take on greater significance.

RELIGION

In answer to the question: "The job requires work on Saturday. Is there anything to prevent you from making this commitment?" the candidate says: "Well, frankly, I'm not available for work on Saturdays because of my religious beliefs. I'm not even available on Friday nights. Does that eliminate me from consideration?"

What do you say?

Let's freeze the interview at that moment, back up a bit, and discuss this as a question of company policy, because that's really where the answer lies. What your organization or department has to consider is whether it is absolutely necessary that this job is performed on Saturday. It might just be tradition that it's done on Saturday. Perhaps it could just as well be done on Sunday, as long as the work is done by Monday morning. If that's the case, then it really is not truly an absolute job requirement, and you shouldn't deny the candidate the job on that basis.

On the other hand, maybe that's not the case. Maybe it has to be done on Saturday because there's no air-conditioning or heat on Sunday or because other people are involved or because you're an international bank and you have to deal with Tokyo, and Tokyo is open on Saturdays. Under those circumstances then, the next question your company must ask itself as a matter of policy is, "Is this already required of all incumbents in that role and all applicants for that role, or are we already giving some current employees special dispensation because of special circumstances?"— "Oh, Bob and Mary, they have new babies in their families so we don't ask them to come in on weekends," or "Roger lives so far away, we don't ask him to come in." If you're already accommodating some employees, it's obvious you can accommodate others, and therefore it would be less justifiable to deny the right to work to anyone who has a legitimate reason for not meeting the requirement. You can obviously reschedule around them as you do with others.

Suppose, however, that you can't reschedule around them. They are absolutely required to be there; everyone is required to be there, and it has to be on a Saturday. You are already short of staff and you can't afford to have someone on the job who cannot share this responsibility. Well, in that case, the candidate is not eligible for the job just as though he or she couldn't come to work on Wednesdays. You're not denying the candidate a job because of religious beliefs, you're denying the candidate a job because of an inability to meet a specific job requirement. It is not illegal to deny someone a job on those grounds, if the requirement is truly necessary, not just a matter of tradition, and you're not accommodating others. There are few jobs whose requirements are that rigid, but there are some. In those cases you would be justified in not hiring someone who was unable to meet specific job requirements.

Therefore, under those circumstances, I would say to the candidate: "Well, it is absolutely required for everyone in this role. We really need someone who is available on Saturdays, and we're not making any accommodations for anyone else because we're short-staffed."

If, on the other hand, you are in a position to say: "Well, we're already accommodating some employees, we'll take that into account, even though there is some Saturday work. If we were able to work it out so you could work Sundays rather than Saturdays, would you be willing to accept that? Because there is definitely weekend work, and people have to do their fair share, so you may be assigned more Sundays rather than Saturdays. Is there any reason to believe you wouldn't be able to make that commitment?" And if it turns out the candidate just doesn't want to work weekends at all, well that's no longer an EEO issue.

AGE

As a technical matter the law does not permit you to ask a person's age. You can ask candidates whether they are over eighteen because of the legal complications—work permits in some states, mandatory school attendance—which attach to minors. Up until recently it was permissible to ask if a person was over seventy, but this is no longer true.

In any event, determining candidates' approximate age without asking is not difficult, and asking their age is seldom the issue. The issue is to what use you put this knowledge. You will probably be unable to avoid knowing their approximate age by looking at them, reviewing their background, seeing dates of graduation from school and of their various jobs. It's hard to be blind to a person's age. But your task is to base your decisions exclusively on job-related matters. If someone is fifty-eight and shows evidence of a declining energy level and is unable to do several things at once and the job requires that, then you won't want to put that candidate in that very demanding job. On the other hand, a twenty-eight year-old candidate who is unable to sustain high levels is just as inappropriate for the job. It's not because one's fifty-eight and the other's twenty-eight. It's not because of your assumption about fifty-eight year-olds—it's because of identifiable behaviors that are or are not present. There are some fifty-eight year-olds that have twice as much energy as someone aged twenty-eight. Look around at your friends and the people you work with. Age alone is not the deciding factor. Maybe it was true 50 years ago, that when you got past fifty-five or sixty years of age you shouldn't rock too hard in that rocking chair because you might fall and break something. But people are living longer and staying productive longer nowadays. Therefore, if you were to assume that someone who is forty-eight or fifty-eight or sixty-two is over-the-hill, there is a big chance that you'd be wrong, even if you were allowed to use their age as the basis of your decision.

Another point to consider is the investment a company makes in an employee (an ostensible reason for wanting them young): Fifty years ago the average length of stay for an employee was eight to twelve years; some stayed forty or fifty years on a job and some left earlier, but the average was eight to twelve years. Nowadays the nationwide average stay on a job is three to five years. Therefore, there's no evidence to support the conclusion that a candidate who's twenty-five or twenty-eight or thirty is going to be around longer than someone aged fifty-eight. Evaluate a person in terms of their immediate contribution in the foreseeable future—the job at hand and one level up—because that's all you can predict accurately anyway.

Measure the candidate against the job criteria. If you can demonstrate that you did not hire an individual who's fifty-two years old because of the Can Do, Will Do, and Fit factors, that's perfectly legitimate; you're not denying the candidate the job because of their age. But, on the other hand, do not disqualify the candidate just because usually the people who apply for this particular job are in the twenty-two to twenty-five age range, coming out of college or graduate school. Perhaps a candidate is starting a new career, went back to graduate school, and is now applying for a job. If there's talent here, you don't want to miss it. It's neither smart nor fair to deny this candidate access to the job.

APPEARANCE

You can use appearance as part of your job criteria and deny a candidate the job based on appearance, providing you can make a case that your decision is job-related, not based merely on your personal reaction to the individual's appearance. Say Jeff, who is being considered for a job working in the catacombs of your building entering data into a terminal, has a slight blue streak across one side of his head. While this may personally offend you, if he is otherwise qualified for the job this is not a reason to deny Jeff the right to work. On the other hand, that appearance might enter into the job requirements if this employee is going to represent you to the public, or to other organizations, or to other departments. If this employee will be an auditor going into other departments, having the appearance often referred to, in the banking and financial community, as "executive presence" might be a legitimate job requirement.

In the course of doing a job analysis for a client, the people with whom I was meeting started talking about the need for executive presence. I pressed them by asking, "Well, does that mean that a person with a turban need not apply?" They thought about it a minute and said, "Well, they have to go to another department and convince the manager of that department that they know what they're talking about, that they can make a contribution, and that they're really an expert in that area—if they can do that and do that quickly with their verbal skills, then the turban would not be an issue."

Remember that "appearance" has been used as a code word for racial or religious background for many years, and was used routinely to deny people fair access to jobs. It's important not only to be professional in your own personal reaction to a candidate's appearance, but also not to act on assumptions that other people might be unwilling to accept that individual. For many years blacks were denied access to many jobs because it was reasoned that they wouldn't be accepted by customers. So, if an air-conditioning repair person would have had to go into a white community, blacks were routinely denied access to this job. As we know now, it turns out that when the air-conditioner isn't working and it's 107 degrees out, people don't care who fixes it; they just want it fixed. A person is accepted into a home in the capacity of a professional or a technician. The same logic applies to the initial resistance to sending women to the Far East or Latin America; it is often possible to make these things work even though it might not be easy at first. Beware of automatically denying somebody the right to work without testing your assumptions; an evaluation based on your momentary reaction may not be justified.

Attractiveness

Let's consider appearance as personal qualities. If a person is going to work, for example, as a receptionist, then we might require that he or she be reasonably groomed and attired for the job. Much depends on the details of this particular position. Would it be a very public and visible position? Then one might be stricter about appearance. We're not talking about young and cute now, we're talking about having a businesslike, well-groomed appearance that would be pleasant to others—it doesn't justify hiring people based on your personal preference.

A cosmetic company was routinely not hiring people whose skin or hair were not up to the high standards they set. Their defense for this practice was, "Well, this is a cosmetics company." Ah—but they were applying that standard to candidates for operations areas, back where employees don't meet the public. It's inappropriate to deny somebody the right to work based on some artificial standard.

ARRESTS AND CONVICTIONS

In France, if you are accused of a crime, your attorney must prove that you're innocent; absent of that proof you go to jail. Greece, Mexico, Turkey, lots of other countries in the world have that system, which is based on the Napoleonic Code.

Here in the United States we have a different system, based on the British system of justice, which we share with Canada and Australia and a few other countries in the world. Under this system of justice you are innocent until you are proven guilty. The prosecutor must prove your guilt beyond a reasonable doubt. In the absence of that proof you are not guilty in the eyes of the law.

In the spirit of our system you cannot inquire into arrests per se and you cannot deny somebody the right to work merely because of an arrest that has not subsequently been followed by a conviction. If they've been convicted, however, it legally establishes that they did it, and they're responsible for it. You can ask about it on an application, you can ask for details, and on a case-by-case basis you can evaluate the circumstances of the conviction against the job requirements; it is part of your mix of information about that candidate. Note that— leaving aside bondability and security clearance for the moment—you cannot automatically eliminate somebody solely because of a conviction, but the circumstances of the convictions must be weighed on a case-by-case basis.

BONDING, SECURITY CLEARANCE, AND U.S. CITIZENSHIP

If a person in this position has to be individually bonded or has to have a security clearance, those investigations are exempt from the EEO rules and regulations—ah, but not you the interviewer—you are still bound by the same rules. The investigation will yield a result—the candidate is bondable or not, gets a security clearance or doesn't. You don't get back the dossier, you only get back the conclusion. You don't have access to the information behind it. What you can say is: "This job will require you to be bonded. Have you ever been bonded before? Is there any reason why you cannot be bonded? Because you cannot function on the job without it." You can say the same thing with respect to a security clearance. Those are legitimate areas of inquiry. If the job requires the person to be a U.S. citizen, as it does for many positions at a defense contractor, you may ask: "This job requires you to be a U.S. citizen. Are you a U.S. citizen?" For all other employers a legitimate question is,

"Do you have the legal right to work in the United States?"
And you are required to have them produce documentation.

DRUG TESTING

Drug testing is an area of great controversy now, but for the
moment EEO rules and regulations are not applicable. The
privacy act may eventually become the applicable statute
here, but the thing to take into account is that where there
is a clear justification that public safety is involved by drug
testing (employees for a nuclear power plant, for example,
or railroad engineers), there isn't much quibbling.

The issue is murkier when it comes to jobs the everyday
performance of which do not affect directly public safety—
this is currently an area of controversy, and in time the
courts will decide. Still, many employees are required pre-
employment drug tests as a condition of employment.

EDUCATION AND WORK EXPERIENCE REQUIREMENTS

I don't mean to imply that you can't ask about Work
Experience or Education! It means that you have to make
sure the requirements you establish are reasonable and
necessary. It is legitimate to require a college degree in a
specific subject matter area that is related to the job—for
example, to require a degree in computer science or mathe-
matics for a programming position. For a position in the
finance area, requiring a degree in accounting, business, or
even economics is unchallenged.

What has been challenged is the practice of requiring a
college degree with no particular subject matter attached:
Some companies, as a matter of policy, have not cared what
candidates studied, so long as they had a college degree. In
particular, a life insurance company was challenged and
came to the realization that you might not need to be
a college graduate to be an insurance agent. You might

need to have certain qualities. The insurance company's rationale had been that a college degree represented a certain baseline of qualities—verbal fluency, numerical ability, breadth and depth of knowledge, a certain sophistication, awareness, and things of that sort (a walk through a college campus nowadays might lead you to challenge that assumption!). In response to this argument the courts ruled that a college degree can be required providing that those individuals who did not have a college degree, but did have all the qualities necessary, would not be excluded. Nowadays ads say: college degree or equivalent experience.

By the way, from a business standpoint it's also smarter to do that. Suppose I interview Jane who has 116 credits from college (4 short of the 120 necessary) but didn't graduate because she had to leave in her last semester. But Jane is an incredible programmer, or engineer, or salesperson, or whatever. Do I want to deny myself this talented person because of four credits? Probably not.

While these topics do not exhaust the issues that could be raised in this chapter, they do represent the most common areas of concern raised in my seminars. I have tried to avoid merely listing "Title VII" and legal technicalities. You will find that if you apply the practical principle of stating the job requirement and asking a closed-ended question and embed your inquiry in the structure covered in this book you will not even make a technical EEO error, let alone a substantive one.

ABOUT THE AUTHOR

W‍ILLIAM S. SWAN, Ph.D., a nationally recognized expert in interviewing, conducts selection interview seminars and workshops for major corporations and government agencies. He has trained over 14,000 managers to conduct more effective interviews. Dr. Swan established Swan Consultants, Inc. in 1980 to provide selection and campus interview training programs, and materials on all aspects of the hiring process.

Prior to establishing his own consulting firm, he was Senior Vice President at Drake Beam Morin, Inc. and a Senior Trainer with The Psychological Corporation. There he designed and conducted training programs in selection interviewing, campus recruitment, performance appraisal, and communications skills, as well as providing general consulting services to a broad range of clients, both in the United States and overseas.

Before joining The Psychological Corporation, Dr. Swan was the Assistant Dean of the New York School of Psychiatry. He has had extensive administrative experience through positions as program director at Albert Einstein Medical Center and Kingsboro Psychiatric Center. He is a New York State licensed psychologist, and has served on the faculty of Temple University, John Jay College, and Clarkson University.

Dr. Swan served two terms as President of the New York Metropolitan Chapter of the American Society for Training and Development, and served on the chapter's Board of Directors. He is also a member of the American Society for Personnel Administration and the American Psychological Association.

Dr. Swan earned his Ph.D. in clinical psychology from Temple University, his M.A. from St. John's University, and his B.S. from Manhattan College.

INDEX